Interviewing
for Solutions

Peter De Jong, Ph.D., is Director of Social Work at Calvin College in Grand Rapids, Michigan. He teaches courses in interviewing skills and practice with individuals and families. He has worked as a practitioner in community mental health. He also conducts workshops and consults with public and private agencies interested in adopting a solution-focused approach to clients and services. Besides several articles, he has written a training package for the Family Independence Agency of the State of Michigan that is being used to prepare workers in a strengths-based, solution-focused approach to interviewing clients.

Insoo Kim Berg, M.S.S.W., is a co-developer with Steve de Shazer of the solution-focused approach and the co-founder of the Brief Family Therapy Center of Milwaukee, Wisconsin. She is the author of *Family Based Services* and co-author (with S. D. Miller) of *Working with the Problem Drinker*. She has also written many articles and is well known for her videotaped interviews with clients. She lectures, conducts workshops, and consults with agencies and organizations in the United States and abroad. Her current professional passion is working with the Family Independence Agency of Michigan to develop efficient and effective ways to help families and children in the child welfare system.

Interviewing for Solutions

Peter De Jong
Calvin College

Insoo Kim Berg
Brief Family Therapy Center

Brooks/Cole Publishing Company

I⟨T⟩P® An International Thomson Publishing Company

Pacific Grove • Albany • Belmont • Bonn • Boston • Cincinnati • Detroit • Johannesburg • London
Madrid • Melbourne • Mexico City • New York • Paris • Singapore • Tokyo • Toronto • Washington

Sponsoring Editor: Lisa I. Gebo
Marketing Team: Jean Thompson, Margaret Parks, Deanne Brown
Editorial Assistants: Terry Thomas, Shelley Bouhaja
Production Editor: Jamie Sue Brooks
Manuscript Editor: Bernard Gilbert
Permissions Editor: Carline Haga

Interior Design: TBH/Typecast
Cover Design: Laurie Albrecht
Cover Photo: Peter Griffith, Masterfile
Typesetting: TBH/Typecast
Cover Printing: Phoenix Color Corp.
Printing and Binding: Maple-Vail Book Manufacturing Group

For more information, contact:

BROOKS/COLE PUBLISHING COMPANY
511 Forest Lodge Road
Pacific Grove, CA 93950
USA

International Thomson Editores
Seneca 53
Col. Polanco
11560 México, D.F., México

International Thomson Publishing Europe
Berkshire House 168–173
High Holborn
London WC1V 7AA
England

International Thomson Publishing GmbH
Königswinterer Strasse 418
53227 Bonn
Germany

Thomas Nelson Australia
102 Dodds Street
South Melbourne, 3205
Victoria, Australia

International Thomson Publishing Asia
221 Henderson Road
#05–10 Henderson Building
Singapore 0315

Nelson Canada
1120 Birchmount Road
Scarborough, Ontario
Canada M1K 5G4

International Thomson Publishing Japan
Hirakawacho Kyowa Building, 3F
2-2-1 Hirakawacho
Chiyoda-ku, Tokyo 102
Japan

Library of Congress Cataloging-in-Publication Data

DeJong, Peter
        Interviewing for solutions / Peter De Jong, Insoo Kim Berg.
            p. cm.
        Includes bibliographical references and index.
        ISBN 0-534-23160-8
            1. Social case work.   2. Interviewing.   3. Short-term counseling.
        4. Solution-focused therapy.   I. Berg, Insoo Kim.   II. Title.
    HV43.D45 1998
    361.3'22—dc21   97-8713
                                                              CIP

Contents

Chapter 4. Getting Started: How to Pay Attention to What the Client Wants   43

Chapter 5. How to Amplify What Clients Want: The Miracle Question   67

Chapter 6. Exploring for Exceptions: Building on Client Strengths and Successes 94

Chapter 7. Formulating Feedback for Clients 107

Chapter 8. Later Sessions: Finding, Amplifying, and Measuring Client Progress   134

Chapter 9. Interviewing in Crisis Situations   165

Foreword

Few approaches to interviewing have had so much impact on how we work with clients today as has the solution-focused approach developed by Steve de Shazer, Insoo Kim Berg, and their colleagues at the Brief Family Therapy Center in Milwaukee. This small group of thoughtful, independent-minded clinicians became concerned about the incongruity between how they approached their work with clients and how their clients in fact used their services. While de Shazer, Berg, and their colleagues expected treatment to take a long time—perhaps a year or more—most clients came to treatment for only a few sessions and then left. And while the clinicians expected that clients would make fundamental personality changes, their clients seemed more interested in small but concrete changes in their day-to-day lives. This growing cognitive dissonance prompted these pioneering clinicians to look for a better way of working with their clients—a way that would be more consonant with how clients use professional services to make positive changes in their lives.

Embarking on a journey that would eventually lead to the development of the solution-focused approach, the Milwaukee group began to reexamine some of the givens in practice wisdom. They experimented with new ways of thinking about change and new ways of interviewing, prompted by their careful observation of how clients used professional services to make desired changes. As these clinicians discovered more effective ways of working, they incorporated the new techniques into their approach; they made systematic observations to see if the innovations were useful to their clients in the change process. The Milwaukee team discovered that change occurs in small steps and that small changes often lead to larger, lasting change. They discovered that it is not always necessary to delve into problems to bring about change; focusing on the desired change from the start is often more effective. What's more, they found that, in many cases, clients were already beginning to make the changes they desired—even before the first session! What began as a courageous enterprise three decades ago evolved into a revolutionary new way to work with clients, one that views the client as competent and in charge, helps the client to visualize the changes he or she desires, and then builds on the effective aspects of what the client is already doing.

De Jong and Berg provide here a highly readable description of this new way of working. De Jong's expertise as a teacher and writer combine with Berg's expertise as a clinician and consultant to produce a clear and authoritative account of solution-focused interviewing. They present a constructionist view of the change process, along with key concepts and techniques of solution-focused interviewing. Generous excerpts from actual interviews conducted by the authors illustrate the solution-focused techniques and add realism and concreteness to the authors' account.

Readers of this text might easily get the impression that solution-focused interviewing is simple and straightforward. In a sense, it is. The theory of change is direct, and the techniques for setting goals and bringing about change are also simple. In each session, the practitioner needs to carry out only a few tasks (summarized in the protocols in the Appendix) to help the client stay focused on positive change. Yet, even after practicing solution-focused interviewing for more than a decade, I occasionally find it difficult to stay solution-focused in my work with clients. Some clients seem to feel entirely hopeless, as though change is not possible; talk about change seems useless and even silly to these clients. Other clients may believe that they need to understand the problem before change can occur; for them, talking about change before analyzing the problem makes no sense. Yet purposeful change happens only when the client begins to visualize the change he or she desires. Engaging the client in change talk—setting clear goals, focusing on what the client can do and is already doing—is essential for the change process to unfold. Thus, while the concepts and techniques of solution-focused interviewing are simple and straightforward, they will not always be easy to implement. And you, dear reader, should not give up when you have difficulty putting them to practice! Not giving up—believing that change is possible, even when the client feels hopeless—is perhaps the most important thing you can do as a professional change consultant to help your clients be successful in their efforts to change.

And so it is with pleasure and anticipation that I introduce De Jong and Berg's text on solution-focused interviewing. If you find some of their ideas challenging, use this as an occasion to reexamine your assumptions about change. If you find solution-focused techniques difficult to implement in your interviews, keep trying; the training many of us received taught us to focus on problems rather than change. Change in how you interview and how you think about interviewing will come only with practice.

Finally, I urge you to exercise in your work the same intellectual inquisitiveness and professional integrity that spurred the team at Milwaukee 30 years ago to question their accepted ways of working. Careful and systematic observation of what you do that works for your clients, along with a willingness to examine your work from new perspectives, will help you develop your interviewing skills and maximize your professional effectiveness. Reflect on the ideas presented here. Try out the techniques that seem useful. And, above all, take note of what works as you help your clients change.

Wallace Gingerich
Case Western Reserve University

Preface

This is a book about how to interview clients. It offers a set of skills for basic interviewing in the helping professions. In most respects, these skills are unique. First, they are intended to assist the client in developing a vision of a more satisfying future. Second, they direct both client and practitioner towards a deeper awareness of the strengths and resources that the client can use in turning vision into reality. These skills are based on the belief that it is essential to work within each client's frame of reference.

We have chosen to call this way of interviewing clients *solution building,* in contrast to the problem-solving approach that undergirds most other interviewing approaches. In problem solving, practitioners gather information from clients to assess the nature and seriousness of client problems, and design interventions that will solve or alleviate problems. This approach relies heavily upon professional expertise for its assessments and interventions.

Our students and workshop participants who are making the change from problem solving to solution building have told us that this change is similar to the switch from doing things with your right hand to doing them with your left hand; it takes some getting used to. They also report that understanding the differences between the two approaches in theory is easier than effectively putting the skills into practice. Consequently, we wanted to produce teaching materials primarily aimed at enhancing practice skills.

The purpose of this book, then, is to teach you, the reader, how to build solutions with clients. We devote most of the book to describing and illustrating the requisite skills. Because solution building occurs through the words that pass between practitioners and clients, many dialogues from our actual interviews with clients are included. They are quoted at sufficient length to give you a clear sense of the ways in which solution-building conversations unfold; such conversations tend to be full of starts and stops and twists and turns.

To complement this book an Instructor's Resource Manual and a Learner's Workbook are available. The supplementary materials are organized around the belief that those new to solution building will learn it most quickly and effectively by practicing it. The materials include instructional ideas, in-class exercises, scenarios for practice outside of class, sample test items, and tools for solution building with clients.

In addition, videotapes—available through the Brief Family Therapy Center, PO Box 13736, Milwaukee, WI, USA (414-785-9001)—present examples of interviews with individual clients and with a family and include teaching comments by ourselves that highlight different aspects of solution building and clients' responses to them.

The chapters in this book are organized as follows. First, two chapters provide a context for the skills. In these chapters, we explain that the problem-solving approach to helping clients may be traced to the rise of modern medicine and its impressive accomplishments. We outline concerns about the assumptions of problem solving as applied in the helping professions, and describe solution building as an alternative. Second, in Chapters 3–9, we present the skills used in solution building. The sequence of presentation reflects the order in which the skills are used in first and later sessions of solution building; in other words, their presentation follows the process of solution building from beginning to end. This organization, we believe, will make it easiest for learners to eventually apply the skills to their own practice. Third, in Chapters 10–13, we give information that relates more generally to the place of solution building in agency practice and the helping professions. We present outcome data and address the extent to which solution building reflects the most cherished values of the helping professions, including a commitment to diversity-sensitive practice. We provide examples of adaptations of the approach to small-group and organizational practice. Lastly, we discuss the theoretical implications of these skills and clients' responses to them.

We believe that this book can be useful to a wide audience. Along with the videotapes, Instructor's Resource Manual, and Learner's Workbook, the book can be used to teach interviewing skills to undergraduate and graduate students enrolled in beginning practice courses in counseling, psychology, pastoral counseling, psychiatric nursing, and social work. We also believe that it will be useful to counseling centers, family service centers, mental health centers for children and adults, and other social service agencies interested in training their staff in solution-building skills. We have used this material with a wide range of audiences, who have encouraged us to organize it into a book, videotapes, a manual, and a workbook.

As you will soon discover, the book is written in an informal, conversational style. We have avoided technical words, and we make frequent use of first- and second-person pronouns. When referring to past experiences particular to one of us, we identify the person involved as Insoo or Peter. Informality is more natural to us. This style more accurately reflects the way we work with our clients, students, and workshop audiences, and we believe that it allows us to communicate our experiences and ideas more clearly.

This book offers a map to practitioners who wish to help clients build solutions within their own frames of reference. We believe that clients empower themselves by envisioning alternative futures and working hard to turn those visions into realities; as practitioners, we can contribute to their solution building. When purposefully and meaningfully applied, the skills presented in this book represent the practitioner's contribution to client empowerment. To participate in this process is invigorating and gratifying. Welcome to the exciting world in which clients make something different happen in their lives.

Our thanks to the following reviewers: Shirley Clark, Chattanooga State Technical Community College; LaVonne Cornell-Swanson, University of Wisconsin—Whitewater; Harold Engen, University of Iowa; Lorraine Gutíerrez, University of Michigan; Andy Horne, University of Georgia; Twinet Parmer, Central Michigan University; Kathleen Perkins, Louisiana State University; David E. Pollio, Washington University; and Linda R. Qualia, Collin County Community College. We also benefited greatly from the reviews and comments of Steve de Shazer, Brief Family Therapy Center, and Cheryl Brandsen, Calvin College. Our thanks, too, to our students, workshop participants, and clients.

Peter De Jong
Insoo Kim Berg

To order *books,* call Brooks/Cole at 1-800-354-9706

Interviewing for Solutions ISBN 0-534-23160-8
Learner's Workbook for Interviewing for Solutions
    ISBN 0-534-35432-7

Instructor's Resource Manual for Interviewing for Solutions
    ISBN 0-534-35021-6
    (available to instructors adopting *Interviewing for Solutions;* call 1-800-423-0563)

To order *videotapes,* contact

Brief Family Therapy Center
P.O. Box 13736
Milwaukee, WI 53213-0736
414-785-9001

CHAPTER *1*

From Problem Solving to Solution Building

> Assessment is a critical process . . . for the nature of goals and the selection of relevant interventions are largely based upon the assessment. Indeed, the effectiveness of selected interventions, and ultimately the case outcome, depend in large measure upon the accuracy of the assessment.
>
> (Hepworth & Larsen, 1993, p. 192)

> The client constructs his or her own solution based on his or her own resources and successes.
>
> (de Shazer, 1988, p. 50)

Cheryl, a colleague of Peter's, teaches an introductory course to one of the helping professions. In order to demonstrate to her students that all of us have preexisting ideas about how to help others—even before we begin our professional education—she engages her students in a role-play exercise. On one occasion, she role-played Rosie, a character based on one of her clients.

The professor told her students that Rosie is 23 years old and has never married. She is five months pregnant and has four children: two boys (ages 8 and 6) and two girls (ages 3 and 2). She subsists on welfare benefits, including Food Stamps, and Medicaid. Cheryl then asked her students to collectively interview Rosie—that is, to ask the questions they thought necessary to help Rosie. Here are the questions that they asked, along with Rosie's answers:

STUDENT: How do you feel about being pregnant again?

ROSIE: I don't like it; I'm sick all the time and I don't have any energy. I really want an abortion, but I didn't find out about being pregnant soon enough to have one on Medicaid and, now that I'm five months along, I can't get a doctor to do one, so I'm stuck with another child.

STUDENT: It sounds like you didn't want to get pregnant again. Were you using birth control?

ROSIE: No, I wasn't. Birth control costs a lot, and I guess I didn't have the money.

STUDENT: Did the baby's father use a condom?

ROSIE: Look, I make some extra money by having men over, and if I asked all of my clients to use rubbers I wouldn't have any business. Yes, I know I shouldn't have men over, especially with little kids around, but welfare doesn't go very far with four kids, and the extra money from the men helps and, besides, I need things too.

STUDENT: What can we do for you here today?

ROSIE: I'm going crazy with all the things I have to do for my kids. I'm always tired, and I'm afraid that my two boys are gonna be put in a foster home again because I have trouble getting them to school in the morning.

STUDENT: How did you feel about your children being taken away?

ROSIE: Terrible! Horrible! I cried a lot.

STUDENT: What was your childhood like?

ROSIE: Terrible. I was oldest of six kids. I had two younger brothers always hanging around the house and trying to get the older boys to carry a beeper and deliver drugs because it pays good. I tell my boys not to get into that because it won't get them anywhere.

STUDENT: But yet you prostitute yourself for money.

ROSIE: That's different.

STUDENT: How is it different?

ROSIE: [glowering] It just is!

STUDENT: Tell me about the difficulty you have with getting your boys to school.

ROSIE: They don't want to get up in the morning and fix their breakfast. I try to, but I'm not feeling well with this pregnancy. When I do get up before them and make them breakfast, then things go better. But usually they just want to lay around and watch TV. They say school won't do them any good anyway and that they can earn more working for their uncles—delivering goods.

STUDENT: Did you know that most schools have attendance officers that can come to the house and get your kids for you if they don't show up at school? Maybe that would help. You could get another adult with you to help get them out the door.

ROSIE: Maybe.

STUDENT: Rosie, how motivated are you to help yourself?

ROSIE: I'm motivated, but I'm not sure about how you plan to help me.

STUDENT: Have you ever thought about placing the baby for adoption?

ROSIE: No. If I give birth to it, I'm going to keep it. No way am I going to give it to strangers.

STUDENT: Adoption really isn't like that at all. Wouldn't you be interested in hearing more about how adoption works these days—for your benefit and your child's?

ROSIE: No.

STUDENT: How much education do you have?

ROSIE: I went through the eight grade. I dropped out when I got pregnant the first time.

STUDENT: How did you feel about having to drop out?

ROSIE: OK. I didn't like school much anyway.

STUDENT: Would you like to go back to finish high school?

ROSIE: Well, um, sure, but who will watch my babies, and how will I get there?

STUDENT: There are programs that offer childcare, and you could take the bus. Do you have any people around who could help you, like your neighbors or your parents?

ROSIE: My neighbors are in the same boat as me; I don't know who my father is; my mom is sick and she is always worrying about her other kids.

STUDENT: Tell me about your relationship with your mother.

ROSIE: It's OK now—better than when I was a kid. My mom used to shout at us and hit us a lot. There was a lot of fighting. I always had to take care of the younger kids. She got real angry at me when I got pregnant and kicked me out of the house.

STUDENT: That must have made you sad.

ROSIE: Yeah, life stinks sometimes. But I can see now how tough it is to take care of kids and why she treated us the way she did.

STUDENT: Do you find that you often make the same mistakes in parenting as your mother?

ROSIE: Yeah, I yell, and sometimes I hit them.

STUDENT: How do you feel when you treat your kids this way?

ROSIE: I feel lousy, OK? But I get tired and I can't help it.

STUDENT: Have you ever thought about taking parenting classes?

ROSIE: Yeah, it's probably a good idea, but it seems like a lot of work right now.

The interview ended at this point, in part because the students ran out of questions to ask, in part because Rosie did not want to continue. We'd like to make several observations about this interview, especially about the types of questions that the students chose to ask Rosie. These questions reveal how the students assumed they could be most helpful. Undoubtedly, the students were eager to assist Rosie.

First of all, note that the students chose to ask a lot of questions of Rosie, rather than, for example, to make observations about her or to give her instructions. This focus suggests that the students believed they needed more information about Rosie in order to assist her. What kinds of questions did they ask?

- **Questions about problems.** Some questions zeroed in on possible problem areas in Rosie's life. The students asked Rosie about being pregnant again, prostituting herself, not getting her boys to school consistently, dropping out of school, not having a job, and mistakes in parenting.

- **Questions about mistakes.** The students also asked Rosie—sometimes directly, sometimes by implication—whether she had taken certain actions. These questions were directly related to the problem areas that the students had identified: "Were you using birth control?" "Did the baby's father use a condom?" "Do you find that you often make the same mistakes in parenting as your mother?" An apparent implication of this type of question is that, had Rosie chosen to do something different than she did, she would not be having these problems right now, or the problems would not be as serious.

- **Questions about causes.** We might also think about those questions that searched for Rosie's past mistakes as attempts to get at immediate, practical *causes* of her problems—such as not using birth control and dropping out of school. The interview also contains questions about more remote causes: "What was your childhood like?" "Tell me about your relationship with your mother." The students are acting as though they must know *why* Rosie's problems are occurring before they can be helpful to her.

- **Questions about solutions.** A fourth group of questions implied possible solutions. These questions generally came on the heels of those that sought to identify Rosie's problems and their causes: "Wouldn't you be interested in hearing more about how adoption works these days?" "Would you like to go back to finish high school?" "Have you ever thought about taking parenting classes?" Given that these questions consistently follow those about problems and their causes, it seems that these student interviewers are acting as though possibilities for solutions will flow from *the interviewers' understandings* of Rosie's problems and their causes.

Looking back over the four types of questions we have identified to this point, we can make a couple of observations. First, two-thirds of the questions that the students asked fall into one or more of these four categories. Second, the students asked the questions in an identifiable sequence: questions about problem areas, followed by questions about immediate and remote causes, followed by questions about possible solutions. On the basis of these observations, we believe that these students have already absorbed a *problem-solving* approach about how best to help others. One final type of question remains.

- **Questions about feelings.** Most of the remaining questions were about Rosie's feelings: "How do you feel about being pregnant again?" "How did you feel about your children being taken away?" "How do you feel when you treat your kids this way?" These students somehow believed that getting Rosie to express her feelings was an important part of helping her.

Helping As Problem Solving

The approach to helping implicit in the questions of these beginning students is very similar to the basic approach found in many textbooks about professional practice in counseling, psychology, and social work. These textbooks frequently organize their content around the stages of the problem-solving approach. This term sometimes appears in their titles, for example: *Problem Solving in the Helping Professions* (McClam & Woodside, 1994) and *The General Method of Social Work Practice: A Problem-Solving Approach* (McMahon, 1990). The stages of problem solving essentially systematize and elaborate the approach taken by Rosie's interviewers.

The Stages of Problem Solving

McMahon's (1990) formulation includes the following stages:

- **Description of problem(s) and data collection.** Here, the client describes those concerns for which relief is sought. The practitioner asks follow-up questions to obtain a more detailed understanding of the client's problem(s) so that a professional assessment can be made.
- **Problem assessment.** Once the problem is described, the practitioner makes a determination of the nature of the client's problem and its seriousness. The practitioner draws from a profession's acquired knowledge base—its categories, theories, research findings, and practice wisdom—to make the assessment.
- **Intervention planning.** Together with the client, the practitioner develops a list of goals and designs a set of interventions intended to solve or to reduce the negative consequences of the problem(s). Again, the practitioner relies on the profession's knowledge base to participate in developing the plan.
- **Intervention.** The problem-solving actions (interventions) intended to alleviate the problem are carried out.
- **Evaluation and follow-up.** As problem-solving actions are taken, the client and professional monitor the consequences. The information from the monitoring is used to decide if the actions taken have been successful. If not, adjustments in the level of intervention are made or new actions are taken. Once the problem is deemed solved by the client and practitioner, the process is finished, and the client stops services.

Often the practitioner and client make arrangements for follow-up contacts, to make sure that the problem does not recur.

A Caveat: The Importance of Trust Development

The helping professions are aware that professional helping cannot be reduced to problem solving alone. Practitioners long ago recognized that establishing a relationship of trust with their clients is very important in the helping process. Professionals know that, without trust, clients will be unlikely to contract for services or follow through on recommendations. Consequently, those who write about and teach professional helping commonly add a step to the helping process before problem solving begins; this step is called relationship building or engagement. They also add a final step named termination. In these steps, the practitioner pays special attention to sensitivity, warmth, and empathy, in order to establish and maintain a trusting relationship with the client.

The Medical Model

Problem solving in the helping professions has been strongly influenced by the medical model (Conrad & Schneider, 1985; Goldstein, 1992; Weick, 1992). This model arose as a result of the impressive achievements in the field of medicine in the late 19th and early 20th centuries. During that period, researchers such as Louis Pasteur discovered that many contagious, life-threatening diseases may be traced to bacteria. This new knowledge led to a practice model of diagnosis and treatment. Physicians tried to help patients by *diagnosing* which diseases were causing their symptoms and then administering appropriate *treatments* (antidotes). By the early 20th century, death rates from contagious disease were falling dramatically. The causes of tuberculosis, cholera, tetanus, diphtheria, and typhoid were known; hope was running high that the devastating effects of diseases could be controlled. These achievements prompted great confidence in scientific knowledge as a basis for medical practice and also in the medical model of diagnosis and treatment.

Problem Solving: The Paradigm of the Helping Professions

Kuhn (1962) defines a *paradigm* as an overarching model; it guides theory, research, and professional practice in a field. We believe that problem solving has been the dominant paradigm of practice in the helping professions.

During the 20th century, the application of the medical model has not been confined to physical illness. Biomedicine's impressive progress in quelling infectious diseases, where a specific cause could be identified, quickly influenced the way both professionals and the public came to view mental illness, emotional problems, interpersonal difficulties, and social problems. Over the past century, scientists have conducted research about the nature and sources of problems at every level of human existence, in the belief that, once we come to understand the causes of these problems, we can better devise strategies to solve and control them. The helping professions now abound with classifications of problems. The psychiatric profession's *Diagnostic and Statistical Manual of Mental Disorders*—DSM IV, for short (American Psychiatric Association, 1994)—is one such classification; others include Freud's (1966) categories of psychopathology, Satir's (1982) categorization of discrepancies between levels of messages in interpersonal communication, and Germain and Gitterman's (1980) list of psycho-social-environmental stressors.

The helping professions have become highly diversified. They differ in the types of problems that they address, and they prefer different explanations of problems and solutions. Despite their differences, however, the helping professions share some equally important commonalities. These commonalities, which derive from the medical model, together make up the basic features of a problem-solving paradigm. Let's take a look at these commonalities.

Commonality One: A Problem Solving Structure

Since the appearance of the medical model, most helpers follow the same basic *structure* when providing assistance to clients.[1] They work from the premise that, before the client can be helped, the practitioner must figure out what the client has. This is true whether the practitioner thinks in terms of assessing problems or diagnosing disorders. The heart of this premise is that there is a necessary connection between a problem and its solution. Because different problems demand different solutions, the practitioner must make an accurate assessment in order to select the particular intervention that will be most effective in each individual case. It is clear that this premise has found its way into popular thinking. When clients finish describing their problems and symptoms, they commonly ask the practitioner, "What do you think it is? I just can't figure out what it is."

This problem-solving structure is based on the medical model, which prescribes that the physician must diagnose the patient's disease before being able

---

[1] The work of practitioners like Milton Erickson, Steve de Shazer, and others moved in another direction, as we will see later in this chapter.

to treat it effectively. Different diseases require different treatments, and each disease has a different cure.

Another aspect of the medical model is the idea that the client's problem and whatever gives rise to it are objectively real, just as organ malfunction, disease process, and bacteria are objectively real. As we have seen, professions have developed extensive categorizations of problems, with associated assessment techniques and intervention techniques, just as modern medicine has generated categories of disease, diagnostic procedures, and treatments. Moreover, for much of the 20th century, the helping professions have regarded the factors that give rise to a client's problem as operating in a linear, cause-and-effect manner, just as bacteria attacking the organs of the body cause a disease.

Although seemingly diverse, most viewpoints within these professions work from the premise that problem and solution are somehow connected. (This is even true of the systems viewpoint, which simply adopts a circular, rather than a linear, model of causation.) They differ mainly in their categorizations of problems, assessment procedures, and intervention techniques. For example, clinical psychologists look for different problems using different assessment procedures than do generalist social workers. Clinical psychologists typically find a problem by psychological testing and proceed to assign it to a category found in the *Diagnostic and Statistical Manual of Mental Disorders*. Generalist social workers, on the other hand, find a problem by means of assessment tools such as genograms and ecomaps and then classify it in terms of system transactions of one sort or another. The problems found and the names given to them are different, but the *structure* of helping remains the same. [2]

Commonality Two: Reliance on Scientific Expertise

The second commonality is an extension of the first. If different problems demand different solutions, then it is important for professional helpers to be knowledgeable about various problems, procedures for assessing them, and techniques for intervening with them. Moreover, as the problems of clients are thought to be objectively real (that is, to have an existence separate from the knower), they can be studied scientifically. Therefore, once science has gained knowledge about them, this knowledge can be taught to professional helpers as

---

[2] The problem-solving structure is less readily discernible in some parts of the field than in others. For example, the counseling profession, reflecting the assumptions and goals of humanistic psychology, is less focused on linking diagnosed psychological disorders to particular treatments than is clinical psychology. Counselors work to foster the self-directive, developmentally healthy tendencies of their clients, whom they assume to be essentially normal people. In a general sense, however, the problem-solving structure is still there in their work. When asked about the source of a client's current difficulties, counselors point to developmental issues in the client's past. Also, they regularly ask questions about a client's developmental past; in so doing, they imply that it is important for clients and themselves to understand these developmental issues as an aid to treatment.

the foundation for helping clients. This scientific knowledge about different problems and their different solutions, along with the art of applying this knowledge in professional contexts, is what constitutes the expertise of a helping profession.

Helping As Solution Building

The generic structure of problem solving—first determining the nature of the problem and then intervening—influences the content of the interaction between practitioners and clients. Practitioners characteristically ask clients to spend significant amounts of time describing (and sometimes analyzing) the who, what, when, where, and why of their problems, in order to gain sufficient information for accurate assessment of the problems. In this process, clients often fill out long intake forms about themselves, their families, their occupational histories, and other aspects of their lives. They may be asked to list the problems they have been experiencing and to complete assessment inventories such as personality tests and family-interaction questionnaires. (In employing such assessment tools, practitioners are attempting not only to be as thorough as possible but also to protect themselves against charges of negligence.) Once problems are assessed, most practitioners, again drawing on their expertise about problems and related interventions, shift the interaction toward making interventions. As a result, the interaction between clients and practitioners focuses on problems.

Concerns about the Problem-Solving Paradigm

Increasingly, over the last 15 years, writers are expressing deep concerns about the field's emphasis on problems and scientific expertise. Let's look at some of these concerns.

Client Problems Are Not Puzzles

Julian Rappaport (1981) boldly states that many—if not most—of the difficulties brought by clients to helpers bear little resemblance to the diseases for which the medical model was designed. Diseases, which are a consequence of physiological processes such as the workings of bacteria or the effects of environmental contaminants, are more like the scientific problems that natural scientists study than the client difficulties that helping professionals try to address. Diseases and the analytic problems of natural science resemble puzzles. Puzzles can be exceedingly complex when they are made up of many intricate pieces but, because all their pieces exist, solutions can be discovered. This is true whether the solution is discovering a bacterial agent for chicken cholera, unraveling the DNA code, or predicting the precise path of the planets around the sun. Rappaport (1981) states that the type of research and reasoning best suited to solving such puzzles *converges* on the solution; that is, over time, increasingly rigorous and ingenious investigations offer various solutions that gradually converge toward the right answer. Experimental research is an example of convergent reasoning and has proved very successful in solving scientific and medical puzzles.

The problems encountered by practitioners in the helping professions are different from puzzles. Most often, these problems do not have a single correct solution. For example, a family may seek professional assistance because it is experiencing conflict between the parents and their children. Perhaps both parents are employed and the children are getting into mischief after school and seem to want more attention from their parents. The practitioner may be tempted to recommend that one of the parents work fewer hours in order to devote more time to their children. However, this solution may jeopardize that parent's job performance and, consequently, make the parent more anxious, which, in turn, may have its own negative impact on parent-child interaction in this family.

In thinking about such a case, the practitioner soon realizes that the appropriate solution will depend on the parents' individual needs at this point in their lives, their past experiences with parenting, and their cultural values regarding job and childrearing. Because individual people and their perceptions about life are so diverse, there is no single solution for such a problem. Consequently, Rappaport (1981) maintains that *divergent* thinking is more appropriate in the helping professions. In divergent thinking, the practitioner surveys several different perspectives about the problem and searches for potential workable solutions. With the goal of being useful to clients, divergent thinking gives as much weight to the perceptions of clients as to the expertise of the practitioner.

Focusing on Empowerment and Client Strengths

The mission of the helping professions is to *empower* clients to live more productive and satisfying lives. Rappaport (1981, 1990), Saleebey (1992), Schon (1983), and Weick, Rapp, Sullivan, and Kishardt (1989), among others, emphasize that the field's dominant emphasis on client problems and expert solutions detracts from this mission.[3] If practitioners focus on categories of problem or pathology, clients may become discouraged and feel that they are victims of some disease or dysfunction, such as alcoholism or the dysfunctional family syndrome. Empowering clients, on the other hand, means "help-

---

[3] Not all approaches put equal emphasis on expert solutions. The nondirective approach, for instance, deemphasizes such solutions. It relies on unconditional positive regard by the practitioner and self-direction by the client.

ing people discover the considerable power within themselves, their families, and their neighborhoods" (Saleebey, 1992, p. 8).

Saleebey calls his version of empowerment the *strengths perspective*. Summarizing the work of several like-minded writers, he identifies its basic assumptions:

1. Despite life's struggles, all persons possess strengths that can be marshalled to improve the quality of their lives. Practitioners should respect these strengths and the directions in which clients wish to apply them.
2. Client motivation is increased by a consistent emphasis on strengths as the client defines them.
3. Discovering strengths requires a process of cooperative exploration between clients and helpers; expert practitioners do not have the last word on what clients need to improve their lives.
4. Focusing on strengths turns practitioners away from the temptation to judge or blame clients for their difficulties and toward discovering how clients have managed to survive, even in the most difficult of circumstances.
5. All environments—even the most bleak—contain resources.

Saleebey's notion of empowerment and the assumptions on which it rests present a clear contrast with the traditional problem-solving approach. Instead of focusing on problems, Saleebey calls for practitioners to discover, in mutual exploration with clients, those personal strengths and resources that clients can bring to bear on their concerns. He believes that clients' frames of reference and perceptions about what would be most useful to create more satisfying lives for themselves should count for as much as—if not more than—scientific expertise about problems and solutions. In short, he wants to replace a focus on problems with a focus on client strengths. At the end of his book, Saleebey (1992) makes this challenge to practitioners:

> At the very least, the strengths perspective obligates workers to understand that, however downtrodden or sick, individuals have survived (and in some cases even thrived). They have taken steps, summoned up resources, and coped. We need to know what they have done, how they have done it, what they have learned from doing it, what resources (inner and outer) were available in their struggle to surmount their troubles. People are always working on their situations, even if just deciding to be resigned to them; as helpers we must tap into that work, elucidate it, find and build on its possibilities. (pp. 171–172)

This is a daunting challenge; the field has long worked and generated practice techniques to fit problem solving. If Saleebey's challenge is to be met, new practice techniques must be developed, taught, and used with clients. To date, the literature about empowerment and the strengths perspective is comprised mainly of philosophy, practice principles, and general areas to explore for possible strengths. Some empowerment advocates who do address how to determine client strengths recommend using an inventory of potential areas of strength (Rapp, 1992; Cowger, 1992) based upon a set of categories that the worker brings to clients. However, these categories may or may not reflect the categories that clients use to organize their experiences. Notably lacking is an interviewing approach that fosters empowerment by more fully working within clients' frames of reference. This book, we believe, offers such an approach—the *solution-building* approach.

History of Solution Building

The solution-building approach was pioneered through the work of Steve de Shazer (1985, 1988, 1991, 1994), Insoo Kim Berg (1994), and their colleagues. De Shazer, who has written extensively on solution-focused therapy, has been intrigued throughout his career by the early work on communications by Gregory Bateson (1972; Bateson, Jackson, Haley, & Weakland, 1956) and by the approach to psychotherapy of Milton Erickson (Haley, 1973; Zeig & Lankton, 1988). He and Insoo have spent their professional careers working with individuals, couples, and families to resolve a wide variety of difficulties. They have also trained many other professionals in their procedures at the Brief Family Therapy Center in Milwaukee, Wisconsin and around the world.

De Shazer and Insoo are unusual in that they have always believed that holistically observing and reflecting on the actual process in which they work with their clients will teach them more about how to be effective than will traditional scientific research, which attempts to break the therapeutic process down into components and then gathers and interprets data about these. They have not been content to accept prevailing ideas about how therapy ought to be conducted. While working at a community agency during the 1970s, they and their colleagues installed a one-way mirror to observe themselves and other therapists at work. Their hope was to make observations about which therapist activities were most helpful to clients. The agency, however, was uncomfortable with the mirror and instructed them to remove it. Rather than give up a tool that they believed was necessary to make advances in their understanding of their work, they established their own agency in the mid-1970s. Since then, they and their associates have been innovatively working with their clients, carefully observing the therapy process, researching outcomes, and teaching their procedures to other practitioners around the world.

This brief history highlights a key aspect of the way in which De Shazer, Insoo, and their colleagues developed their procedures. They worked *inductively,* by observing individual interviews and simply paying attention to what was most useful. In the process, they tried to set aside any preexisting ideas about the nature and origin of client problems. Most other procedures in the field, by contrast, were developed deductively; they were deduced from an existing theory regarding the nature and causes of client problems. De Shazer and Insoo have pointed out that they know less about why their solution-building procedures work than they know about what is useful to clients. However, now that the procedures are well developed and their usefulness is being documented, de Shazer, in particular, has begun to think and write about the nature of therapeutic process (de Shazer, 1991, 1994).

De Shazer first hit upon the idea that there is not a necessary connection between problem and solution in 1982, when working with a particular family (Hopwood & de Shazer, 1994). As usual, de Shazer and his colleagues asked, "What brings you in?" In response, family members kept interrupting one another until, by the end of the session, they had listed 27 different problems. Since none of the 27 were clearly defined, de Shazer and his colleagues were unable to design an intervention. Still, wishing to encourage the family members to focus on something different from their problems, de Shazer and his colleagues told them to pay careful attention to "what is happening in your lives that you want to continue to have happen." When the family returned, two weeks later, they said that things were going very well and they felt their problems were solved. According to the assumptions of the problem-solving approach, the family should not have improved so dramatically, because the practitioner had not yet been able to isolate and assess the patterns and nature of the problems. Their experience with such cases led de Shazer and his colleagues towards a solution focus in place of a problem focus. They and many others (Dolan, 1991; Furman & Ahola, 1992; Miller & Berg, 1995; O'Hanlon & Weiner-Davis, 1989; Walter & Peller, 1992; Weiner-Davis, 1993) have been continuing to work out the implications of this shift ever since.

Solution Building: The Basics

The most useful way to decide which door can be opened to get to a solution is by getting a description of what the client will be doing differently and/or what sorts of things will be happening that are different when the problem is solved, and thus creating the expectation of beneficial change.

(de Shazer, 1985, p. 46)

We now give an overview of solution-building procedures, so that you can see how different they are from problem-solving procedures. Let's begin by returning to the case of Rosie.

A Second Interview with Rosie

In Chapter 1, we presented an interview in which Peter's colleague Cheryl role-played a 23-year-old client of hers named Rosie. We saw that Cheryl's students, in their attempts to help Rosie, asked a number of problem-solving questions. In contrast to her students, Cheryl herself had asked several solution-focused questions in her work with Rosie. To introduce you to the uniqueness of solution building, here are some excerpts from Cheryl's first interview with Rosie:

CHERYL: How can I be of assistance?

ROSIE: Well, I've got some big problems. First thing—I'm pregnant again. I already have two babies, two little girls who are 3 and 2 [years old], and I have two boys who are in school. I'm going crazy with all I have to do, and I'm afraid that my two boys are gonna be put in a foster home again because I have trouble getting them to school in the morning. They don't wanna get up in the morning. They just wanna lay around and watch TV. They say school won't do them any good, and they can make more delivering goods for their uncles.

CHERYL: "Delivering goods"?

ROSIE: Yeah, drugs I think. I tell them that is no good and they're gonna get into trouble, but they don't listen to me. I feel better when they're in school, because at least then they can't be with Lamar and Brian [the uncles]. But they won't get up and I'm so tired because I'm pregnant again.

CHERYL: [empathically] Wow, I can see you really have your hands full. Handling four kids by yourself is really tough to start with, but to be pregnant on top of all that . . .

ROSIE: Yeah, it is, and I don't want my boys to be taken away again. But they fight me on school, and I'm so tired with everything I have to do and being pregnant.

Rosie continued to give details about her problems, including information about her involvement in prostitution to supplement AFDC payments for basic needs and her pregnancy, which may have resulted from unprotected intercourse with a client. Cheryl then moved to a different area:

CHERYL: So you have several big problems—getting your boys to school, getting enough money, being pregnant and very tired. Let me ask you a different kind of question about these; it's called the miracle question. [pause] Suppose that you go to bed as usual tonight and, while you are sleeping, a miracle happens. The miracle is that the problems you've been telling me about are solved! Only you're sleeping, and so you do not know right away that they've been solved. What do you suppose you would notice tomorrow morning that would be *different*—that would tell you, wow, things are really better!

ROSIE: [smiling] That's easy; I would have won the lottery—$3 million.

CHERYL: That would be great wouldn't it. What else would you notice?

ROSIE: Some nice man would come along who has lots of money and lots of patience with kids, and we'd get married. Or I wouldn't have so many kids and I would finish high school and I would have a good job.

CHERYL: OK, that sounds like a *big* miracle. What do you imagine would be the first thing that you would notice which would tell you that this day is different, it's better, a miracle must have happened?

ROSIE: Well, I would get up in the morning before my kids do, make them break-fast, and sit down with them while we all eat together.

CHERYL: If you were to decide to do that—get up before them and make them breakfast—what would they do?

ROSIE: I think maybe they would come and sit down at the table instead of going and turning on the TV.

CHERYL: And how would that be for you?

ROSIE: I'd be happier because we could talk about nice things, not argue over TV. And my babies won't start crying over all the fighting about the TV.

CHERYL: What else? What else will be different when the miracle happens?

Rosie and Cheryl went on to explore and develop other parts of Rosie's miracle picture. Cheryl then moved on to questions about a related topic:

CHERYL: Rosie, I'm impressed. You have a pretty clear picture of how things will be different around your house when things are better. Are there times already, say in the last two weeks, which are like the miracle which you have been describing, even a little bit?

ROSIE: Well, I'm not sure. Well, about four days ago it was better.

CHERYL: Tell me about four days ago. *What* was different?

ROSIE: Well, I went to bed about ten the night before and had a good night of sleep. I had food in the house, because I had gone to the store and to the food pantry on Saturday. I had even set the alarm for 6:30 and got up when it rang. I made breakfast and called the kids. The boys ate and got ready for school and left on time. [remembering] One even got some homework out of his backpack and did it—real quick—before he went to school.

CHERYL: [impressed] Rosie, that sounds like a big part of the miracle right there. I'm amazed. How did all that happen?

ROSIE: I'm not sure. I guess one thing was I had the food in the house and I got to bed on time.

CHERYL: So, how did you make that happen?

ROSIE: Ah, I decided not to see any clients that night and I read books to my kids for an hour.

CHERYL: How did you manage that, reading to four kids? That seems like it would be really tough.

ROSIE: No, that doesn't work—reading to four kids at the same time. I have my oldest boy read to one baby, because that's the only way I can get him to practice his reading; and I read to my other boy and baby.

CHERYL: Rosie, that seems like a great idea—having him read to the baby. It helps you, and it helps him with his reading. How do you get him to do that?

ROSIE: Oh, I let him stay up a half hour later than the others because he helps me. He really likes that.

Cheryl continued to explore, in detail, what was different about the day that resembled Rosie's miracle and how it happened—especially what Rosie did to make it happen. Then Cheryl asked some scaling questions in order to better understand how Rosie viewed herself in relation to her problems:

CHERYL: I'd like you to put some things on a scale for me, on a scale from 0 to 10. First, on a scale from 0 through 10, where 0 equals the worst your problems have been and 10 means the problems we have been talking about are solved, where are you *today* on that scale?

ROSIE: If you had asked me that question before we started today, I would have said about a 2. But now I think it's more like a 5.

CHERYL: Great! Now let me ask you about how *confident* you are that you can have another day in the next week like the one four days ago—the one which was a lot like your miracle picture. On a scale of 0 to 10, where 0 equals no confidence and 10 means you have every confidence, how confident are you that you can make it happen again?

ROSIE: Oh, . . . about a 5.

CHERYL: Suppose you were at a 6; what would be different?

ROSIE: I'd have to be sure that I always had food in the house for breakfast for the kids.

Cheryl continued to explore with Rosie what else she could do to increase the chances of her miracle happening in the future. She ended this first interview with some final feedback for Rosie, which included pointing out to Rosie what she was already doing to make her miracle happen and suggesting that she do some of the additional things that might make miracle-type days more likely to occur.

Solution-Building Interviewing Activities

The questions that Cheryl asked Rosie were intended to assist her in building solutions to her problems. And, while there is more to the solution-building approach than its interviewing questions, these questions go a long way toward identifying the uniqueness of the approach.

Solution-building interviews are organized, in large part, around two useful activities (De Jong & Miller, 1995). The first is the development of well-formed goals within the client's frame of reference; the second is the development of solutions based upon exceptions (de Shazer, 1985). After clients have had an opportunity to describe what in their lives they would like to see changed as a result of meeting with the practitioner, solution building moves on to these two activities.

There are several characteristics of well-formed goals. Among other things, well-formed goals are important to the client, small, and concrete and represent the beginning of something different rather than the end. (See Chapter 5 for more details.) Many of the questions that Cheryl asked were intended to help Rosie develop a sharper vision of what her life would be like when her problems were less serious. Thus, Cheryl asked Rosie the miracle question and related questions to assist her in developing a detailed and vivid picture of a more satisfying life, especially in those areas where she was having problems. With the aid of the questions, Rosie was able to work her way to the point of describing several concrete things that both she and her children might be doing and feeling differently when her problems were solved.

The second solution-building activity that Cheryl used was exploring for exceptions. *Exceptions* are those occasions in clients' lives when their problems could have occurred but did not—or at least were less severe. In solution building, the practitioner focuses on the who, what, when, and where of exception times in clients' lives, instead of the who, what, when, where, and why of problems. In Rosie's case, Cheryl opened up the exploration for exceptions by asking: "Are there times already, say in the last two weeks, which are like the miracle which you have been describing, even a little bit?" Since Rosie was able to identify a specific day that was better, Cheryl went to work exploring, in detail, what was different about the day and what Rosie did that made the day better. The exploration revealed that Rosie already had successes and strengths to her credit; seeing those successes and strengths made her more hopeful that her life could improve.

Solution-building practitioners use information about exceptions to help clients devise strategies that solve or reduce their problems. Ideally, client exceptions should be related to client goals. That is why Cheryl chose to work on well-formed goals before asking about exceptions.

The Stages of Solution Building

Cheryl's work with Rosie reflects the solution-building paradigm that we discussed in Chapter 1. In particular, it is consistent with de Shazer's observation that clients can usually build solutions to their problems without either clients or practitioners assessing or understanding the nature of the problems. Given this view of problems and solutions, the structure of solution building differs markedly from that of problem solving. The basic stages of solution building are as follows.

DESCRIBING THE PROBLEM. This step resembles the first step of problem solving in that clients are given an opportunity to describe their problems. We ask, "How can we be useful to you?" Clients generally respond by describing a problem of some sort, and we ask for some details.

In solution building, however, we spend much less time and effort here than in the problem-solving approach. We ask for fewer details about the nature and severity of client problems, and we do not ask about their possible causes. Instead, we listen respectfully to clients' problem talk and think about ways to turn the conversation toward the next step, which initiates solution talk.

DEVELOPING WELL-FORMED GOALS. Here, we work with our clients to elicit descriptions of what will be different in their lives when their problems are solved.

We do this work at the point where a practitioner who follows the problem-solving approach would be doing assessment.

EXPLORING FOR EXCEPTIONS. At this stage, we ask about those times in clients' lives when their problems are not happening or are less severe. We also ask about who did what to make the exceptions happen.

This step substitutes for intervention planning in the problem-solving approach.

END-OF-SESSION FEEDBACK. At the end of each solution-building conversation, we construct messages for our clients that include compliments and usually some suggestions. The compliments emphasize what clients are already doing that is useful in solving their problems. The suggestions identify what clients could observe or do to further solve their problems. The feedback is based upon information that clients have revealed to us in the conversations about well-formed goals and exceptions. It always focuses on what the clients, given their frames of reference, need to do more of and do differently in order to enhance their chances of success in meeting their goals.

We construct and give feedback at the point where problem-solving practitioners would be doing the interventions indicated by their prior assessments.

EVALUATING CLIENT PROGRESS. In solution building, we regularly evaluate with our clients how they are doing in reaching solutions satisfactory to them. Customarily, this is done by scaling—by asking clients to rate progress on a scale of 0 to 10. Once client progress has been scaled, we work with clients to examine what still needs to be done before they feel that their problems have been adequately solved and they are ready to terminate services.

As with the problem-solving approach, solution building may be thought of as including an engagement step at the beginning and a termination step at the end. In these steps, issues of relationship and trust between client and practitioner are very important. As we will show in later chapters, the two approaches handle these issues in different ways.

The Client As Expert

As we explained in Chapter 1, the helping professions in the past have largely committed themselves to working with their clients through the application of scientific expertise—accumulated scientific knowledge about problems and solutions. One consequence of this is that, wittingly or unwittingly, the helping professions have encouraged practitioners to believe and act as though their perceptions about their clients' problems and solutions are more important to the helping process than are the clients' perceptions. In fact, the professional literature teaches that clients' perceptions often get in the way of professional practice because they are the source of client resistance, which practitioners must work hard to overcome.

In solution building, by contrast, we insist that clients are the experts about their own lives. We rely on their frames of reference in three ways to move the process of solution building along.

1. We ask them what they would like to see changed in their lives; they customarily answer with a description of their problems. We accept these client definitions of problems and the words (categories) that clients use to describe them.
2. We interview clients about what will be different in their lives when their problems are solved. We listen carefully for, and work hard to respect, the directions in which clients want to go with their lives (their goals) and the words they use to express these directions.
3. We ask clients about their perceptions of exceptions to their problems. We respect these perceptions as evidence of clients' inner resources (strengths) and as sources of information about useful outer resources that exist in the contexts in which they live.

Consequently, in all of this work, we do not view ourselves as expert at scientifically assessing client problems and then intervening; instead, we strive to be expert at exploring clients' frames of reference and identifying those perceptions that clients can use to create more satisfying lives.

By drawing on clients' frames of reference in these ways, we find that client resistance ceases to be a concern (de Shazer, 1984). We also find that we can work equally well with diverse clients and with a wide variety of problems. We will return to these topics in our final chapters.

Our next step is to examine how we build solutions with clients. That topic is the heart and soul of this book. To begin, we consider how to listen to clients with solution-building ears.

Skills for Not Knowing

*Curiosity leads to exploration and invention of alternative views
and moves, and different moves and views breed curiosity.*
(Cecchin, 1987, p. 406)

If, as a practitioner, you wish to put clients into the position of being the experts about their own lives, you will have to know how to set aside your own frame of reference as much as possible and to explore those of your clients. In other words, you will have to learn how to adopt the posture of *not knowing*. This useful term belongs to Anderson and Goolishian (1992), who maintain that a practitioner never knows a priori (by virtue of an expert frame of reference) the significance of the client's experiences and actions. Instead, the practitioner must rely on the client's perceptions and explanations. The best way to do this, they write, is to take a position of not knowing:

> The not-knowing position entails a general attitude or stance in which
> the therapist's actions communicate an abundant, genuine curiosity.
> That is, the therapist's actions and attitudes express a need to know
> more about what has been said, rather than convey preconceived opin-
> ions and expectations about the client, the problem, or what must be
> changed. The therapist, therefore, positions himself or herself in such a
> way as always to be in a state of "being informed" by the client. (Ander-
> son & Goolishian, 1992, p. 29)

Learning how to take and maintain this posture takes commitment and practice; it is a life-long process. In this chapter, we will present the basic communication skills that allow us to be informed by the client. Some of these skills are unique to solution building. Most are not but, as you will see, solution building has its own slant on how the practitioner can most usefully apply them.

Basic Interviewing Skills

Listening

Insoo likes to say that practitioners who are accomplished at solution-building have learned how to listen to the client with solution-building ears. They are able to hear the client's story without filtering it through their own frame of reference. Commonly, when we listen to others tell us about themselves, we not only listen but also react to what they are saying. Suppose you are listening to a 15-year-old, who tells you that, angry at his parents about a 10 P.M. curfew, he called them "old fashioned jerks" and then stayed out until 3 A.M. While listening to his story, you might think, "Calling his parents names is unlikely to get his curfew lifted." Or perhaps, "Developmentally speaking, staying out until 3 A.M. is an immature and unproductive way to handle anger." Such evaluative thoughts come from your frame of reference and interfere with careful listening. They interfere, first, because it is difficult to listen and evaluate at the same time; while you are thinking about the first thing the speaker said, it is difficult to absorb the next. Second, such evaluation could easily lead you to premature problem solving, as exhibited by the students who interviewed Rosie (Chapter 1). Evaluating Rosie's situation from their own frames of reference, they asked Rosie about the possibilities that they thought made sense in her situation.

Most of us find it very difficult to suspend our own frame of reference and to hear the client's story from the client's point of view. We are used to filtering what others tell us through our own experiences and beliefs. Education in the helping professions reinforces this approach by its emphasis on listening as a means of gaining assessment information.

To address this problem, Peter teaches a first course on listening and responding skills in which students develop skills by role-playing. He and his students have struggled to find ways to listen more carefully. They find that the most useful place to begin is to listen first for who and what are important to the client. In their efforts to describe what assistance they need, clients talk about those people, relationships, and events that are significant to them. In our example of the 15-year-old, the important people are his parents, and the important events include the imposition of a 10 P.M. curfew and the night he stayed out until 3 A.M. Peter and his students have found that listening for these important players and events has three important consequences: First, it immediately gets the practitioner focused on some important parts of the client's frame of reference; second, it hinders the tendency to evaluate what the client says; and, third, it helps to prevent early problem solving from the listener's point of view.

Practitioners' Nonverbal Behavior

We have noticed that most of our clients are very sensitive to whether or not we are listening carefully and respectfully. This is especially true at the beginning of our work with them. They seem to come to a conclusion about whether we are listening carefully by watching us and listening to our verbal responses. According to Okun (1992, p. 24), research bears out this observation. She states that clients rely on the following nonverbal behaviors of practitioners to judge whether or not they are being heard and respected:

- a tone of voice that matches the client's
- eye contact
- occasional head nodding to show that the practitioner is tracking what the client says
- varying facial expressions in response to what the client says
- smiling at appropriate points to demonstrate warmth and understanding
- occasional hand gesturing
- sitting in close physical proximity to clients
- using a moderate rate of speech
- leaning slightly toward the client to indicate interest and concentration
- occasional touching

Some practitioners stress the importance of nonverbal skills. Peter has a colleague who instructs students at length about body posture, head nodding, the use of smiles, and the forward lean. While we acknowledge that your nonverbals are important, we believe that what you choose to say is more important in demonstrating to your clients that you are respectfully listening. Moreover, your nonverbal skills will tend to develop naturally as you learn to quiet your own frame of reference and listen more carefully to who and what are important to your clients.

Nevertheless, effective nonverbals can contribute to setting an attentive, respectful atmosphere in a professional interview. Little or no eye contact, inappropriate smiling or facial expressions, unusual gestures, an unpleasant tone of voice, and a rate of speech that is too fast or too slow can all be distracting (Okun, 1992). Consequently, it is useful to videotape your interviews periodically so that you can review how your nonverbals are affecting your interactions with clients.

Echoing Clients' Key Words

Clients use language to describe their relationships and experiences. Often, although their language is very meaningful to them, it may be vague to you. One way to clear up ambiguity is to simply repeat or *echo* key words used by the client. Key words are those that clients use to capture their experiences and the meaning they attribute to these experiences. For example, a client might say to you: "My life is a mess." If you wish to know more about what that means to the client, all you need do is to echo "a mess" with a rising intonation, or simply ask, "What do you mean by 'a mess'?" The client almost always takes that as an invitation to say more about what is happening in his or her life.

Clients' use of language is the primary means by which they convey their frames of reference. It is crucial to solution building, then, that you listen carefully for and explore each client's choice of words. Exploring the client's words is also an important way of demonstrating respect for the client. In this connection, we believe it is disrespectful, and undermines client confidence, to reframe the client's key words into professional jargon.

Like any of the basic skills that we discuss, echoing can be misused by practitioners. In his course on beginning interviewing, Peter notices that many students have difficulty in picking out key words. In their early interviews, they may get into a thoughtless and mechanical pattern of echoing. Or they may echo in a way that suggests they are skeptical of what they are hearing or disapprove. We believe that most of these misapplications arise when the interviewer's frame of reference shapes what he or she hears. Learning to echo effectively is usually hard work, but Peter has found that, with role-play practice and feedback, nearly all students learn to do it comfortably and authentically within one semester.

Open Questions

We ask questions throughout the solution-building process. Although we ask some closed questions, we prefer open ones. As Benjamin (1987) explains, closed questions narrow the client's focus, while open ones widen the client's perceptual field. Closed questions also tend to ask for hard facts, while open ones request the client's attitudes, thoughts, and feelings. Lastly, closed questions more often reflect the practitioner's frame of reference, while open ones ask for the client's. Here are some examples of closed questions:

- "Do you like your parents?"
- "Did you ask your parents for a change in your curfew before you decided to break it?"
- "Do you want to patch things up between you and your parents?"

The following are examples of open questions:

- "Can you tell me something about your relationship with your parents?"
- "I'm wondering what happened between you and your parents the night you stayed out until 3 A.M.?
- "If things were to get better between you and your parents, what would be different?"

Do not confuse open questions with vague questions or questions that do not request specific information. All of the open questions in our examples are intended to elicit specifics from the client. When used with echoing, they provide a very effective means of exploring for the details of who and what are important to clients.

We also prefer open questions (or equivalent statements such as "Please, tell me more about that") because they are more consistent with our commitment to not knowing. We want to do whatever we can to cast our clients into the role of experts about their own lives. Open questions, when asked with genuine curiosity, transfer both control and responsibility to our clients, because, in comparison with closed questions, they give clients more choice about what to say about themselves and how to say it. Using open questions is one way to respect and promote client self-determination.

Summarizing

Peter teaches the solution-building process to students who have had little or no formal training in professional practice. The first basic communication skill he teaches is summarizing, which is essential in order to treat each client as different from every other. You will use this skill right from the beginning and throughout solution-building work with clients.

In summarizing, you periodically state back to the client his or her thoughts, actions, and feelings. You use this technique after you have gotten a detailed description of a part of the client's story, with the judicious use of echoes and open questions. To illustrate, let us go back to the case of the 15-year-old at odds with his parents over his curfew. With Tom as the client and Peter as the practitioner, the interview unfolded this way:

PETER: [*open question*][1] How were you hoping that I could help you?

TOM: My parents are such old-fashion jerks; I can't believe it!

PETER: [*genuinely curious and echoing*] "Old-fashioned jerks"?

TOM: Yeah. Like one thing is that they have this ridiculous rule that I have to be in by ten during the week. They say I need to get to bed on time so I can do well in school, instead of running around with my friends. [cynically] Yeah, right! Just because they're getting old and have to get to bed so early.

PETER: So you don't see it the way they do.

TOM: I sure don't. In fact, the reason they made me come here to see you was because I got mad last week and stayed out past my stupid curfew.
[Tom pauses and stares sullenly into the distance, with his arms folded across his chest.]

PETER: [*open question*] Can you tell me more about what happened that night?

---

[1] In the dialogues in this book, italicized words or phrases within brackets usually identify the skills or procedures being used by the practitioner. On occasion, they indicate what the practitioner noticed or was thinking at that point in the interview.

TOM: [sighing] It was the same old thing. I told them that a bunch of us were going out to the $2 movies and then a fast-food place or to one of my friends. They told me I had to be home by ten and I said I couldn't, and then we started yelling at each other. They told me my grades were falling and I shouldn't even go; I should be studying. I told them I was doing OK and to chill. They ordered me to stay home, and I got mad and left and stayed at my friend's house overnight after the movie. His parents were gone on vacation.

PETER: [*summarizing*] OK, let me see if I've got this correct. You're here because your parents made you come. You argued with them recently about your curfew, got angry about what they said, and stayed out past curfew without permission by sleeping overnight at your friend's house.

TOM: Yeah, that's right. We fight about this almost every week. They're so old-fashioned; none of my friends have a 10 o'clock curfew like that. You'd think they could get with it; we're living in the 1990s, you know.

The summary that Peter gave in this dialogue was intended for both Tom's and his own benefit. The summary reassured Tom that Peter was listening carefully; it also reassured Peter that he had heard Tom accurately. Peter used some of Tom's words and phrases in the summary as a way of respecting the way Tom chose to describe his own experience and as a way of getting as clear an idea as possible of Tom's frame of reference. If they are descriptive and are offered in a spirit of openness, summaries usually have the effect of inviting the client to say more—to correct, revise, and add to the practitioner's summary. Because they are essentially reflective, summaries are an effective way for you to put your clients in control of how to describe their experiences.

Carl Rogers, who is well known among therapists for his role in introducing nondirective therapy techniques, strongly advocates the use of summaries throughout work with clients, because they promote an understanding of the other person's frame of reference; they block the listener's tendency to evaluate when trying to listen. They also help the listener to remain composed when the speaker is talking about ideas, behaviors, or reactions that the listener would normally find foreign or offensive. To demonstrate the effects of summarizing, Rogers (1961, p. 332) suggests the following exercise:

The next time you get into an argument with your wife, or your friend, or with a small group of friends, just stop the discussion for a moment and for an experiment, institute this rule. "Each person can speak up for himself only *after* he has first restated the ideas and feelings of the previous speaker accurately, and to that speaker's satisfaction."

Rogers also points out that successful summarizing requires careful listening, which tends to take the emotion out of a discussion or conversation, by making differences among participants more rational and understandable.

Paraphrasing

The essence of paraphrasing is to "feed back to the client the essence of what has just been said by shortening and clarifying client comments" (Ivey, 1994, p. 100). Paraphrases are briefer than summaries and hence do not interrupt the clients' train of thought to the same extent. They are very useful in demonstrating to your clients that you are really hearing them. When you paraphrase, you offer your clients an invitation to clarify and expand their stories. As in summaries, we recommend that, when you paraphrase, you include your clients' key words.

As an example, let's return to the case of Tom. Instead of summarizing, Peter might have chosen to simply paraphrase what Tom had said: "So, you got fed up with your parent's 'old-fashioned' curfew and stayed out all night." Tom would then have had a chance to modify Peter's understanding.

You can use paraphrasing to move the conversation between you and your clients in a direction that you think more useful. As we saw in the previous chapter, once clients have described their difficulties, we explore what they would like to have different in their lives. Another paraphrase that Peter might have used with Tom would be: "So, you're not happy with the way things are going in your relationship with your parents; you want to see something different." This paraphrase would demonstrate to Tom that he was being heard and also serve as an invitation to begin thinking about an alternative, better future with his parents.

Our observations of students and workshop participants have shown us that, as practitioners become more experienced in solution building, they use more paraphrases and fewer summaries. With more experience, they seem to need fewer words to demonstrate that they are listening carefully and to invite clients to move in new directions.

The Use of Silence

Most beginning practitioners are very uncomfortable with silent pauses in interviews. Our experience is that silences tend to make new practitioners freeze. Freezing, a kind of performance anxiety, is the most common difficulty experienced by those learning interview skills, according to research by Epstein (1985); it seems to be tied to an inner sense of not having the ability to help clients. Epstein states that, in such circumstances, the beginner is apt to engage in destructive self-talk: "I can't do it. I'm making a fool of myself. Worse yet, the client knows that I don't know what I'm doing."

Writers about basic communication skills point out that what silence means to the client is almost always different from what an anxious practitioner takes it to mean. According to Benjamin (1987), silence may mean that the client is sorting out his or her thoughts, is confused or angry about the situation just described, or is simply taking a short breather from the work at hand. Benjamin believes it is important to respect client silences.

We agree. The solution-building approach calls for practitioners to increase their toleration for client silences. In Western societies, silence makes people uncomfortable. After five seconds, most people feel pressure to fill a silence by saying something—almost anything! If that is your tendency and you want to work with a solution-building approach, you have work to do. The questions that you will be asking—about clients' experiences, what they want to have happen differently in their lives, and what is already going well—require clients to do some hard thinking before they can put their responses into words. Often clients will be silent for a time, then say, "I don't know," and then fall silent again. If you give in to a tendency to fill the silence with your observations and suggestions, you will be resorting to the sort of questioning that the students used with Rosie in Chapter 1. If, on the other hand, you can tolerate the silence for a while—10, 15, or even 20 seconds sometimes—you will be surprised by clients' capacities to come up with answers. They will often surprise themselves, because they really did not know their answer until you asked the question. By remaining silent, you gave them an opportunity to work on the answer. Sometimes clients will interrupt the silence by saying, "That's a tough question." We recommend that you simply respond sympathetically, "Yes, it is; I know," and then continue your silence. At times, you can also compliment them for their hard work, and encourage them to continue working by asking additional questions.

Clients are also uncomfortable with silence. You can utilize that discomfort in your efforts to encourage clients' solution building. If you develop your capacity to remain silent, clients will soon learn that you do not intend to answer the questions for them, and they will feel pressure to struggle for their own answers.

There may be circumstances in which allowing the silence to continue is not productive. On rare occasions, by virtue of being human, you will do something in an interview that confuses or even offends the client; you might make an odd facial expression or ask a carelessly worded question. In response, the client may remain silent. On other occasions, you may be meeting with a mandated client—that is, a person pressured to be there against his or her wishes. Such a client may also be silent, especially at the beginning of the interview. In those situations, you may wish to use one or both of the two skills we discuss next.

Noticing Clients' Nonverbal Behavior

As we have seen, most clients take the measure of their practitioners partly by paying attention to their facial expressions, gestures, tone of voice, and eye contact. As an attentive practitioner, you will likely observe the same signals in your clients, because they too will convey meaning through nonverbal behavior. Clients who respond to a comment by smiling, or rolling their eyes, or looking off into space, or slouching down in the chair, or heaving a sigh, or crossing their legs and arms, or changing their tone of voice, or falling silent are communicating through these nonverbals as surely as if they were using words. When you are in tune with your clients, you will notice these nonverbals, the context in which they are used, the various patterns in which different clients use them, and any changes in those patterns. Having noticed such nonverbal signs, you can choose whether or not to mention them and explore their meaning.

Clients tend to use nonverbals in their own individual patterns and, therefore, the meaning of nonverbals must always be discerned in context. Note that, according to research, the nonverbals of clients cluster somewhat according to cultural group. Lum (1992), for example, states not only that people of color differ from the white population in their use of nonverbals such as eye contact and tone of voice but also that African Americans, Asian Americans, and Latinos exhibit distinctive patterns of nonverbal behavior. In our experience, it is useful to know these cultural patterns but, when you work with specific clients, you need to be aware that there are many differences within each cultural group as well. More generally, we believe that the possible meaning of client nonverbals is best understood within the client's total self-presentation, verbal and nonverbal. Most of us intuitively respond to others in a holistic fashion; that is, we respond on the basis of our interpretation of all their verbal and nonverbal messages. The same is true when we work professionally with clients. Ideally, we decide whether to explore a client's nonverbal cues, including their silences, on the basis of our sense of what the cues mean within the overall context of what the client is communicating at that point.

Self-Disclosing

If, as a practitioner, you employ self-disclosure, you "discuss your own personal observations, experiences, and ideas with the client" (Ivey, 1994, p. 280). There is wide variation among practitioners in their use of this technique. Some practitioners disclose their own feelings and experiences as a way to motivate and educate their clients. Others shy away from such practices, in the belief that they interfere with client self-determination and undermine client self-confidence.

We do not recommend that you tell clients about your own experiences. The notion behind solution building is that the first place—and usually the only necessary place—to look for solutions is within the client's frame of reference and past experiences. However, that does not mean that we think you ought never to reveal to clients what is on your mind; sometimes it is important to tell clients what you are thinking. For example, to the client who abruptly stops talking, you might say, "I notice that you have stopped talking; can you tell me what that means?" Likewise, if you hear a contradiction in what the client says, you might comment on it: "Earlier, you said things were pretty good between you and your mom. Just now, you said you are sick of her. I'm confused; can you explain to me how those two fit together?" Appropriate use of such self-disclosures can help us understand how clients are experiencing the interview and clarify clients' perceptions about their lives.

In summary, we believe that self-disclosure is best understood to mean using your senses, critical-thinking capacities, and thoughts as instruments in the solution-building process; it does not mean telling your clients that, for instance, you too broke curfew as a teenager or you too were sexually abused. While some practitioners argue that the latter type of self-disclosure enhances rapport, we believe it is unnecessary and impairs clients' ability to build their own solutions. It is also based on the questionable assumption that those who have experienced a particular tragedy can be most helpful to clients who are struggling with the same tragedy.

Noticing Process

As we noted in Chapter 1, practitioners in the helping professions have long emphasized that the first order of business in working with clients is to establish a relationship of trust with them. Several authors in the field explain that client trust is tied to perceived practitioner understanding (Benjamin, 1987; Carkhuff, 1987; Ivey, 1994). Unless clients believe that practitioners really understand what they are trying to say, they are unlikely to believe that the practitioners have their best interests at heart or can be of use to them.

Those authors also emphasize that understanding clients involves grasping both the content and process of client communications. *Content* refers to clients' verbal messages—the information they pass on about their struggles and the important people and events in their lives. *Process* refers to the way in which clients express the information—that is, to the affect or feelings that clients convey when they give information. This affect can be revealed by, for example, a client's posture (erect or slumping in a chair), degree of eye contact, pace of speech, use of silence, capacity to stay focused on the subject at hand, facial expression, and tone of voice.

Often client content and process match, and the helper paraphrases and summarizes the content for the client, to make sure that the two share the same understanding of the client and his or her situation. Sometimes, however, client content and process do not match. For example, a client who is estranged from her husband may say that her husband no longer matters to her, but have tears welling up in her eyes. When practitioners notice such apparent discrepancies between content and process, they can choose to address them through paraphrasing, summarizing, and self-disclosing, or just file them away in the back of their minds for the moment, perhaps to be addressed later in the interview. Practitioners' decisions about what to do should always be based on how best to help the client—that is, how to proceed so that the client feels the interview is moving in a constructive direction.

Noticing how a client presents information to you is important for another reason. All clients have their own interpersonal style. Some clients will demonstrate impressive clarity and organization of thought; others will have sparkle and a sense of humor; others may have a warm and caring manner. When you notice client qualities that might be useful to the client, it is a good idea to mention them. This skill, which we call complimenting, is our next topic.

Complimenting

Clients have personal qualities and past experiences that, if drawn upon, can be of great use in resolving their difficulties and creating more satisfying lives. These qualities—such as resilience in the face of hardships, a sense of humor, an organized mind, a capacity for hard work, a sense of caring toward others, the ability to see things from another's point of view, a willingness to listen to others, an interest in learning more about life and living—are *client strengths*. Useful past experiences are those in which the client either thought about or actually did something that might be put to use in resolving the current difficulties. These experiences are the client's *past successes*.

As an example of complimenting, consider the following interview between Peter and a young mother who was at risk of having her children taken from her by Protective Services because of suspected neglect:

PETER: I understand that Protective Services is investigating your home situation to see if they are satisfied that you are taking good care of your children.

ELLEN: That's true, and I'm really scared about it. I have four children: Bill who is 4, Stacey who's 3, and my twins who are 10 months. They are an incredible amount of work.

PETER: I'm sure they must be. It must be difficult for you having four preschoolers.

ELLEN: It is; I feel like I'm buried in diapers and dishes, and sometimes it seems like they all need me at the same time. What makes it even worse is that my husband is just starting out in business and is always gone.

PETER: [*complimenting*] You seem to be a mother who cares very much for her children, trying to get each of them what they need.

ELLEN: [tearfully] I do, but sometimes I just can't keep up, and things get pretty messy. But I try to take a little time with each one separately; every child needs to know that they're special.

PETER: [*continuing to compliment*] You seem to be working really hard at being a good mother. I'm interested in this idea of yours that each child is special. It seems like an important one to you. Did you figure this out on your own, or did you pick it up somehow from someone else?

ELLEN: My mom had lots of kids, and she got really sick with depression and had to be hospitalized. She never had time for us, much less for each one of us separately. So, I decided a long time ago that it would be different when I got my own children; I was going to pay separate attention to each one of them.

PETER: [*complimenting again*] I can see that you have done a lot of thinking about this. Tell me about exactly what you do when you treat each of your children as a special child.

Complimenting should not be motivated by a desire to be kind to clients. Instead, it should be *reality-based,* in the sense that it is derived from what the client communicates to you through words or client process. As you can see from Peter and Ellen's conversation, compliments are often used to reinforce in the client's mind what is important to the client.

When complimenting was first introduced at the Brief Family Therapy Center (BFTC) in Milwaukee, compliments were mainly used at the end of the interview, to draw clients' attention to strengths and past successes that might be useful in achieving their goals. Little by little, however, practitioners turned to complimenting throughout sessions, because the procedure seems to help clients grow more hopeful and confident. As you will likely find for yourself, in-session complimenting also helps to uncover more information about client strengths and successes. If complimented, a client usually nods in agreement, which tells you that he or she shares this perception. You are then in a position to follow up with more questions about what else has happened in the client's life that supports the compliment.

There are several types of compliments. A *direct compliment* is a positive evaluation or reaction by the practitioner in response to the client. An example of a positive evaluation is Peter's comment to Ellen in their dialogue: "You seem to be a mother who cares very much for her children." If a client who is struggling to stop drinking tells you that he or she has not had a drink in four weeks, you might yell "Wow!" That reaction is also a direct compliment. We prefer to use positive evaluations sparingly and positive reactions frequently. Both types of direct compliments are best used when they reflect what the client values.

An *indirect compliment* is a question that implies something positive about the client. One way to indirectly compliment is to ask for more information about a desired outcome stated by the client. For example, Peter might ask Ellen, "How have you managed to make the household so calm?" Another is to imply something positive through a relationship; that is, the practitioner asks the client to answer a question from the vantage point of another person or persons. Peter might ask Ellen: "If your children were here and I were to ask them what you do to be a good mother to them, what do you suppose they would say?" And a third is to imply that the client knows what is best, as Peter did when he asked Ellen: "How did you know that it is important for you to treat each of your children as though they are special?" Indirect complimenting is preferable to direct complimenting because its questioning format leads clients to discover and state their own strengths and resources.

Finally, clients may use a *self-compliment.* They might say: "I decided to quit using cocaine because I got smart." Or: "I decided that, since I was going to school, I might as well do some studying." Your job as a practitioner is to recognize such compliments as possible signs of progress and to reinforce them with indirect compliments: "Did it surprise you that you decided to do that?" "Is that new for you?" "Has it been difficult?" "Is that something you can continue to do?"

Many clients accept compliments easily; others downplay or even reject them. When practitioners begin to give more compliments, it is common for them to feel awkward and anxious about how their clients will respond. If you feel anxious, remember that the first goal in giving compliments is for clients to notice their positive changes, strengths, and resources; it is not necessary for clients to openly accept the compliments.

Affirming Clients' Perceptions

Felix Biestek (1957), a well-known writer on the development of trust, long ago formulated several important principles of relationship building. One of the principles he writes about is the purposeful expression of feelings. Biestek believes that every request for professional help is accompanied by feelings that the client needs to purposefully express if he or she is to feel understood and come to trust the practitioner.

Many in the field have taken this principle and made it the centerpiece of their work with clients. Here are some quotations from basic texts about the importance of understanding clients' feelings in order to help them:

> Underlying clients' words and behaviors are feelings and emotions. The purpose of reflection of feeling is to make these implicit, sometimes hidden, emotions explicit and clear to the client. (Ivey, 1994, p. 119)

> Responding to feelings is the most critical single skill in helping. (Carkhuff, 1987, p. 99)

> The skill of reflection of feeling is aimed at assisting others to sense and experience the most basic part of themselves—how they really feel about another person or life event. (Ivey, 1994, p. 119)

Implicit in these quotations is the belief that feelings represent the core aspect of human beings and that clients must come to understand their feelings before they can move on to solve their problems. Practitioners of this persuasion, therefore, consistently try to tune in to clients' feelings and to label them: "You seem angry"; "You seem really scared." Such practitioners also note whether clients can express their feelings with appropriate intensity or whether they repress them. In addition, these practitioners pay attention to whether or not clients can own their feelings as authentic ways of reacting to the important people and events in their lives or whether they shift responsibility for their feelings to the provocations of others: "My mom makes me so mad because she criticizes all my friends."

Contrary to this view, we have not found that our clients regularly need to focus on and own their feelings (especially so-called repressed feelings) in order to feel understood or to make progress. However, we have found that they need to be asked about their perceptions, including those related to the nature of their problems; what attempts they have made to overcome their problems; what they want to have happen differently in their lives; what has worked for them already; and what has not. *Webster's New World Dictionary* (1974, p. 1054) defines perception this way:

> 1. a) the act of perceiving or the ability to perceive; mental grasp of
> object, qualities, etc. by means of the senses; awareness; comprehension
> b) insight or intuition, or the faculty for these 2. the understanding,
> knowledge, etc. got by perceiving, or specific idea, concept, impression,
> etc. so formed.

So defined, a perception is some aspect of a person's self-awareness or awareness of his or her life. This awareness is achieved through the senses, the person's capacity to think and feel, and his or her intuition. Perceptions, then, are holistic; they include a person's thoughts, feelings, behaviors, and experiences. Practitioners learn about a client's perceptions by asking the client to describe them, in words. Consequently, we believe that the client's descriptions of his or her perceptions may productively be thought of as the interplay between the client's experiences and frame of reference (that is, the concepts the client uses to organize and give meaning to his or her experiences).

Clients not only need to be asked about their perceptions in order to feel understood. They also need affirmation of their perceptions; they need some indication that the practitioner can understand how the clients think, feel, act, or experience life. Insoo had this point dramatically reconfirmed to her recently, when she was interviewing a young prostitute who was dying of AIDS. The woman told Insoo that staff members at the AIDS clinic where she was receiving treatment were pressuring her to confront her brothers for their past sexual abuse of her. She, on the other hand, wanted to concentrate on dying well, which, to her, meant getting her mother to understand that she was a good person and spending her last days in her own tiny apartment instead of the hospice that the clinic staff preferred. Insoo explored and affirmed the perceptions that led her to these wishes and explored with her how she could go about making her wishes happen. She eventually chose to write her mother a letter, because she was too weak to travel, and stayed in her apartment until she died.

If you wish to affirm your clients' perceptions, you can do so in several ways. You might simply demonstrate acceptance through nods and short statements ("uh-huh," "sure," "of course"), or you might choose an unmistakable affirmation: "From all that you have told me, I can understand why you want to spend your last days in your own apartment."

In reflecting on Biestek's principle of the purposeful expression of feelings, we have come to the conclusion that, although feelings are an important part of client perceptions, they are no more important than client thoughts, attitudes, beliefs, or past behaviors. Rather than separating out and labeling any particular aspect of a client's perceptions, we have found it more useful to ask about, and listen to, their perceptions as holistically as we can. Once we have grasped their perceptions, we proceed to affirm these perceptions as meaningful. We believe that, if you choose to do the same, you will be demonstrating respect for client perceptions, treating each client as an individual, encouraging your clients to value and trust their ways of experiencing their lives, and leading them to trust you and enter into a productive working relationship with you.

Exploring and affirming clients' perceptions, as clients describe them, constitutes a major share of what is done in solution-building interviews. Consequently, almost every interview excerpt that we present in this book illustrates this skill. In fact, the excerpt from Peter's interview with Ellen is an example of how compliments may be used to affirm client perceptions. Reread that dialogue and look for examples. Notice, too, how Peter continuously asks Ellen to expand on her statements and give more description of both her situation and how she has chosen to deal with it. We believe that these requests for more description, in and of themselves, are a further example of affirming the client's perceptions; by simply asking for a client's perceptions and then accepting them as information, a practitioner affirms their importance. Finally, the examples of empathy in the next section also illustrate how to affirm the client's perceptions.

Before moving on, we must address a question that often arises in our workshops and classes. The question is usually posed this way: "Do you always affirm client perceptions? What if a client is contemplating suicide as a way to escape a grinding depression? Or threatening to beat up a romantic rival? Or considering hitting a misbehaving child?" The implication of this question seems to be that the questioner cannot conceive of affirming anything at all related to such client thoughts and would be inclined to immediately use education and confrontation in order to turn the client away from transforming such thoughts into actions. We will discuss our approach to clients who are contemplating such extreme actions at much greater length in Chapter 9. Our basic principle is that, even in such cases, we would proceed from a posture of not knowing. We have found that clients considering extreme actions—suicide, beating up a rival, or hitting—do so within a context of several associated perceptions. When explored and understood, these perceptions help both us and them to make sense of what is prompting them to talk this way. Therefore, we recommend that, when you meet with such clients, you respectfully ask them to provide information about their extreme perceptions. For example, to a client who thinks of hitting a child, you might say, "What's happening in your life that tells you that hitting might be helpful in this situation? What else? How would doing that be helpful? Does it work?" And you could continue: "If you were to decide to do that, what would be different between you and your child? What would be different between you and your other children? What would be different between you and the courts?"

As we have said, such questions serve to make sense of what is driving the client to talk about such extreme actions. When we have heard the client's story, we often find ourselves saying: "After what you have just told me about what is going on around your house, I can understand how you might feel like hitting your child at times, even though you are saying it doesn't work for you." Many practitioners might assume that affirming such a client perception could increase the chances of the client taking such action or that we are condoning behavior such as hitting a child. Ironically, though, we have found just the opposite. As clients are respectfully asked about the perceptions that surround possibilities such as suicide and beating up or hitting others, they usually are more able to relax, and they themselves turn the conversation toward working on less extreme possibilities.

Empathy

Another principle of relationship building formulated by Biestek (1957) is that the practitioner must be capable of controlled emotional involvement, which Biestek defines as being sensitive to the client's feelings, understanding the meaning of these feelings, and responding appropriately. This principle calls upon the practitioner to communicate at the level of feelings as well as thoughts. For example, to a client who has described the ways in which her spouse relentlessly ridicules her for being overweight, the practitioner might say: "His comments must really hurt; they must cut you to the bone." Many beginning practitioners—and, for that matter, many who are experienced—find developing and using this skill very challenging. Some practitioners are never able to connect with clients at that level; this inability is thought by many in the field to be a deficiency.

Biestek's principle comes closest to what other writers (Keefe, 1976; Benjamin, 1987) refer to as empathy. Empathy is an elusive quality; it seems to defy precise conceptualization. (Some authors, including Benjamin, prefer to illustrate its meaning by means of stories.) Empathy is thought to be a consequence of imaginatively entering the client's world of thinking, feeling, and acting. It is not the same thing as sympathy, which means having the same feelings and concerns as the client; in other words, it does not mean that the practitioner identifies with the client and becomes lost in the client's world. Rather, the practitioner works to explore and adopt the client's frame of reference, without ever losing the inner sense that he or she is a separate person from the client. According to Carl Rogers (1957, p. 99), to feel empathy is "to sense the client's private world as if it were your own, but without ever losing the 'as if' quality" and "to sense the client's anger, fear, or confusion without getting bound up in it."

All of those who write about empathy emphasize that being empathic with another requires practitioners to feel or be moved by the client's story; this brings us back to Biestek's idea of controlled emotional involvement. Practitioners must do more than cognitively comprehend what the client communicates; they must also understand the client's story with all of their being—emotions as well as thoughts. (Some practitioners refer to empathic statements as "from the heart" statements.) The more practitioners can achieve such empathic understanding, the more natural it will be for them to respond to the client with empathic statements. And, as many in the field emphasize, the more practitioners are able to use empathic statements, the more the client will feel cared about and fully understood.

Lambert and Bergin (1994, p. 164) state that there has long been virtual unanimity in the field that "accurate empathy, positive regard, non-possessive warmth, and congruence or genuineness" are essential for building a "working alliance" with clients and for client progress in general. However, while research findings continue to confirm the importance of accurate empathy, they are becoming "more ambiguous than once thought" (Lambert & Bergin, 1994, p. 165). The findings do indicate that practitioner empathy is positively related to client satisfaction with the practitioner-client relationship. In addition, findings indicate that empathy is positively related to client progress when progress is measured by clients' estimates of progress. However, when progress is measured by some more objective means—for example, a standardized test or direct observation of client change—practitioner empathy seems less important.

We believe that empathy, like any other skill, can be overemphasized. We definitely do not recommend that you use the type of empathy that is sentimental or that tends to amplify negative feelings. For example, we do not recommend that you repeat statements such as: "You're really hurting now; this seems to be a deeply discouraging time in your life." We have found that such statements tend to drive clients further into those aspects of their lives that are least useful for generating positive change. On the other hand, we are persuaded that a demonstration of empathic understanding is required and helpful on many occasions when clients are describing events and their personal reactions. At these times—for example, when a client is describing what is difficult and painful in a particular relationship—we recommend an empathic affirmation such as: "I can see that things between you and him are very discouraging right now." You can then move on to explore what the client is doing to mobilize his or her strengths in order to get through this difficult time. The exchange between Peter and Ellen earlier in the chapter provides another example of this approach to empathic understanding.

As a practitioner, you can demonstrate empathic understanding of your clients in many ways—for instance, by a knowing nod of your head; by paraphrases and summaries that convey your understanding of the significance of what the client is saying; by respectful silences; and by adopting a compassionate tone of voice. You can find examples of verbal empathic skills throughout this book; nonverbal skills are illustrated on videotapes produced to accompany this book.

We have discussed empathy here as though it is a separate skill. You should understand, however, that its presence or absence in your work with clients is inseparable from the other skills described in this chapter. Your nonverbals, paraphrases, and affirmations of client perceptions can all convey a sense of empathy or the lack of it. Empathy, like any other aspect of the client-practitioner interaction, is best thought of as one ingredient existing among many. Client-practitioner interaction is like a cake. Once the cake is baked, we cannot separate the sugar from the flour. What is more, the taste of the cake depends upon the combination of all the ingredients. Likewise, the taste of the interaction for the client—the client's sense of whether or not the practitioner really understands and is being useful—largely depends on the combination of skills used by the practitioner.[2]

Returning the Focus to the Client

Experience at BFTC—and at other facilities around the world where the procedures described in this book are in use—confirms that many clients are able to create more satisfying and productive lives. They do so by developing well-formed goals and taking steps to turn these goals into realities. In both parts of this process, the client does the work; usually, the client needs to do something different than in the past.

Our observations also indicate that practically all clients, when describing their problems and attempting to articulate what they want to achieve through their relationship with the practitioners, talk about what they would like *others*

---

[2] Of course, what the client brings to the interaction also influences how the client perceives the practitioner's responses. But practitioners who have integrated the listening and responding skills into their way of being with clients will listen for, and attempt to respond appropriately to, these differences among clients.

to do differently. They tend to talk as though they are powerless in their circumstances and at the mercy of others. They make statements like these:

- "My kids are lazy. They don't want to get up in the morning and they lay around a lot during the day just watching TV. They don't seem to realize that I need help sometimes."
- "I wish my parents would join the 1990s; I'm 15 and they still have this ridiculous curfew that I have to be in by 10 o'clock at night during the week."
- "My child is doing very poorly in school. I think a lot of it has to do with the fact that he has special learning needs which his teachers don't know how to handle."
- "If my boss would only stop talking down to me. Sometimes he treats me like I'm a child."
- "My husband has a horrible temper and, when he loses it, he hits out. I think it is because he was kicked around a lot when he was growing up. When he gets mad like that, I get really scared because I don't want to get hit."

We think it is important to listen to and respect these perceptions, because they represent how clients view these parts of their lives at the time they are speaking. But we also think that, in order to move from a sense of powerlessness to a sense of empowerment, clients will have to shift their focus. They will have to focus less on what they do not appreciate about other people and their current circumstances and more on what they want to have happen differently in the situation and how they see themselves participating in a solution. As practitioners, we can often help clients make this shift. Here are several sample questions you can ask to invite your clients to return the focus to themselves:

- "What gives you hope that this problem can be solved?"
- "When things are going better, what will be happening differently? What will others notice you doing differently?"
- "What's it going to take to make things even a little bit better?"
- "If your boss were here and I were to ask him what you could do differently to make it just a little easier for him not to talk down to you, what do you think he would say?"
- "Suppose a miracle happened tonight while you were sleeping and the problem we are talking about was solved by tomorrow morning. Assume, too, that you didn't know that the miracle had happened, because you were asleep. What is the first thing you would notice that would tell you that things were better? What would others notice about you that would tell them you were doing better?"

- "Are there times already in your life which are like this miracle you are describing?"

Some of these questions explicitly ask clients to shift their focus to themselves, while others do so implicitly. Because inviting clients to make this shift is such an important part of what de Shazer (1994) calls the change from problem talk to solution talk, you will find many examples of such questions throughout this book.

Amplifying Solution Talk

Solution talk between client and practitioner addresses what aspects of life the client wants to be different and the possibilities for making those things happen. Much of the rest of this book will illustrate in detail how you can engage in solution talk with your clients. At the end of the previous section, we provided some examples of questions that invite clients to engage in a conversation around building solutions. You will find that some clients more readily accept the invitation than others. Clients who are reluctant are more insistent on returning to problem talk, which focuses on what they do not like about their lives and other people. Most clients, however, will begin to participate in solution talk when you lead in that direction. Your task is to notice this switch to solution talk and to encourage the client to provide as much detail as possible. In the following example, Insoo invited a young man (Kenrick) to amplify what would be happening differently in his life after his problem (using drugs) was solved:

INSOO: So when your problem is solved, what would be different?

KENRICK: I wouldn't do drugs at all.

INSOO: So what would you do when you have these cravings?

KENRICK: Do something constructive so I won't think about it, which is just do anything, play basketball, just run and just do something just to get it off me, or just go talk to somebody, you know.

INSOO: That helps?

KENRICK: Yeah.

INSOO: [recalling his comment that he was drug-free during a previous stay in the hospital] Is that what helped when you were in the hospital?

KENRICK: Yeah, you know, just make jokes or something.

INSOO: Making jokes helps?

KENRICK: Yeah, when you sit there talking to a bunch of people and everybody is laughing 'cause [of] something you said, you know, it makes you feel good; then it's like you don't need no drugs to do that.

INSOO: I see. Do you have a good sense of humor?

KENRICK: Yeah.

INSOO: Is that what other people tell you?

KENRICK: Yeah.

INSOO: Really? Have you always been that way?

KENRICK: Yeah.

INSOO: Ah-ha. And you are saying that helps you?

KENRICK: Yeah, it helps me.

INSOO: What else helps you to cope with the cravings?

KENRICK: My kids.

INSOO: Your kids? How do they help you?

KENRICK: 'Cause they remind me of my craving. It's like when I be around them, you know, I be thinking about some dirty stuff to do, to go get some drugs, and my oldest son he talks to me—you know, when these cravings come up —and it's like I look at him and pay attention to him, and then I do something constructive with him and then while we do something it's like . . . [silence]

INSOO: Like what? What constructive thing?

KENRICK: We write his name, we do numbers, ABCs, you know.

INSOO: Do you? You teach him how to?

KENRICK: Yeah.

INSOO: Oh, OK. That helps?

KENRICK: Yeah.

INSOO: And you like doing that?

KENRICK: Yeah.

INSOO: [*noticing affection in his voice*] He likes that, apparently?

KENRICK: Yeah. He does.

INSOO: You must love him very much.

KENRICK: Yeah, I love all my kids very much.

In this dialogue, Insoo invited Kenrick to talk about what his life would be like when his problem was solved. Noticing both that he had some ideas about how his life would be different and that he was putting the focus on *what he would be doing differently,* she worked hard to have him amplify these differences. She was not content with his statement that his life would be different because he would not be doing drugs. She asked for more information: What would he do when he had cravings? Kenrick answered in more detail and more concretely: He would "play basketball," "run," "talk to somebody," and "make jokes." Insoo asked further how doing these things—in particular, making jokes—would be helpful. Kenrick responded by amplifying more; he explained that, when others laugh at his jokes, he can feel good without using drugs. Insoo also asked, "What else helps you to cope with the cravings?" Kenrick was able to add even more information, this time about doing constructive things with his children.

In solution building with clients, you must work very hard to amplify any solution talk that your clients offer. Solution talk is very useful to counter the sense of powerlessness that many clients are experiencing when they first come for services. At first, clients focus on their problems and how difficult these make their lives. Once the practitioner invites clients to talk in detail about what they want to have different in their lives and how that might happen, they become more hopeful and even confident about their possibilities. To a certain degree, then, empowerment is a matter of perception; it is a state of mind that is heightened by clients' solution talk.

Finally, you should reread the dialogue between Kenrick and Insoo and look for examples of the basic skills we have discussed in this chapter. There are examples of careful listening, echoing, open questions, paraphrases, noticing the client's nonverbals, compliments, affirming the client's perceptions, empathy, and keeping the focus on the client. Even in this brief segment of dialogue, Insoo integrates practically all of the basic skills into her work.

Leading From One Step Behind

We have noted repeatedly that we try to work in ways that allow clients to be the experts about their own experiences and what these mean. However, we are not encouraging you to be passive with your clients and to wait patiently for them to express themselves. Quite emphatically, we believe that you can be most useful to your clients when you are active and, in a certain sense, lead your clients. However, we also believe that you will lead best when you *lead from one step behind* (Cantwell & Holmes, 1994). In other words, you must adopt a posture of not knowing and develop interviewing skills that allow clients to provide information about themselves and their situation. We have covered several of these basic skills in this chapter. In our experience, practicing these skills promotes client trust, confidence, and hopefulness about the future.

CHAPTER *4*

Getting Started: How to Pay Attention to What the Client Wants

Tell me and I'll forget. Show me, and I may not remember.
Involve me, and I will understand.
(Native American saying)

In Chapter 2, as you may recall, we identified several stages of the solution-building process: describing the problem; developing well-formed goals; exploring for exceptions; formulating and delivering useful feedback to clients; and measuring and amplifying client progress. In Chapters 4–9, we will proceed sequentially through these stages and discuss the skills appropriate to each. We will demonstrate the skills with dialogues from cases we have encountered.

In this chapter we focus on how you can get started with clients. We limit our discussion to the conversation between a practitioner and a client. We believe it is unnecessary here to describe the intake information forms that agencies ask new clients to complete. Many parts of these forms are self-explanatory; other parts are so tailored to the needs and outlooks of particular agencies that a textbook description of them is of limited value. No matter what agency you may work at, your orientation to that agency will include a discussion of its intake forms.

When You First Meet Your Client
Names and Small Talk

As a practitioner, you would rarely meet a client for the first time without having at least some information about the client and his or her concerns. Typically, you would get a completed intake form or some referral information before seeing a client. That information minimally would include the client's name and some data about the client's family, school, and work contexts. Different practitioners use that information in different ways; we think it is important to use it in ways that set a tone of respect and empowerment right from the beginning. As a result, when introducing ourselves to clients, we ask them how they would like to be addressed. We also tell them that we would be comfortable being called Insoo or Peter. We think it is a good idea in the beginning to ask some questions about how clients spend most of their workday time. While some practitioners view such questions mainly as icebreakers, which make it easier for the client and practitioner to get started together, we have also found that they begin to uncover useful solution-building information. Often, in answering these questions, clients begin to reveal what and who are important to them, as well as some areas of strength. Here is an example of how Peter began with a client we will call Christine.

PETER: Hello. Welcome. [motioning toward one of the empty chairs] Please take a seat over here.

CHRISTINE: Thanks.

PETER: [looking at the intake form in his hand] I see from what you wrote down here that your name is Christine Williams. To start out with, what would you like me to call you? Christine? Ms. Williams? Something else?

CHRISTINE: Well, my friends call me Christi; I like that.

PETER: OK. And I'd be comfortable if you would call me Peter. Is that OK with you?

CHRISTI: Yeah, I think I could do that.

PETER: OK, that's settled for now anyway. We can make changes on it later if we decide we want to. So, Christi, tell me, how do you like to spend your time?

CHRISTI: Ah, well, a lot of my time goes to my college classes, but right now that is not what I enjoy doing. I like to travel, going to different places. I like to socialize. I like to read. [an embarrassed laugh] I like pleasure reading, not the reading for my courses right now. And I like the outdoors, biking and playing tennis. Mostly, right now, I like to socialize.

PETER: Socialize? You mean with friends?

CHRISTI: Yeah, both with friends and my family. Right now, I'm spending a lot of time with my friends, maybe too much.

PETER: So you like to talk with people. Is that something you are good at?

CHRISTI: [laughs] Yeah, people like to talk to me, both about fun things and their problems. They seem to want to come to me and discuss what's bothering them. I try to help them.

PETER: Is that right?

CHRISTI: Yeah, I don't put them down for their problems, and I think I'm a pretty good problem solver.

PETER: Is that right? Do they tell you that?

CHRISTI: [smiling] Yeah, they do; they thank me too. I guess that's a main reason that I want to be a social worker.

PETER: Yeah. Already I can begin to understand what you say; you seem to have a real cheerful and easy way about you. I can see that you would be easy to talk to.

CHRISTI: Thanks, but that's part of the reason I'm here; I'm spending too much time with other people and not enough with my school work; that's what I really want to talk about.

Peter's interview with Christi occurred in a professional setting. Sometimes, however, you might find yourself interviewing clients on their turf—for example, in their homes. Insoo has written about how to get started with clients in this setting (Berg, 1994, pp. 22–23). She suggests that, once invited inside a client's home, the practitioner can take notice of something nice or attractive or something the client has clearly put a lot of effort into. The practitioner can also ask questions about the family pictures that he or she might see. Such observations and questions put the client into the role of expert and, at the same time, demonstrate respect for the client and uncover interests and strengths. Often, meeting clients where they live makes it easier to begin work, because the items on display will reflect what interests the clients and the practitioner can immediately begin to ask questions about those items. Usually, clients are also more relaxed, because they are in a familiar place.

Clarifying How You Work

Before you get too deeply into the client's concerns, it is a good idea to clarify how you prefer to organize your work-sessions with clients and to check out if that organization is acceptable. Adopting the approach developed at BFTC (de Shazer et al., 1986), we have found it useful to organize sessions by first interviewing clients about their concerns, goals, exceptions, and strengths. Once this information has been gathered, we like to take a 10-minute break, so as to formulate some end-of-session feedback based upon the information obtained. Sometimes we work with a team (with the prior permission of the clients); in that case, the team observes the interview through a one-way mirror and can help in developing the feedback. More often we work alone, and the break time allows us to collect our thoughts and decide what feedback would be most useful to the clients in building a solution. In either case, we regularly inform the clients how we prefer to work:

PETER: Before we get into your concern, let me tell you how I like to work and see if that is OK with you. What I'd like to do today is talk with you for about 30–40 minutes and then take a 10-minute break to think about what you told me.

During the break, if you want, you can get something to drink from the waiting area or you can stay here if you prefer. After 10 minutes or so, I'll be back with some feedback and possibly a suggestion or two for you. Is that OK?

CHRISTI: Sure, that's fine.

In our experience, clients are very accepting of how we wish to proceed. We will have more to say about the advantages of this approach in a later chapter.

Problem Description
Asking for Client Perceptions and Respecting Client Language

We want to remind you of the central message of Chapters 1–3, because it is critical to solution building. In order to work within the client's frame of reference, you must assume a posture of not knowing. You must ask for, listen to, and affirm the client's perceptions; as you do so, you take note of the words that the client uses.

We offer this reminder here because we are about to discuss how to explore the client's concerns. At this stage, it is especially tempting for practitioners to listen to clients with the ears of an expert. The helping professions, with their emphasis on problem solving, have all generated elaborate categorizations of possible client problems. Once educated in these, we can easily apply them and lose our focus on exploring the client's frame of reference. In the following dialogue, Peter works at taking a posture of not knowing in exploring Christi's concern:

PETER: So, how were you hoping I could help you? You said earlier that you came here today because you are spending too much time with other people and not enough with your school work.

CHRISTI: Well, ah, I have this disease that a lot of people tend to get in their fourth year of college—senioritis. That's what I have.

PETER: What tells you that you have senioritis?

CHRISTI: Um, I can see the change from my past three years; in this year, I'm just not motivated. I'm interested in my classes this year because they are my major classes, but it's like I'm tired and bored with the whole study process. So that's how it is; I'm just tired of it.

PETER: Um hum.

CHRISTI: Like, last year when I had a test or a paper, like, I would get really, really stressed out and devote all of my time to studying, or reading, or being on top of things. This year I don't get stressed out. It's not like I don't study but . . . but I don't study as much. . . . I guess I just don't care as much.

PETER: Uh, does that pretty much say it, or is there more? Is senioritis—your getting bored, not being motivated, not studying as much—or is there more?

CHRISTI: [slowly] I guess that's about it.

How Does the Problem Affect the Client?

As we said earlier, it is very tempting to assume that you know what the client's perceptions and experiences mean to the client. In the dialogue with Christi, it would be easy for Peter to assume that senioritis is a problem for her because she is studying less and getting poorer results and so she wishes that she were working as hard as she did last year. However, it is important to always go the next step and make sure the client tells you how this problem is a problem for him or her. Peter got some unexpected and important information when, instead of making assumptions, he asked further questions:

PETER: So, how is your senioritis a problem for you? [*checking out his assumption that Christi is probably doing worse*] By the way, are you doing worse in school this year or better?

CHRISTI: [laughing] That's what's weird; I'm doing the same. I can't figure it out. But it's not like I don't study at all; it's more like I'm not as into it as I used to be.

PETER: Yeah, that confuses me too. In what sense, then, is this a problem for you?

CHRISTI: Well, just because I feel guilty that I'm not stressed out about this—because, like, I'm getting this expensive education and I should be putting in as much time and getting as much out of this as I can. And I think last year I really did, and this year I'm just trying to get by or whatever.

PETER: So, part of what you would like to have different as a result of our talking is for you to get more out of this education?

CHRISTI: [hesitating] Well, yeah. Well, maybe I'd just like to maybe make the guilt go away.

PETER: Well, ah, what's more important? Is it more important to make the guilt go away or is it more important to get more out of the education?

CHRISTI: I think they are combined because, if I get more out of the education, then I think I won't be feeling guilty feelings.

PETER: Is there anything else that you can tell me that you would like to get out of coming here, besides what you already told me?

CHRISTI: Um, no.

Besides checking out his assumptions, Peter's questions serve a second purpose. They give Christi a chance to reflect carefully on her perceptions—at this point, perceptions about just how her problem affects her. We have found that client perceptions about anything are more or less fluid and shifting. Given time and open questions, clients regularly reflect, explore, rethink, struggle to put their thoughts into words, and sometimes shift their perceptions. Christi, for example, seems to have shifted—or expanded—her sense of her problem from lowered motivation for her studies to guilt. She feels guilty because she is not "getting as much out of this as I can" and because of the cost of college. (Later in the interview, she reported that her parents are paying for much of her tuition.)

Peter did not cause Christi's shift in the perception and definition of her problem by the interviewing techniques he used. Rather, we believe, her perception shifted as a result of the interaction between the two of them. Many clients seek help with problems or complaints that are poorly articulated; it is useful to them, and clarifying for us, to interact around the meaning of their problems. Peter's part in the interaction with Christi was to engage her in a conversation about how senioritis was a problem for her. His questions were an invitation to interact around the meaning of her problem. Her part was to accept the invitation and work to put her sense of senioritis into words. Their interaction led her to expand or reshape her definition of senioritis.

What Has the Client Tried?

It is a good idea to ask clients what they have tried so far to solve their problems. Clients usually have taken some steps to redress their problems, and these attempts generally have been more or less successful. Asking the question sends the message that we think that clients are *competent*—that is, they have the capacity to make some good things happen. Clients sometimes can tell us in concrete terms what they have done to try to make a difference. By adopting the posture of not knowing, we can learn about their successes and the strengths that they used to make the successes happen. Sometimes, clients describe a few things they have tried but indicate that nothing has worked very well. At other times, they say nothing has worked and they are at the end of their rope. Christi fell somewhere between the extremes:

PETER: Have you tried anything to cure yourself of this disease?

CHRISTI: Yeah, yeah. I don't really go to the library a lot anymore. Like, last year I used to go to the library every night, and this year I go maybe once a week. But I try to study in different places.

PETER: Is that helpful—to study in different places?

CHRISTI: Yeah, yeah, it is. I don't, like, try and say that I'm going to study, like, six hours tonight. Instead, if I feel like reading, I'll read; but if I don't, I don't make myself.

PETER: And if you don't make yourself, what's different?

CHRISTI: Well, I don't study.

PETER: Um hum, and does that help with the disease?

CHRISTI: Yeah, because before, when I didn't feel like studying, I would make myself, even though I didn't like it. But now, I just don't.

PETER: Hum, and you're doing about as well as you did last year. [she nods her head] So, I'm wondering again, how is this a problem for you?

CHRISTI: I guess because of the guilt. I'd like the guilt to go away. . . . I guess I really haven't done anything to make the guilt go away. . . . Maybe I could study more, but I don't feel like it.

PETER: Is there anything else you've tried?

CHRISTI: Uh, I can't think of anything else; I really should do something about this.

By this time, the dialogue had come full circle. Although Christi said that she had tried studying in different places, she was unable to identify how this was helpful. If she had, Peter would have spent time exploring this as a success and asking where she got the idea to do this and how she went about making it happen. Instead, having come back to the guilt and having heard there was nothing else that she'd tried, Peter chose to move on.

What Is Most Important for the Client to Work on First?

We frequently encounter clients who, when asked, will lay out problem after problem, until our heads are spinning. Usually this problem description is mixed in with theories about where the problems come from and how they are interconnected. It's little wonder that clients can feel overwhelmed. With such clients, there are several things a practitioner can do. We usually acknowledge how difficult things seem to the client and then simply ask, "Which of these is the most important to work on first?" When the client gives an answer—and practically all do—we follow up by asking, "What is happening in your life that tells you it's important to work on that first?" These questions illustrate again how solution building both works with client perceptions and respects client self-determination.

How To Work with Clients on What They Might Want

If practitioners ask how they can help, most clients, like Christi, respond by giving a description of their concerns or problems. In solution building, however, we are more interested in exploring what clients want to be different in their lives. Sometimes, clients begin to specify what they want to be different as they talk about their problems. Christi, for example, said she wanted to make the guilt go away and to get more out of her education. These statements are not well-formed goals yet, but they begin to articulate what differences she would like to see in her life.

Very often, however, clients talk about their problems in ways that give little or no indication of how they would like their lives to look when their problems are solved or partly solved. Instead, they seem intent on giving a detailed description of how horrible or difficult these problems are. They may also talk at length about what others are doing to make their lives difficult. Many clients are unable to specify strategies that they have tried to remedy their situation; when asked about what they have tried, they quickly return to problem description and the fallout for their lives. De Shazer (1994) calls this *problem talk*. By contrast, talk about what clients want to have happen differently in their lives is one aspect of *solution talk*. As a practitioner, you will first encounter the challenge of inviting your clients to shift from problem talk to solution talk at the point where they have had enough time to describe their problems in order to feel heard. For us, that point is usually 10–15 minutes into the first session.

Opening and sustaining a dialogue around what the client might want can be difficult in practice, especially if the client is being coerced by someone else to meet with you. Experience at BFTC and many other agencies suggests that three types of relationship may develop between yourself and your clients when you invite them to discuss what they want (de Shazer, 1988; Berg & Miller, 1992). As we examine each in turn, we will give examples of how the practitioner can respond in each situation.

Customer-Type Relationship

Definition and Illustration

In this type of relationship, the client and practitioner jointly identify a problem and/or a solution picture to work toward. "In addition, the client indicates that he sees himself as part of the solution and is willing to do something about the problem" (Berg & Miller, 1992, p. 22). We have found that we most readily develop this sort of relationship with clients who have chosen of their own accord to come to us for services. Such clients have often thought about what they want from their work with us and realize that getting what they want will require effort on their part.

The relationship that developed between Christi and Peter appears to be of this type. In their dialogue, Christi and Peter were successfully engaged in jointly identifying a complaint—senioritis. They also jointly identified an initial statement of a goal—making the guilt go away. However, we cannot tell from this dialogue whether Christi sees herself as a part of the solution—that is, whether she perceives what she might do differently to begin building a solution to her senioritis. Nevertheless, Christi and Peter have made a good beginning on this type of relationship; they have started a transition into solution talk by identifying, in general terms at least, what Christi wants. Moreover,

Christi does not view others as the source of her senioritis. Instead, she seems to view herself as part of any solution when she says, "I really should do something about this."

How to Respond

Peter did nothing out of the ordinary to invite Christi to begin solution talking. He first asked Christi for descriptions of her concerns and what she had already tried. While she was giving information, he listened carefully, to ascertain whether Christi was identifying a complaint or concern and whether she might want something different. When he heard that senioritis was her concern, he turned the dialogue toward her current perceptions of the meaning of senioritis. As she described these, he kept wondering to himself what the implications of these perceptions were for what she might want different in her life; he did not begin a detailed problem assessment. Together, they figured out that she did not necessarily want to study more or get higher grades, but rather was more interested in working on making the guilt go away. Having determined that Christi wanted something from their relationship, Peter knew they were now at a point where they could begin to develop well-formed goals. This is the next stage of solution building; we consider it in detail in the next chapter.

A Word of Caution

We want to emphasize that we are writing about a type of *relationship* between Christi and Peter; we have not chosen to label Christi as a particular type of client. For example, we chose not to describe or diagnose Christi as a cooperative or voluntary client. Although we have found it more likely that we will establish customer-type relationships with so-called voluntary clients than with involuntary clients, we cannot predict what will happen in any particular case. More importantly, thinking about clients as voluntary or involuntary or as cooperative or uncooperative can set up inaccurate expectations in practitioners' minds about the relative abilities of different clients to build solutions. We have found that we remain more hopeful about the possibilities for our clients when we resist thinking about them in such categories. It is more useful for our clients—and more empowering to us as practitioners—to think about what sort of a relationship is developing between us and our clients.

Complainant-Type Relationship

Definition and Illustration

This relationship develops between practitioner and client when they are able to jointly identify a complaint or problem but are not able to identify a role for the client in building a solution. Their dialogue reveals that the client can often describe in detail a problem and the importance of finding a solution; however, the client does not yet perceive that he or she is a part of the solution. Instead, the client usually believes that the solution will require changes on the part of someone else—perhaps a spouse, child, employer, friend, or co-worker. Here is an example:

INSOO: How can I help you?

ALICE: I sure hope there is hope for my son. He has never been what you would call a motivated child, but he has been worse lately. He is a smart kid, but does he study? No; he has always been on the lazy side. His father was like that—no ambition in life. Only thing he cared about was to hang out with his buddies and being wild. I'm afraid that my son is turning out to be just like his father. He won't come home on time, won't do anything to help out around the house. Now skipping school is all he does.

INSOO: So, how can I be of help to you?

ALICE: I don't know what to do with him any more. Whenever he doesn't come home, I'm a wreck worrying about him. There is lots of violence out there on the street. Mothers worry about stuff like that. Of course, his father is another story. When he ran off with that woman, all he saw was the woman. His kids didn't matter to him. I begged him to think about the kids, but does it matter? Hell, no. Now I'm stuck with working to keep the family together, but he doesn't appreciate anything I do.

In this example, Insoo and Alice are developing a joint understanding of a problem—the low motivation of Alice's son and his negative behaviors. However, there is nothing here yet to suggest that Alice sees what she can do differently to begin building a solution. At this point, she seems to feel powerless in the situation and problem talks about her son and his father.

Initially, conversations between us and our clients often resemble the Insoo-Alice dialogue. Indeed, as we first start to work with our clients, a complainant-type relationship is more likely to emerge than a customer-type relationship. This is not surprising; people who already perceive themselves as a major part of any solution are more able and likely to take steps on their own. What this means for you as a practitioner is that you have to be able to work with clients in the complainant-type relationship.

How to Respond

In a complainant-type relationship, the client will often want the practitioner to change the person (or persons) to whom the client attributes the problem—whether a spouse, a child, or a co-worker. If the problematic person is not already present, the client may ask whether the practitioner thinks it would be a good idea to meet that person. In other words, the client wants the practitioner to fix the other person.

In many situations, however, it is not realistic or possible for the troublesome party to come in for services. In that case, the client may want instruction from the practitioner on how to change the problematic person. Lastly, it is possible that the client only wants to express frustration and disappointment with the important people in his or her life and is not really looking to see anyone or anything changed. The client only wants the practitioner to listen.

It is a common belief in the field that clients who do not take responsibility for creating change in their lives need to be educated that blaming others is not going to solve their problems. Egan (1994, p. 161) writes that practitioners must learn "to challenge" clients' "failure to own problems" and "failure to define problems in solvable terms." We disagree. In our experience, challenging or confronting clients' current perceptions is not the most useful approach. We prefer to employ the skills outlined in Chapter 3. With these skills, we attempt to respect the client's current perceptions but at the same time to shift the focus from the problematic others to the client and any role that he or she might feel able to play in any positive change. In other words, through our questions, we invite the client to shift from problem talk to solution talk. Here is how Insoo began this process with Alice:

INSOO: I can see that you have a very serious problem on your hands, and I wonder what, do you suppose, needs to happen so that your son will be a little bit easier to live with?

ALICE: He has to go to school first. I keep telling him that he won't get anywhere in life without an education.

INSOO: That's a big one. I don't know how he is going to do that, but suppose, just suppose, that somehow he goes to school and stays in school. If that were to happen, what would your son be saying about how you are different with him now?

ALICE: He wants me to not nag him so much. That's what he probably would say—not nagging him and maybe even talking to him nice. Actually, once he starts going to school and doing what I tell him to do, there is no reason why I should nag him. He has no idea how much I worry about him.

INSOO: I'm sure you do. You seem to care about him very much.

Notice that Insoo did not challenge Alice's perception of the problem or who needed to do the changing. She accepted Alice's perception that it would be helpful to Alice if her son would do things differently. She then attempted to bring the focus of the conversation from what is wrong with the son (problem talk) to Alice herself, by asking Alice to suppose that her son were indeed different in the ways that she wanted. As Alice began thinking about this possibility, Insoo asked what differences Alice's son might see in her behavior toward him in that situation. Alice accepted the invitation to begin solution talking by saying she would probably "not nag him so much."

The first segment of Alice's conversation with Insoo was all problem talk. It suggests that a complainant-type relationship is in the making. We might expect that, at the end of the session, Alice would want Insoo to see her son and fix him. Or she might want nothing beyond verbalizing her frustrations. However, in the second segment, Alice accepts the invitation to put the focus on herself. It seems possible that, with more exploration, Alice might perceive some things she could do differently with her son, as steps toward a solution— things like nagging him less and "talking to him nice." The next task for Insoo would be to pick up on the solution talk and invite Alice to say more about precisely what it means to her to nag less and talk nice more and how she might conceivably go about doing this. This is a matter of developing well-formed goals, which we will address in the next chapter.

The Type of Relationship Can Change

As we have seen, Alice and Insoo at first develop a complainant-type relationship. However, when Insoo invites Alice to focus on herself, she responds favorably; this suggests the possibility of a shift to a customer-type relationship. We do not know for certain yet, because the solution talk is just beginning. However, Alice's responses do suggest that she may see some connection between what she does and what her son does. It is important to recognize that the type of relationship between practitioner and client can shift. In our view, that shift will depend as much on what the practitioner does in conversation with the client as on anything that the client may bring to the relationship. This point will become clearer when we discuss the visitor-type relationship.

What If the Client Refuses the Invitation to Solution Talk?

Students and workshop participants often ask us, "What do I do if the client does not accept my invitation to solution talk and continues to criticize and blame others for his or her problems?" This is an important concern, because many clients do just that.

There are several things you can do. One is to bring the focus back to the client periodically, by asking: "What is happening that tells you that this problem might be solved?" You can also ask: "How were you hoping I could help you with this problem?" Another possibility is to ask the client what the chances are of finding a solution, on a scale from 0 (no chance) to 10 (every chance), and then to ask the client to explain the scale value chosen. If the client seems overwhelmed by his or her problems, you can turn to coping questions. We will consider these ways of responding in later chapters, especially Chapters 7–9.

Visitor-Type Relationship

Definition

In this relationship the worker and client are not able to jointly identify a complaint or goal on which to work (Berg & Miller, 1992). The client does not perceive a problem on which he or she wants to work with the practitioner or feels that someone else has a problem. Frequently, clients who have been pressured into services—for example, by the courts, Protective Services, the schools, or parents—are predisposed to develop this type of relationship.

Practitioners regularly tell us that their most difficult cases are those in which a visitor-type relationship develops. The practitioners feel frustrated that they and their clients do not even agree on what the problem is, much less what to do about it. In visitor-type relationships, our focus as practitioners remains the same—to find out what the client might want from the relationship with us. The best way to describe how we think and work in these situations is to look at a case.

Beth: Background Information

Recently, Insoo was asked to consult on the case of a 15-year-old, whom we'll call Beth Visser. Even before Insoo met the client or was given any background information about the case, she was told that both social services and her parents had had it with Beth. The social worker told Insoo that Beth had "burned all her bridges," that she would most likely "end up in a treatment center for a long time," and that she certainly needed it. Clearly, the worker was very frustrated with Beth and unsatisfied with how the case was turning out, despite the countless hours she had devoted to problem solving with Beth.

The social worker described Beth as having a core problem—being "uncontrollable, impulsive, and manipulative." The worker also described the many things she had tried—with considerable expertise—from her problem-solving perspective to change Beth's core problem. She had "tried to talk some sense into" Beth by pointing out her mistakes; reasoned with her; pointed out inconsistencies between Beth's claims and the facts; threatened to send her into residential treatment; cajoled her; recommended probation and seen her placed on probation for a year; arranged for individual therapy with a psychologist; arranged for in-home treatment with another therapist, who worked with the whole family; and placed her in a treatment foster home. These increasingly restrictive and costly measures brought no real success in helping Beth stop her destructive behavior. The social worker was understandably frustrated and discouraged.

The social worker and others involved in Beth's case believed that all these attempts failed because of Beth's lack of cooperation. Moreover, they agreed that her destructive behavior itself was caused by an underlying depressive tendency. Consequently, they believed that the only remaining treatment option was long-term, intensive individual therapy in a residential setting.

Accordingly, when Insoo encountered the case, the worker was seeking approval and funding from the court to pay for this expensive, long-term service. She was hoping to place Beth in an out-of-state institution known to treat difficult adolescent cases. The worker favored an institution that was far away and relied on restrictive measures, because Beth had a history of running away and threatening suicide.

The latest crisis in Beth's case had occurred the previous evening, when police called at the Visser home after Beth reported child abuse at the hands of her father. Mr. Visser was handcuffed, taken into police custody, finger-printed, and finally released on bond. In the meantime, Beth was taken to the hospital emergency room, examined, and released. She showed no evidence of physical abuse, such as broken skin or bruises. The worker decided that Beth would stay with a friend overnight until something more permanent could be worked out. The next day, Mr. and Mrs. Visser requested out-of-home placement for Beth—immediately!

Insoo was invited to accompany the worker to Beth's school, where the worker planned to interview Beth about the previous evening's events. The interview took place in the principal's office; the social worker took the lead:

SOCIAL WORKER: So I understand there was another big fight with your parents last night. Your parents are pretty upset with you. What happened?

BETH: It's not my fault. My father pushed me against the wall for no reason. He always pushes me around. My friend was there, and she saw it too. You can ask her. My mom always sides with my dad but I'm telling you the truth. My dad pushed me against the wall for no reason at all. All I said was I wanted to go out and wanted some money. That's no reason to push me so hard that my head is busted open. I think it's child abuse.

WORKER: I saw the police report, and that's not what it says. Now, why do you think your dad hit you?

BETH: See, nobody believes me. Everybody says it's my fault.

WORKER: You know, Beth, you said there was blood on your head, but the police and the hospital reports say there is no medical evidence that your skin was broken.

BETH: [starting to cry and burying her head in her hands] Everybody is against me and nobody believes me. Even my grandma says it's my fault, but I'm telling you that my dad pushed me. Ask my friend, Melodie, she was there and saw the whole thing. My dad pushed her, too.

WORKER: Well, it's hard to believe you. You don't always tell the truth and, this time, the hospital report says there is no evidence of blood anywhere. Well, you can't go home now, and we will have to find a temporary place for you to stay.

BETH: [continuing to cry] Everybody is against me. Now I have no place to go, and I am not going to a foster home again. They treated me like I was a pet or something.

WORKER: Don't you think you should be more honest about what happened? Remember how much trouble you got yourself into when you lied about the rape? Wouldn't it be better to be honest about what happened? So, what did really happen?

BETH: Nobody believes me. I am telling you the truth. This time my dad pushed me so hard my head cracked open, and I had a towel against my head and I saw the blood on the towel. He hit me with a closed fist on this side of my head. [pointing to the right side of her head]

WORKER: That's not what the report says. The police report says your dad admitted hitting you with an open hand.

BETH: That's a lie. You've got to believe me. I had to have a towel on my head [putting her right hand on the right side of her head] and, when I took it off, there was blood on it.

WORKER: Beth, you have to be honest about these things.

BETH: [starting to cry again] See, everybody is against me. Nobody believes me, but I'm telling you the truth. You've got to believe me because I'm telling you the truth.

WORKER: I don't know what to believe anymore. Besides, I will have to find you a place to stay temporarily until we figure out what's best for you.

BETH: I want to go home, but I know my parents won't take me back. They are mad at me just because I stood up for my rights. I had to call the police, but my grandma says I shouldn't have done that. She won't even talk to me now. Everybody blames me now. Nobody cares about me.

WORKER: I'm trying to do what is best for you, Beth. And your parents say they don't want you home anymore. It means we have to find a place for you.

BETH: I don't want to go to no foster home. If I end up in a foster home again, I will run away or kill myself.

As the exchange continued, Beth became increasingly defensive and stuck with her original story. The more defensive she became, the more the worker pointed out the facts from the police and hospital reports. Soon the exchange felt more like a tug-of-war than a useful conversation. Clearly, neither Beth nor the worker felt understood, and both became increasingly frustrated as they remembered that their talks had ended in the same way before.

How to Respond: Pay Attention to the Client's Perceptions

Cases such as Beth's—long-term cases that practitioners traditionally label as chronic, multiproblem, or difficult cases—present an enormous challenge. Despite the most careful assessments and the best practitioner intentions, such clients often seem uncooperative. They do not follow through on the interventions that practitioners have carefully designed. Consequently, most practitioners now expect resistance from many clients, and it has become standard practice in the field to write textbooks that teach beginning practitioners how to recognize and deal with client resistance. Beth's social worker was following one of the accepted procedures for handling client resistance by confronting (Hepworth & Larsen, 1993) or challenging (Egan, 1994) Beth's claims of child abuse, which ran contrary to the facts of the police and hospital reports.

We approach such clients in another way. As we stated in Chapter 3, we work from the posture of not knowing. When we begin to work with a client, we assume that the client's self-perceptions and perceptions about his or her circumstances make sense within the client's frame of reference at that point in time. Our job is to respectfully ask questions about the client perceptions that do not yet make sense to us. We assume the client is competent even when he or she reports information or observations that seem implausible to us.

How to Respond: Hold Clients Accountable for Their Perceptions

While respecting the client's perceptions as meaningful, we also hold the client accountable for those perceptions. If a teenage client, for example, were to say, "I do better in school when I study less," we would begin to ask exploratory questions: "What is happening that tells you that you do better when you study less?" "How does studying less help you?" While such questions give the client responsibility for explaining his or her perceptions to the practitioner, they do so in a respectful fashion; they imply that the client is competent to perceive accurately and to make meaningful statements about those perceptions. Paradoxically, even though such responsibility amounts to pressure on the client, we have found that, as de Shazer (1985) wrote, client resistance fades away.

Whenever we begin a case, there are at least two matters that we are genuinely curious about: (1) clients' perceptions about themselves and their circumstances; and (2) clients' perceptions about what they might want. We are equally concerned about both, whether clients come to us by their own choice, as did Christi, or are required to meet with us, as in Beth's case.

In cases like Beth's, where clients are pressured or coerced to meet with a practitioner, the clients' perceptions of their circumstances and what they might want from the professional relationship are profoundly influenced by how the clients got to the practitioner. That's our next topic.

How to Respond: Pay Attention to How the Client Got to You

The manner in which a client enters the system of professional services affects the client's relationship to the practitioner during the beginning phase of their work together. From the very beginning of that relationship, we pay careful attention to when and under what circumstances the client entered the system and to how it is that the client comes to us for services at this particular time. This information will tell us much about how to proceed with the client. In Beth's case, we see that Beth is not the only client. The social worker, Beth's parents, the court, and the school all want certain things to happen. When Insoo first encountered Beth's case, she had a better idea about what these collaterals in Beth's case wanted than about what Beth might want. You might say that, initially at least, the collaterals were the real clients. By paying attention to how Beth got to her, Insoo saw that Beth might be very unmotivated to follow through on what the collaterals wanted and that she knew very little, if anything, about what Beth might want.

Paying attention to how the client gets into services is crucial, then, because it can play such an important role in how the client views what the problem is and what and who needs to change. It may be that, in Beth's view, the problem is not her charges of child abuse, her strained relationships with the courts and school, or her threats of running away and suicide. To Beth, the problem may be that her father is abusive and the system is intrusive. Her definition of the problem will affect her demeanor, what she might want to work on, and hence the sort of relationship she is willing to enter into with her practitioner.

Clients who are required to meet with practitioners by some collateral have usually been given some sort of mandate for what they are to accomplish from the relationship—to stop drinking, get a job, be a good parent, go to school and stay off the street, stop being abusive, and so forth. These clients usually feel that they have not been given a choice about the goal or the methods used to achieve it. Not surprisingly, they frequently see this mandate as punishment for no good reason, as unfair, or as evidence that "someone is out to get me." In these contexts, as Haley (1987) points out, collaterals expect practitioners to perform a social control function. We can add that most coerced clients are aware of this and, therefore, expect their practitioners to listen more carefully to what collaterals want than to what they want.

The natural response to being coerced is defiance, resistance, and a desire to subvert others' attempts at control. Human beings somehow sense that they are being robbed of their dignity when they permit themselves to be controlled. Perhaps this is why, across history and cultures, resistance movements are a common response to oppression. This perspective allows us to make some sense of Beth's reaction to her social worker.

Beth and Her Worker: A Visitor-Type Relationship

In a visitor-type relationship, as we have seen, practitioner and client are unable to jointly define a complaint or goal on which to work together. The exchange between the social worker and Beth is typical of a visitor-type relationship. Return to that exchange, and notice that the two were unable to jointly identify a complaint: Beth perceived child abuse, whereas the worker perceived Beth as stretching the truth—if not outright lying—about the previous evening's events. Nor were they able to jointly settle on a goal: Beth said that she wanted to go home, while the worker did not think this possible and said she would have to find a place for Beth.

Without a joint view of a goal or even the problem, the client in a visitor-type relationship is unlikely to be invested in making changes—at least not the changes that others want for her. When meeting a practitioner, the client is simply visiting. As we noted earlier, many in the field believe that workers should confront or challenge a client's denial, and help the client to correctly perceive the problem and the need for change. For example, Ivey (1994, p. 189) states: "Although all counseling skills are concerned with facilitating change, it is the confrontation of discrepancies that acts as a lever for *the activation of human potential*." Ivey's view is that, in a visitor-type relationship, when the facts seem not to support the client's perceptions, the practitioner should try to get the client to change his or her view of the problem or goal through confrontation. However, changing another person's perceptions by confrontation is very difficult. It is little wonder that Ivey, like other writers, calls confrontation an advanced skill.

Let's now return to Beth's case and see how Insoo went about paying attention to the client's perceptions and to how the client got to her, as they jointly worked on defining what Beth might want.

How to Respond: Insoo's Conversation with Beth

Recognizing that she and Beth were repeating the same frustrating pattern of interaction, the social worker turned to Insoo and inquired whether she had any ideas about how to proceed. Insoo asked Beth whether she would be willing to answer a few questions about some matters that were not clear to Insoo. This is the dialogue that took place:

INSOO: I have been sitting here and listening to how frustrated you are, Beth. How do you want your life to be different, if you could have your way?
BETH: [irritated] I told you, I want to go home. Nobody will let me go home.

By simply asking Beth what she wanted to have different in her life, Insoo established that what Beth really wanted was to go home. Already, it seemed to Insoo that Beth and she might be able to develop a customer-type relationship around going home, instead of the visitor-type relationship that had formed between Beth and the social worker around Beth telling the truth. Consequently, Insoo proceeded to further clarify what Beth might really want.

INSOO: I am confused, Beth. What about going home is so important to you?
BETH: Because I want to live with my parents, not in a foster home. I already have a home.
INSOO: I can see that it is important to you that you go home. Do you think your parents know that? I mean, do you think they know how important it is for you to live with them?

BETH: I love my parents and they should know that.

INSOO: Do you think they do? I'm not sure they do. What would it take for them to know how much you love them and how much you want to live with them?

BETH: Well, I want to go home.

INSOO: OK, I can see that you really want to go home. So, what would it take for you to go home? I mean, what has to happen first so that you can go home, do you think?

BETH: My parents will have to say I can come home. But they won't say that, because they are mad at me because of last night.

Insoo here has invited Beth to expand on her wish to go home and to live with her parents. As the conversation developed, Insoo became more convinced that this was what Beth really wanted. Consequently, she invited Beth to begin a dialogue on what it would take for that to happen. Notice how Insoo stayed with Beth's perceptions throughout; she asked for more information from a genuine posture of not knowing. She did not give Beth suggestions or advice, because she realized that Beth would reject these just as Beth rejected the social worker's advice. Instead, Insoo asked Beth to expand on her perceptions, so as to gain the clearest possible understanding of Beth's point of view. Even though this represented a lot of work for Beth, because she might not have thought it through this way before, she seemed motivated to do it. We think this is because it was work around what she wanted to have happen.

INSOO: Well, I guess I can understand how angry they are at you today. So what would your parents say has to happen so that you can go home?

BETH: They think it's all my fault. But my dad really hit me.

It would have been a mistake here to become distracted by Beth's apparent attempt to return to the previous night's events and who was to blame. The social worker had already been through that and, as usual, it led to an impasse. Beth, like many clients who have no choice about seeing another practitioner, has probably had many years of experience in debating the facts with adults, social workers, foster parents, psychologists, counselors, and many others who have tried to help her. Such debates about what really happened, why it happened that way, and whose fault it really is rarely lead to solutions; instead, they usually lead to frustration and feelings of misunderstanding and hurt. It is more useful to circumvent such problem talk by acknowledging the client's perception of the facts and refocusing the conversation on what clients want and what they think it might take for that to happen. That is what Insoo chose to do with Beth:

INSOO: I can see that you believe that your dad really hit you. [with genuine curiosity] So, what has to happen so that you can go home?

BETH: My parents will say I have to apologize and promise that I will listen to them.

INSOO: How likely are they going to believe you, if you were to apologize and promise to listen to them?

BETH: I know my dad is really mad at me.

INSOO: So, what would they say it will take for them to let you come home?

BETH: I will have to wait for a few days until he calms down, and then I will have to apologize to them.

Compare the results of the conversation between Beth and her social worker to those of the conversation between Beth and Insoo. Beth and her worker reached an impasse. By contrast, Beth and Insoo jointly identified what Beth wanted and began to work on what it would take on Beth's part to make that happen. Insoo did her part by asking questions about Beth's perceptions from a posture of not knowing and accepting Beth's perceptions as valid and understandable. Throughout, Insoo kept the focus on Beth and invited Beth to return to solution talk when she drifted back toward problem talk. Finally, despite the perceptions of those who were thoroughly frustrated with Beth, Insoo assumed Beth was competent—competent to think and talk about what she wanted in a tense and difficult situation and competent to figure out and draw on those strengths and resources that were available to her.

To sum up, here are some guidelines on how to proceed in a visitor-type relationship:

- Assume that the client has good reason to think and act as he or she does.
- Suspend your judgment and agree with the client's perceptions that stand behind his or her cautious, protective posture.
- Be sure to ask for the client's perception of what is in his or her best interest; that is, ask what the client might want. Accept the client's answer. (Implicit in asking someone a question is your willingness to accept that person's opinion.)
- Listen for and reflect the client's use of language, instead of trying to paraphrase the client's words into your way of talking.

If you ever find yourself at an impasse with a client, you might like to review these guidelines.

What If Clients Want What Is Not Good for Them?

This question usually comes up when we talk to our workshop participants and students about accepting clients' perceptions regarding what they want. In our practice, we rarely encounter clients who insist on wanting what we believe is not good for them. However, it could happen. Let's suppose a client, Bill, tells us he thinks that continuing to use alcohol is good for him and for his family, and that is what he wants. What should we do? It is difficult to answer this question in the abstract, because what a client says at one point in a conversation is tied to what has gone on before. Broadly speaking, however, our response would be the same as in the other situations we have discussed: We would respond from the posture of not knowing. We would assume that the client is competent and ask him to amplify on his perceptions: "What is happening in your life that tells you that continuing to use alcohol is good for you? What tells you that it is helpful to your family?"

We might also invite Bill to think about what he wants from the perspective of his significant others: "Suppose I were to ask your wife about how continuing to use alcohol is helpful to your family. What do you think she would say? What would your children say?" We call these relationship questions; we will illustrate their use in coming chapters.

We believe that it is possible to maintain a respectful posture even when clients seem to be saying they want something that, at first, seems unhealthy or even dangerous. If taken seriously and dealt with respectfully, a large majority of our clients are remarkably sensible about what they want, even in extreme circumstances. Of course, there is always the possibility that the practitioner, however reluctantly, may have to take away client self-determination in certain situations, but we recommend this only after several solution-building procedures have been used. We will return to this topic when we discuss solution building in crisis situations (cases that involve abuse and risk of suicide) in Chapter 9.

What If Clients Don't Want Anything at All?

In a small minority of cases, the client will not seem to want anything at all from the professional relationship with you, even after you have employed several solution-building procedures. In such cases, the client and yourself remain in a visitor-type relationship; clients do not perceive a problem and therefore would not be inclined to work on anything you suggest. If this is the situation at the end of a session with your client, it will influence the type of feedback that you give to your client. We will discuss this situation when we consider feedback in Chapter 7.

Influencing Client Cooperation and Motivation

Nearly every textbook on working with clients—whether in counseling, family therapy, medicine, nursing, psychology, social work, substance abuse treatment, vocational counseling, or other helping professions—discusses methods of reducing client resistance or noncompliance and enhancing client cooperation and motivation. Such discussions originate from a Freudian-influenced medical model of helping people. Implicit in classifying clients as cooperative or resistant is the notion that the experts know what is best for their clients. Moreover, when the client disregards the expert's learned opinion and fails to follow through on the professional's suggested course of treatment, such non-compliance is generally attributed to the client's personal or characterological flaws or to some deep-seated pathology. In the medical model, the professional is rarely, if ever, held responsible for the mismanagement of the professional relationship.

The belief in client resistance is longstanding and runs deep. As we noted earlier in this chapter, practice textbooks consistently teach beginning practitioners to expect client resistance and, therefore, to listen for it when they work with clients. Once they think that they perceive resistance—especially patterns of resistance—they are taught to confront it, because clients are assumed to be incapable of change unless they own their problems.

Our more skeptical side prompts us to point out here that this ideology of resistance and confrontation is self-serving for the field, which has a longstanding commitment to the medical model. The medical model assumes a subject-object relationship between practitioner and client; that is, the practitioner (as subject) is expected to change the client (as object) through the application of expert interventions. Consequently, if the client shows progress, the practitioner can take credit and feel competent. However, if the client does not show progress, the practitioner obviously cannot take credit; practitioner and client may feel doubts about the effectiveness of the practitioner's services. But the notion of client resistance lays most of the blame for lack of progress on the client and allows practitioners to distance themselves from responsibility.

In an article with the dramatic title, "The Death of Resistance," Steve de Shazer (1984) claimed that the field's dominant conceptualization of client resistance more accurately represents the point of view—or construction of reality—of practitioners than any aspect of objective reality. Thinking along very different lines, he proposed that what practitioners took to be signs of resistance were, instead, the unique ways in which clients chose to cooperate. For example, clients who do not follow through on the therapeutic or problem-solving tasks assigned by their practitioners are not resisting but simply cooperating, by telling their practitioners that the tasks do not fit their way of doing things (de Shazer, 1985, p. 21; 1991, p. 126).

Just as the notion of resistance flows from the bedrock assumptions of the medical model, de Shazer's reconceptualization of resistance as a form of cooperation is also bound to his assumptions. De Shazer assumes that clients are competent to figure out what they want (and need) and how to go about getting it. The practitioner's responsibility is to assist clients in uncovering these competencies and marshalling them to create more satisfying and productive lives for themselves—if that is what they choose to do.

As a logical necessity, once we accept the notion of client competence, we are left with a humbling and challenging conclusion: What we once thought of as client resistance is more accurately regarded as practitioner resistance. Impasses and apparent failures in our work do not result from clients' resistance to our best professional efforts to make them well; rather, they result from our failure to listen to clients and take seriously what they tell us.

In solution building, then, we do not seek to enhance client motivation by overcoming client resistance, but by quieting our own frames of reference, so that we listen with solution-building ears and invite clients to participate in solution-building conversations. The Native American saying with which this chapter begins captures this view of motivation well:

> Tell me and I'll forget. Show me, and I may not remember. Involve me, and I will understand.

We believe that this saying could have been written by our clients.

As the case examples in this chapter have illustrated, client cooperation and motivation can change rapidly, depending on what clients see as useful or helpful to them. If the goal of the professional relationship is to be useful to clients, it is only respectful to ask clients for their definitions of problems, what they might want, and possibilities for solutions. For example, it would have been easy to dismiss as unrealistic Beth's wish to live with her family. Instead, Insoo paid attention to Beth's perceptions and proceeded with her respectful questions; Insoo quieted her own frame of reference and opened a dialogue with Beth around what it would take for Beth to go home.

In solution building, the invitation for client participation begins at the first meeting and ends when the client indicates to us that the task is completed. Even someone with Beth's reputation may cooperate with her parents if her voice is heard and she is asked to help shape her own future. Beth might eventually even decide that she needs to stay in a residential treatment facility for a time. If she comes to that conclusion through a respectful dialogue with her practitioner, she will be much more likely to cooperate with the program and much less likely to run away or make suicidal gestures. She will be a stakeholder in thinking through what is best for her and her own treatment. We believe that such participation represents true empowerment.

We would like to return to Insoo's conversation with Beth and to show you how the two of them further developed a workable plan for the short term:

INSOO: It seems like a good idea that you need to wait for a few days until your parents calm down and apologize to them. So, what do you have to do during the next few days while you are waiting for the right time?

BETH: I guess I will have to keep coming to school every day, follow rules, and talk nice to my parents and not demand things from them. I know how to get along with Peggy's mother. I do my chores when I stay with them. Peggy's mom said I can stay there as long as I have to.

INSOO: Wow, you know lots of stuff. I guess they are right about you being smart. So, tell me how is it that Peggy's mom will let you come and stay with her family? Not everybody would want another 15-year-old in their home. [both laugh]

BETH: She is very nice. I like her a lot. I usually help out with the dishes, set the table, and all that stuff. I'm very neat when I stay at Peggy's. Her mom says I can come and stay with her as long as I need to, because she says I help her a lot.

INSOO: Really, I can't believe this. Teenagers are supposed to be messy and all that stuff.

BETH: [laughing] Well, I am! But when I stay at my friends' house, I know how to behave.

This dialogue opens up and affirms a side of Beth that likely never would have emerged had Insoo not asked what Beth wanted and what it would take for that to happen. The conversation clearly reveals that Beth has strengths and past successes that she can draw on in moving toward what she wants. In addition, the longer the conversation continues along these solution-building lines, the more Beth will convince herself that she can be a helpful, neat, organized person. Insoo's task is to keep the solution talk going.

INSOO: Where did you learn this, Beth?

BETH: My mom and grandma.

INSOO: Do your mom and grandma know how much they taught you?

BETH: Yeah, but I don't think they know because I never told them that.

INSOO: What would it take for your mom to know how much she taught you?

BETH: I guess I will have to tell her?

INSOO: How will you do that? I mean, tell your mom how much you learned from her?

BETH: She is mad at me now, but I will tell her in a few days.

Even though, at the beginning of the initial meeting, Beth was in a visitor-type relationship with the worker and in a defensive and noncooperative posture toward services, she gradually changed, in dialogue with Insoo, and came to see herself as wanting something and having the beginnings of a plan to get what she wanted. Clearly, there is much more work to be done with both the collaterals and Beth, but Beth has moved into a customer-type relationship with Insoo around building a way for her to go home.

In this chapter, we have examined the different kinds of relationships that can develop between you as a practitioner and your clients. We have also discussed how to proceed in different types of relationship toward a joint definition of the client's problem and what the client might want. In our experience, working for this joint definition is the best means of enhancing client motivation.

How to Amplify What Clients Want: The Miracle Question

Some people see problems and ask why. I dream dreams and ask why not.
(Robert F. Kennedy)

Only when people start creating scenarios of possibility do they move in directions more satisfying to them, and . . . [their] problems become lost or much less influential.
(Saleebey, 1994, p. 357)

In illustrating his conviction about clients' potential, Saleebey (1994) points to the work of his colleagues (Modcrin, Rapp, & Poertner, 1988) with clients diagnosed as chronically mentally ill, many of whom had a history of previous hospitalizations. These colleagues, assuming the clients' competence and affirming their goal definitions, witnessed amazing results:

> These individuals, almost without exception, began to construct a life—collaboratively—that no one could have predicted. The interesting thing is that they did this "in spite of their illness." In fact, their symptoms may have occurred at the same level, but the other parts of them became part of their unfolding story: "me as employee," "me as piano player," "me as driver," "me as spouse and parent." The symptoms move into the background of a much richer symbolic ecology. (Saleebey, 1994, p. 357)

Our experience with clients has been similar. As de Shazer (1991, 1994) and many others (Berg, 1994; Berg & Miller, 1992; Furman & Ahola, 1992; O'Hanlon & Weiner-Davis, 1989; Talmon, 1990; Walter & Peller, 1992) have found, clients can often make impressive moves toward building more satisfying and productive lives.

To illustrate the process of solution building, consider the analogy of a person who plans a vacation; let's call her Annie. First, caught up in the repetitiveness and pressures of everyday life, Annie thinks that she might like to have something different in her life. She muses: "A trip somewhere might be nice." If the thought stays with her, Annie starts to reflect in general terms about where she might like to go: "I'd like to get far away from here; maybe some place out of the country; maybe even someplace warm, away from all this snow." If, after recognizing that a trip costs time and money, she remains intrigued by the possibility, she will begin to define more clearly where she wants to go and what she wants to do when she gets there. She may talk to friends who have gone to faraway places; she may talk to a travel agent; she may go to the library or bookstore and browse through the travel books. As she reads about the Bahamas, Mexico, Greece, Brazil, and Hawaii, Annie develops a richer sense of what lies in store for her if she decides to go to one of these destinations. The Bahamas have picturesque beaches and snorkeling right off the shore. Greece and Mexico offer monuments of past civilizations. Rio de Janeiro in Brazil seems to have exciting nightlife. As she works to develop a clearer sense of what is there at each of several possible destinations, she becomes attracted to some more than others. In addition, as she thinks about the possibilities, she also has thoughts of how she will get there. The costs of the different options start to occur to her: "I could go by plane; it's faster and cheaper. Or I could go by boat; it's more expensive but relaxing." Thoughts about how to get there could even influence her destination. Annie may decide that the options for getting there are too expensive and change her destination from someplace out of the country to a warmer place within her own country. She may compromise: "At least that way I can drive there and save money."

We want to offer several observations about this process. First, note that Annie worked her way from a general idea of where she might like to go to a more precise vision of what is in store once she gets there. As her vision became more and more developed, she found herself more powerfully attracted to the possibility. Second, considerations of how to get there influenced the choice of destination. Depending on how much time, cost, and work it would take to get there, Annie shifted her perceptions and definitions about the relative attractiveness of different destinations. Third, as a consequence, she discovered that planning a trip can be a lot of work. Fourth, the process was not so much a matter of finding the absolutely perfect destination as of finding a destination that would be sufficiently satisfying to motivate her to make the trip a reality.

In terms of the trip metaphor, we find in our work with clients that thinking about destination should take precedence over mode of transportation. In other words, when clients first start to think about what they want to have different in their lives, it seems to be most useful to have them first begin to conceptualize what will be different, and then move to how they might make that happen. Although these two aspects are often discussed together, with some problem talk thrown into the mix, the what still has logical priority over the how. Thus, in this chapter, building on Chapter 4, we focus on additional interviewing questions that you can use to open and sustain conversations with your clients around what they want different in their lives. In the next chapter, we turn to skills that address the question of how clients can make those things happen.

As we saw in Chapter 4, client motivation often increases dramatically when the conversation between client and practitioner turns to what the client might want to be different. However, most clients must then struggle to define in more detail what they want. Usually, their initial efforts are abstract and vague. They may say, "I'll know things are better when I feel more motivated to study" or, "My problem will be solved when I don't feel so depressed about my life" or, "I'll be getting along better with my parents" or, "I'll have my children back with me and Protective Services will be out of my life." Consequently, once a client has made an initial statement about what differences he or she would like to see, the next task for the practitioner is to open a conversation that transforms abstract and vague definitions into a concrete, vivid vision of what life will be like when the problem is solved. Berg and Miller (1992) call this the process of developing *well-formed goals* with clients. As you will soon see, this process—very much a collaborative one in solution-focused interviewing—involves a lot of work by both clients and practitioners.

Well-formed goals have several characteristics (Berg & Miller, 1992; de Shazer, 1991), as established inductively by solution-focused practitioners. After defining and briefly illustrating each characteristic, we will introduce you to the miracle question, which is a way to open and develop a dialogue with clients around well-formed goals. In this chapter, we are also going to introduce you to two new case studies: Ah Yan and the Williams family. We will return to these cases in subsequent chapters, so that you can follow them through all the stages of the solution-building process.

Characteristics of Well-Formed Goals

Importance to the Client

First and foremost, goals must be important to the client. Whether the goals that the client chooses are those that you as a practitioner believe would be most important for the client is irrelevant. This characteristic reflects the themes in Chapter 4. Unless you make the effort to work with clients so as to identify what they might want, your efforts to be useful to your clients might be defeated before they begin. The case of Beth in Chapter 4 illustrates this truism. When practitioners work hard to understand what clients want for their lives, clients feel respected, are more likely to grow in self-respect, and are more motivated to work on changing their lives (Hepworth & Larsen, 1993; Saleebey, 1992).

Interactional Terms

People live much of their lives in interaction with others, many of whom are tremendously important to them. When clients describe their problems and what they might like to have different in their lives, they regularly include references to their significant others (Mead, 1934): "My problem is that my daughter uses drugs and won't listen to me anymore"; "My husband and I are fighting all the time"; "I'll know that things are going well when my boss and I can talk man to man about a raise."

As an interviewer, then, you must find out who a client's significant others are and weave them into your questions so as to encourage clients to describe their goals in interactional terms. If you do not know who the client's significant others are, it is easy enough to ask: "Who knows you well?" For example, suppose a client says that one thing he would like to have different is to talk calmly to his daughter when she disobeys, instead of losing his temper and yelling at her. You can invite him to bring this emerging goal into his interactional context by asking: "If you were to decide to do that, what would be different between you and your daughter?" You could ask for more amplification along the same lines by asking: "If you were to decide to do that, what might be different between you and your wife?" "What else might be different between you and others in your house?" "What else might be different in your life?" These additional questions come from a recognition that whatever difference develops in the relationship between the client and his daughter might—in his mind—have implications for his relationships to others. Therefore, it can influence whether or not he eventually chooses to do something different in this area of his life. Very often, when the client initiates a positive change in one relationship, a ripple effect leads to positive changes also in other relationships; consequently, when answering such questions, the client tends to reinforce the attractiveness of the original goal. Questions about significant others are called *relationship questions*.

In discussing the metaphor of planning a trip, we saw that the would-be traveller often begins with very vague conceptions of the final destination. The same will be true of your clients as they begin to develop goals. Suppose you ask a client what will be different in her life when her problem is solved. She will most likely answer in broad terms: "I'll feel better about myself" or "I'll have a better attitude about my job." You can invite her to begin to clarify this statement by asking, "When you feel better about yourself, what difference will others notice about you?" You can prompt more detail by asking, "What else will they notice that's different about you?"

Mead (1934) taught that the way in which people perceive themselves—their wishes, strengths, limitations, and possibilities—is greatly influenced by their understanding of how significant others view them. You can put Mead's insight to use by asking relationship questions. For example, suppose a client is totally at a loss about what might be different in his life when his problem is solved. You decide to ask: "If your mother were here, and I were to ask her what would be different when your problem is solved, what would she say." The client may then come up with an answer: "Oh, I think she would say that I'd be watching less TV, that I'd be out looking for a job, that sort of thing." Sometimes, when clients shift from looking at themselves through their own eyes to looking at themselves through the eyes of their significant others, they can generate some possibilities where before there were none.

On occasion, practitioners and students have asked us how to question clients about their interactional context when the clients are socially isolated. Our experience is that it is very rare for a client to be completely isolated. For example, even a single mother with young children can be asked how the children would describe any changes in her if they had the vocabulary and ability to describe what they saw.

Insoo once had a client who took care of her aged father for years and complained of becoming very depressed after he died. She reported that she was not depressed at work, where she was surrounded by friendly co-workers, but that when she came home she "put on a different side of me." In the course of their conversation, the woman revealed that she lived with her dog, who was very sensitive to her mood changes. Insoo asked, "If your dog could speak, what would he say would be different about you when your problem is solved?" Without missing a beat, the woman replied: "He would say I will be bouncy, eager to take him for a morning walk, and that I would talk to him in a cheerful voice."

Situational Features

When clients are discouraged and exhausted from having battled their problems for days, weeks, months, or even years, they commonly describe their problems as if they are happening all the time and everywhere. Therefore, we try to help them to narrow down what they might want to be different to a certain place and setting. Doing so makes developing goals seem more possible. For example, suppose a client complains to you that she is always late for everything and that this is causing problems for her in all parts of her life. Instead of inviting her to develop a goal around never being late for any important activities and events in her life, it would be more useful to ask: "Right now, at this time in your life, what do you least want to be late for?" She might tell you that it is most important to focus on getting to work on time, because she believes that she can better be late with family and friends, who are more forgiving; her employer, in contrast, might fire her.

The Presence of Some Desirable Behaviors Rather Than the Absence of Problems

Just like the rest of us, clients usually begin to describe what they want by describing what they do not want. For example, if you were to ask a woman who has come to see you about family problems what she would like to have different in her family life, she might respond with a lengthy statement:

> I fight with my children way too much. I want to stop yelling and screaming at them because it's no good for them and it's no good for me. Also, I want my son to quit fighting with his sister and to stop stealing money from my purse and lying to me; I want my daughter to stop running away; and I want my husband to get off the bottle so that he can help me more.

A goal description like this is rarely, if ever, useful to a client. Because it is a negative statement, it feeds discouragement, low energy, and a sense of being stuck or trapped. In addition, it focuses what little energy the client may have left on trying to keep this negative something away—a very difficult task. It is usually much easier for people to do something that they perceive as positive. For example, it is usually much easier for clients to lose weight by getting up and taking a walk than by continually reminding themselves not to head off to the kitchen for a bag of potato chips and a soda. Consequently, well-formed goals are described as the presence of something positive rather than the absence of some perceived problem.

De Shazer (1985) has pointed out that there is a straightforward way to respond to a client's negative goal descriptions and begin working toward a description of the presence of something different. All the interviewer has to do is to ask the client what will be there instead when the problem is solved. Here is an example:

JOANNE: I hate it when my son lies to me; I'll know that things are getting better when he stops lying to me. It scares me when he can lie to me with a straight face like that.

INSOO: Of course; I can see that you have good reason to be worried. So, when things are getting better, what will he be doing instead?

JOANNE: He'll be more honest, of course.

INSOO: And what will that look like? What will he be doing differently that will tell you he is being more honest?

JOANNE: Well, he'll admit once in a while that he is lying and apologize for it.

INSOO: And what else will he do?

JOANNE: I don't know, I haven't thought about that. . . . Maybe his voice will be firm and straight, not evasive and mumbling like he does sometimes. . . . And he'll look me straight into my eyes and he will stand straight and tall, instead of all hunched over. He'll be more open with me.

INSOO: I can tell that you know your son quite well. So, he will look you straight in your eyes, his voice will be firm, and he will stand straight and tall. All these make sense. You do know your son quite well, don't you?

JOANNE: Of course; I'm his mother. [laughing] Mothers have eyes in the back of their heads; that's what I tell my Robby all the time.

A Beginning Step Rather Than the Final Result

Contacting a professional is generally a last resort, rather than the first option that clients seek in solving their problems. They may have tried several remedies that are not working satisfactorily, and so they come to an expert for some answers. At that point, clients often want immediate relief.

This hope is wishful thinking on the part of the client. However, that does not stop them from asking for advice, nor does it lift the pressure that you will feel when clients plead for you to relieve their pain. Nonetheless, professionals must not make promises to clients that they cannot keep. In most cases, it is simply not realistic for clients to reach an immediate solution; more often than not, solutions are final results reached only after clients have taken some beginning and intermediate steps to do things differently in their lives. As practitioners, what we have to offer our clients is assistance in finding new ways to begin building more successful solutions.

When you ask your clients how they will know when their problems are solved, expect them to describe the finish line, rather than the first signs of something different. For example, when Insoo asked the mother in our previous example what she would like to have different, she stated the final result— for Robby to be more honest. Insoo then asked what that would look like and she responded: "His voice will be firm, . . . he'll look me straight into my eyes and he will stand straight and tall. He'll be more open with me." This developing definition still sounded more like a final result than a beginning step. Insoo continued the dialogue as follows:

INSOO: You sure know Robby well. Obviously it is going to take more time for him to be honest with you all the time. So what will be the first small sign that will tell you that, "Hmm, he is beginning to be more honest with me"?

JOANNE: Yeah, I guess it will take some time. [smiling] Of course I want him to change yesterday. I guess it will be his looking at me when we talk so that I can see his eyes.

INSOO: So, what will you see in his eyes that you don't see now that will let you know that Robby is beginning to be more honest with you?

In this exchange, Insoo invited Joanne to scale down her wish. Joanne was able to narrow her definition to a beginning: "his looking at me when we talk so that I can see his eyes." By concentrating on a single aspect of her son's change, Joanne will be more likely to notice her son's eye contact when it does occur, and that will increase the chances of a changed interactional pattern with him.

Clients' Recognition of a Role for Themselves

Often, when clients begin their work with practitioners, they feel discouraged about their prospects for something better, because they believe that their problems have been brought on by the actions of others and they feel powerless to do anything about those problems. Consequently, when practitioners ask such clients what will be different when the problem is solved, the clients respond that certain people they know will be different. As we described in Chapter 4, we have found it useful to go with such clients' perceptions and ask for more description of what these significant others in the clients' life will be doing differently. Insoo did exactly that in talking with Joanne:

INSOO: So, tell me, supposing Robby were to look at you more when the two of you talk, how would that be helpful to you?

JOANNE: If that could happen, that would be wonderful! It would make my life so much easier. I wouldn't be so scared—scared that he is doing the same thing to other people, like his teacher, for example. I wouldn't have to worry so much about how he might turn out. . . . I could spend more time at the other things I have to worry about—like doing something about my daughter and my husband.

INSOO: And if he were to do that—look at you more—what would he see you doing differently?

JOANNE: Oh, I don't know. . . . I suppose I wouldn't yell at him as much . . . you know, stay more calm.

With Insoo's guidance, Joanne was able to begin thinking about what she might do differently in the relationship with her son. A lot of work remains to be done around what staying more calm and yelling less might mean, but the solution-focused questions that Insoo asked helped Joanne to begin shifting the focus onto herself. Often, when clients are able to make this shift, they brighten and become more hopeful.

Concrete, Behavioral, Measurable Terms

It should be quite clear by now that helping your clients to articulate concrete, behavioral, and hence measurable goals enables both them and you to ascertain when they are making progress toward satisfactory solutions. In addition, when clients sense that they are making progress, their success fuels continuing efforts to create more satisfying lives. Consequently, we recommend that, instead of accepting vague and sweeping goal statements—such as "I will feel better when the problem is solved" or "I will be happier" or "I will be more productive"—you work with your clients to articulate their goals in behavioral terms. Insoo did exactly that whenever Joanne responded in vague terms. For example, when Joanne stated that she wanted her son to be more honest, Insoo's follow-up questions encouraged her to make that goal more concrete, behavioral, and measurable.

Realistic Terms

Some clients, when asked what differences they would like to see, will respond in unrealistic ways, for example: "My heart condition will disappear" or, "My son will obey me every time I ask him to help around the house" or even, "I'll win the lottery." These outcomes might be wonderful, but the practitioner thinks, "That does not sound like a realistic goal. Certainly this client cannot become more hopeful and create a better future by focusing on unrealistic goals."

Realistic goals are achievable, given the client's capacities and the context in which he or she lives. Since at first you do not know much about the client's capacities and circumstances, you will need to ask about them, in order to get a better sense of whether or not the client's developing goals are realistic. This can be done in several ways. For example, suppose a client tells you that he wants to get along better with his son. Under your questioning, he goes on to define that goal more concretely as spending more time with his son, asking his son more often what he would like to do on Saturdays, and taking his son's answers more seriously. You could then ask: "Is that something which could happen?" Or, "Is that something that you think you could do?" If the client answers yes, you could follow up with other questions: "How do you know you could do that? Are there times already when you have been able to do at least some of these things?" Very quickly, both you and the client get a clearer sense of the client's strengths and past successes and what the client believes can happen in his context.

Another way of encouraging clients to think in realistic terms is to ask them to consider the interactional consequences of any change on their part. For example, suppose that a father tells you that he wants to talk more calmly to his daughter, instead of yelling at her when she does something wrong. You ask him, "If you do that, what will she do differently?" By doing so, you are implicitly asking him if this change on his part is a realistic possibility, given what he knows about his daughter and her ways of reacting.

A Challenge to the Client

At the outset of services, clients often feel discouraged about themselves and their lives. They may feel disappointed—or even ashamed—that they need assistance. Many clients would rather have problems that can be traced to a biological condition and given a medical diagnosis than personal or family problems. Personal or family problems imply that there are flaws in the clients and those close to them for which they bear responsibility; biological conditions are usually regarded as beyond personal control and responsibility.

By suggesting that the client's problems will take hard work to resolve, practitioners strengthen the client's sense of dignity and self-respect, in several ways. First, the client is reassured that coming for professional services makes good sense. After all, if a problem requires hard work to solve, it must be a difficult problem, and so the client is worthy of professional assistance. Second, in cases where the client makes little or no progress, the client does not need to feel a sense of failure; instead, the practitioner's statement focuses the client on the need for continuing hard work. Finally, where the client makes rapid progress, awareness of having solved a difficult problem in a short period of time greatly enhances client self-esteem.

By reminding clients about the necessity of hard work, the practitioner is able to place responsibility for change on the client, without directly saying so. In the beginning, clients often talk as though they want to give their problems over to the professional. The reminder that hard work will be required respectfully conveys that the client will have to participate if change is to occur. We have found that most clients accept these reminders. Though they may wish there were an easier way, they know from experience that some sort of hard work on their part has played an important role in their past successes.

Conclusion

Before moving on, we'd like to make some additional observations about well-formed goals. First, such goals are developed with clients within their own frame of reference. In solution-focused interviewing, the practitioner refrains from making suggestions to clients about what they need or should strive for. Instead, the practitioner persists in inviting clients to conceptualize the goals for themselves and to state the goals in their own words. Second, when they begin their work with practitioners, clients rarely possess well-formed goals; these goals develop over time and in interaction with the practitioner. Goal formulation, like the solution-building process itself, is hard work for clients and requires patience, persistence, and skill on the part of the practitioner.

The practitioner can introduce and sustain a conversation about goals with clients by means of the miracle question. It draws on the client's frame of reference and encourages goal formulation in terms consistent with the characteristics we have discussed.

The Miracle Question

Insoo and her colleagues hit upon the miracle question serendipitously. One day she was interviewing a woman who seemed burdened with the weight of the world: Her children were out of control; the school was calling about their unruly behavior; and her husband of 17 years had been drinking more heavily, with the result that he seemed about to lose his job and, with it, the family's livelihood. The woman was discouraged, and talked as if she could not cope with another day. As was her practice at the time, Insoo asked the woman: "What do you suppose needs to happen so that you could say that the time we are spending together has been useful to you?" The client heaved a long, deep sigh and said: "I'm not sure; I have so many problems. Maybe only a miracle will help, but I suppose that's too much to expect." Committed to picking up on her clients' words and ideas, Insoo asked: "OK, suppose a miracle happened, and the problem that brought you here is solved. What would be different about your life?"

To Insoo's amazement, this woman, who had seemed so overwhelmed and unable to go on, began describing a vision of a different life. She said that her husband would be "more responsible, keeping his job and managing the money better." She said her children would "follow rules at school and at home, doing their chores without putting up such a fuss." And, most of all, she said that she would be different: "I will have more energy, smile more, be calmer with the children and—instead of snapping at them—talk to them in a normal tone of voice. I might even start having normal conversations with my husband, like we used to when we first were married."

In the following weeks, Insoo and her colleagues thought about what had happened in the session with this woman. It occurred to them that, even though we don't normally think of miracles as realistic, this client's description of her life after the miracle had happened was certainly a reasonable and realistic picture of a well-functioning family. In other words, her description of her miracle turned out to be a worthwhile set of goals from her point of view. Thus, the miracle question was born; Insoo and her colleagues began asking it regularly.

The miracle question is useful for at least a couple of reasons. First, by asking about a miracle, it gives clients permission to think about an unlimited range of possibilities. They are asked to think big as a way to get started on identifying what changes they want to see. Second, the question has a future focus; it calls up a time in their lives when their problems are no longer problems. It begins to move the focus away from their current and past problems and toward a more satisfying life.

By now, the miracle question has been asked thousands of times throughout the world. Along the way, it has been refined, as practitioners have experimented with different ways of asking it. The question is best asked deliberately and dramatically. We recommend this approach:

> Now, I want to ask you a strange question. *Suppose* that while you are sleeping tonight and the entire house is quiet, a *miracle* happens. The miracle is that *the problem which brought you here is solved*. However, because you are sleeping, you don't know that *the miracle has happened*.

So, when you wake up tomorrow morning, *what will be different* that will tell that a miracle has happened and the problem which brought you here is solved? (de Shazer, 1988, p. 5)

Asked this way, the miracle question requests clients to make a leap of faith and imagine how their life will be changed when the problem is solved. This is not easy for clients; it requires them to make a dramatic shift from problem-saturated thinking to a focus on solutions. Most clients need time and assistance to make that shift. Experience has taught us that, as a practitioner, you can be very helpful to clients in this process. We recommend the following guidelines when you ask your clients the miracle question:

- Speak slowly and gently, in a soft voice in order to give your client time to shift from a problem focus to a solution focus.
- Mark the beginning of the solution-building process clearly and dramatically, by introducing the miracle question as unusual or strange.
- Since the question asks for a description of the future, use future-directed words: What *would* be different? What *will* be signs of the miracle?
- When probing and asking follow-up questions, frequently repeat the phrase "a miracle happens and the problem that brought you here is solved," in order to reinforce the transition to solution talk.
- When clients lapse back into problem talk, gently refocus their attention on what will be different in their life when the miracle happens.

Remember that the miracle question is an opening gambit; clients usually give an answer that does not fit the characteristics of well-formed goals. The practitioner's task is to pose a series of related questions that help clients express their vision of a more satisfying future in a manner that reflects these characteristics. As an example of this process, let's look at Peter's work with a client whom we'll call Ah Yan.

Ah Yan's Miracle Picture

Ah Yan is a 30-year-old Asian American woman; she is married and has two young children. Peter met her at a public agency where she was seeking assistance. This is how their dialogue began:

PETER: How can I help you?

AH YAN: [very anxiously] I've been feeling . . . I've been having problems. . . . I get nervous—panicky. I just have to sit down and calm down. I'm scared somethin' is gonna go wrong all the time.

PETER: Ah Yan, what's been happening that tells you that you're panicky?

AH YAN: I, I don't know. . . . I just feel all, like, real nervous inside, and my whole body starts shaking. I feel scared and I get all short of breath.

PETER: Umm. That sounds very frightening. [Ah Yan nods in agreement] Is there anything else that's a part of being panicky for you?

AH YAN: Yeah, last year for a while I thought I was crazy or something. I was gonna get up and get out of bed and my hair is falling out and, like, when I took a shower, there's a bunch of hair in my hand. And I went to the doctor and said: "Doctor, why? Why is this?" And they did tests, lots of tests.

PETER: So you went to the doctor and took tests. Was that helpful?

AH YAN: Yeah. Well, the tests didn't show anything, but they tell you how to cure yourself. The doctors said take walks, ride a bike, maybe rest more.

PETER: And has that helped?

AH YAN: I'm not sure. . . . I tried those things. . . . Maybe they helped a little, but I still panic. I hyperventilate.

As we see, Ah Yan was able to describe her problem, but she was not aware of any pattern to it; nor had she found anything that consistently helped. The doctors, too, were puzzled, because they had found nothing physically wrong with her; that's why she came for services. About 10 minutes into their first interview, Peter chose to begin goal-formulation work by asking the miracle question:

PETER: Now, let me ask you an unusual question. Suppose that while you are sleeping tonight a miracle happens. The miracle is that the problem that brought you here today is solved. But, because you are asleep, you don't know that the miracle has happened. When you wake up, what would be the first sign to you that things are *different,* that a miracle has happened?

AH YAN: I don't know. I guess . . . I guess I would just be more myself. . . . You know, smile. . . . I smile but that's on the outside; on the inside, I'm constantly feeling fear—like I'm going to collapse, even that I might die. . . . My fear is of dying.

PETER: You said that you would be more yourself. What's different when you are yourself?

AH YAN: Nothing. . . . I feel . . . I want to go out and walk and just smile. I'm smiling, but inside I can feel scared, like I'm gonna collapse.

PETER: So when the miracle happens, what would be there instead of the fear?

AH YAN: Oh . . . I don't know. I always feel so trapped. That's too hard a question; I don't know.

PETER: Yes it is; it's a very hard question, and I can see that you are really struggling with your fear; it makes your life difficult and miserable at times. I think it makes good sense for you to be here—to see if anything else can be done. [Ah Yan nods]

I'm wondering—the morning after the miracle—what would your husband notice that would tell him that—wow!—things are different, things are much better, something must have happened?

AH YAN: When I talk to him, he tells me . . . that I'm all right and everything is OK. When I'm happy, he's happy.

PETER: So when the miracle happens, you'd be happier? [she nods] So, what would he notice about you that would tell him that you were happier—on the inside as well as the outside?

AH YAN: I'd talk to him. . . . He'd see I was happier. I wouldn't be crying. I'd have something to eat. I'd do more around the house.

PETER: When he sees those things, what would he do?

AH YAN: [becoming less anxious and brightening] He'd be happier because he always worries when I'm scared. He'd hug and kiss me more. He'd ask me if he could help, and we'd make things look better around the house together.

PETER: What else might he do?

AH YAN: That's all. . . . I don't know. . . . Maybe go out together, look around or something. . . . That's all.

PETER: You said you had two children. How old are they?

AH YAN: Di Jia, he's 6; he's the oldest. Then there is Ah Lan, who's 3.

PETER: Wow, two small children; you must be a very busy person. [Ah Yan nods; pause] So, getting back to this miracle, what would your kids notice that's different?

AH YAN: Di Jia—I don't know. He pays attention when I'm sick, like when I'm trembling. He'll tell me, "Mom, tomorrow morning I'll make you soup." You know, he tries to help out.

PETER: So what would be different when the miracle happens?

AH YAN: He'd go outside, play on the swing set, go around on his bike, running in and out.

PETER: And how would that be for you?

AH YAN: I like it. I like it because it's him. I know then he's not thinking of me, but running and playing.

PETER: And Ah Lan, what would she notice?

AH YAN: She's, like, starting to notice things. I . . . think she would . . . She's a huggable person; she likes to be hugging and kissing and saying "I love you." She'd be happy. . . . She'd notice us playing games and doing things together and enjoying it.

PETER: Who else might notice?

AH YAN: I don't know. . . . Maybe my sister-in-law—'cause she knows what I'm going through.

PETER: So what would she notice? What would be the first small thing that would catch her attention, the first thing when she sees you on the miracle morning?

AH YAN: She'd see my smile; she'd say, "Ah Yan, you're smiling!" She'd be surprised.

PETER: And what else would be different around your house when the miracle happens?

AH YAN: I don't know; I don't know any more.

PETER: Well, that's OK; you've already mentioned several things that might be different. Let me ask you this: If you were to decide to do just one part of this miracle tomorrow morning, which part would be the easiest to do?

AH YAN: Oh, I'm not sure. Maybe I could talk to my husband more.

PETER: What might you say to him?

AH YAN: Oh, you know, nothing special. Just say: "Good morning; it's a beautiful day. What are you going to do today?" Things like that. That's all.

PETER: So you can do that? [she nods] What would it take for that to happen?

AH YAN: Just doing it, I guess.

PETER: Really, is that true? If you decide to do something, you can make it happen, just by putting your mind to it?

AH YAN: [nodding] Yes, but it's hard because I can still feel really scared inside and . . .

PETER: Yes, I know; from what you have told me, it's going to take a lot of hard work for you to do that.

In asking the miracle question, Peter invited Ah Yan to enter a conversation with him in which she could work at constructing a hypothetical solution. In terms of the vacation metaphor, he invited her to talk about some possible destinations that, if she eventually chose to work toward them, would make her problem largely a thing of the past. As expected, she started with a very vague concept of what would be different when her problem was solved: "I guess I would just be more myself." Using follow-up questions reflecting the characteristics of well-formed goals, Peter gave her an opportunity to begin shaping a more vivid, more attainable picture. He asked her what would be there instead of her fear (thereby inviting her to describe the presence of something positive). He asked what she would notice that is different when she became more herself (thereby encouraging a concrete, specific, behavioral description and a description of something in which she plays a role). He asked what her husband and children would notice that was different about her (thereby encouraging her to describe possibilities in interactional terms). He asked what other family members would do when they noticed those things that she might do differently (thereby inviting her to think in situational, interactional, and realistic terms). He asked what would be the first thing others would notice (thereby probing for a possible beginning step). He asked what part of her miracle would be easiest for her to do the next morning (thereby inviting her to think about which possibilities were most realistic). Finally, Peter acknowledged that turning parts of the miracle into reality would be hard work.

Ah Yan often responded to Peter's questions initially by saying, "I don't know." As we discussed in Chapter 3, Peter was not surprised by this; he remained silent, so as to give her time to think and put her thoughts into words. His patience and use of silence proved helpful because, during the silence, Ah Yan was able to formulate answers that were meaningful to her.

Most clients find these goal-formulation questions challenging and demanding but, as they work to formulate answers, they brighten and become more hopeful. We have noticed that these questions hold clients' attention; clients work very hard to answer them.

Occasionally, we encounter clients who refuse to work with the miracle question. They might say, "Miracles don't happen"; or, "Things have been so bad in my life for so long that I know there is not going to be any miracle for me." If you find yourself in this situation, you could say, "Well, suppose there were a miracle, even a small one." If the client still insists on returning to how painful the problem is, you might also use the phrase "when the problem is solved or less severe," rather than "when the miracle happens." For example, you could start the shift from problem talk to goal formulation by asking: "What will you notice that's happening differently in your life when your problem is solved or less severe?" You can adapt all of the other questions used to develop well-formed goals in the same way.

If you are not experienced in solution-focused interviewing, it will take time and practice before you feel comfortable opening and sustaining a conversation with your clients around the miracle question. In an effort to help those who are new to this type of interviewing, Peter, his students, and Insoo have put together a goal-formulation protocol and a cribsheet of questions for developing well-formed goals. These tools are used by students in role-playing sessions until they become more familiar with the interviewing questions. We have included them in the Appendix.

The Williams Family

In practice, you will very often be required to meet with and interview several people at once. Although the basic components of solution-focused interviewing do not change under these circumstances, you must get the perceptions of all present and when these perceptions conflict, as they often do, you must work toward a joint definition of goals and a joint solution. To illustrate how this is done, we'll consider a family who came to Insoo for help; let's call them the Williams family.

When developing well-formed goals in a family case, you are working with two or more persons, all of whom may have different definitions of what is wrong and what life will look like when the family's problems are solved. With their different perceptions, individual family members may carry the conversation off in different directions—frequently in the direction of more problem talk from their particular points of view. As always, you must think of such developments as family members' attempts to be helpful, by giving more information about the family's situation, and find ways to return them to the task at hand—developing well-formed goals. Sometimes, you will notice rising tension and conflict among the participants. When this happens, remember to respectfully explore the perceptions of those family members who are stirred up; ask them what they think will be different when the problem is solved. This encourages them to return the focus to the work of developing goals. Finally, as with individual cases, notice what clients are already doing that is useful to themselves and helpful to their significant others and compliment them for those actions.

You will notice how Insoo does each of these things in the lengthy dialogue that follows, which reflects the many starts and stops of goal-formulation work. In the dialogue, as in previous chapters, we indicate periodically the procedures that Insoo used, along with the motivations for her questions.

The members of the Williams family who came for services are 32-year-old Gladys, her four children, and her 28-year-old brother, Albert. Her four children are Marcus (aged 12), Offion (10), Olayinka (8), and Ayesh (7). Having been kicked out by his mother, Albert is currently living with Gladys and her children. When he does not live with Gladys, he lives with other family members or friends. Gladys stated that he is unemployed and bums off people. She also reported that her husband has been in prison for five years. After going over this information about Gladys' household, Insoo began to explore what the family hoped to gain from seeing her:

INSOO: Now, what do you suppose has to happen for you to say, by coming here, that "it was a good idea that we all came to see that lady"?

GLADYS: That my chest pains I'm having now—that they [the doctors] say is stress related—that it goes away. That I can help . . . that you can somehow help me to deal with these problems that I'm having.

INSOO: So when you can deal with these problems, the chest pain will go away?

GLADYS: I hope they do.

INSOO: OK. What else? What else will happen?

GLADYS: My children will start doing things they know they supposed to do and I won't have to shout and holler at 'em and put 'em on punishments.

INSOO: Un huh. So they will listen to you more?

GLADYS: Yeah.

INSOO: [*beginning to work toward something different that is realistic*] Well, they're not gonna always listen. Right?

GLADYS: Right, not always.

INSOO: Not always. Kids at that age.

GLADYS: But sometimes you think they would.

INSOO: OK. You want them to listen to you sometimes.

GLADYS: Yeah, and I could learn or get some help on how to control my actions by saying yes or no to my mom and my relatives, and they would hear me when I say it. It's like, when I say it, they do it anyway.

INSOO: So they would hear you when you say no?

GLADYS: Right.

INSOO: OK. What else?

GLADYS: I don't know. At this time I can't think of nothing else.

MARCUS: We'd all get along.

INSOO: [*respecting the client's words and frame of reference*] "Get along"? What do you mean "get along"? What will you do when you all get along?

MARCUS: Learn to share.

INSOO: OK. Learn to share and get along. What else?

MARCUS: Nothing.

INSOO: Nothing?

GLADYS: But what he says here—he just talking about sharing your things, not his.

INSOO: [to Gladys] So you also agree with that?

GLADYS: Yeah, but he has to learn to share his as well as yours.

INSOO: Right. [to Marcus] I guess you're saying you want to share too. I mean you want to learn to share? Yeah? [Marcus agrees] OK. All right. How about for you, Offion?

OFFION: Make the family come more together. Like at family meetings.

INSOO: So when you have a family meeting you will all come together?

OFFION: We'll have more time together.

INSOO: More time together? Uh huh. More good time together?

OFFION: Yeah. Mostly we're out all day and never get to do anything.

GLADYS: [laughs] He wants to drive me crazy more than what he's doing. It's not enough. He needs to be there more, see.

INSOO: That's not what you're talking about. I mean you're not talking about driving [your] mother crazy; you're talking about getting along.

OFFION: Somewhat.

INSOO: Somewhat?

GLADYS: Hmm. Lord have mercy!

INSOO: [*inviting concrete, behavioral goal description*] So when your family is together and you have a family meeting and the family comes together, what would your family be doing?

OFFION: Playing.

INSOO: Playing together. What else?

OFFION: Having fun . . . and [pointing to Albert, Gladys' brother] not having him around. [Albert laughs]

AYESH: Having him around.

INSOO: You like having him around. And you don't like having him around. [all laugh; *continuing to explore each person's perceptions*] OK. Let me ask you, Albert. Let's say Gladys somehow handles this stress. She has no more chest pain, and she feels calmer with the kids, and she feels that the kids are listening to her and the family is listening to her, and let's suppose all that happens. What will you see different about her that will tell you, "Wow, she is doing better"?

ALBERT: I don't think I'd be able to [laughing] because it's like, well, I might as well tell you, I got a mind that's out of this world, OK? And I don't think I would be able to tell you—ah, to know the difference.

INSOO: Wait a minute. You have a mind that is out of this world?

ALBERT: Yeah. I sit up and I just get to thinking and I talks out loud sometime, and she always laughing, so it like every time I come around I always have her laughing so it wouldn't be nothing different to me.

INSOO: [*focusing on something to build on*] I see. But she likes having you around?

GLADYS: Sometime. Sometime he get on your nerves 'cause he do aggravating things that you tell him not to do, and then he gets the kids to do the same things he do, and they follow.

INSOO: OK. So sometimes it's helpful having Albert around; sometimes it's not.

GLADYS: Yeah. Like tomorrow he got to help move the stuff out the basement, so he can put the furnace and our water heater in. And sometimes I give him money and he buys cigarettes and [pointing to Albert's pants] he bought these pants with the money I gave him.

INSOO: [*complimenting*] So Albert, it seems like your sister's pretty helpful to you, too. You are helpful to her, and she helps you.

ALBERT: You could say that.

INSOO: Yeah, right. So somehow you learned to help each other?

GLADYS: 'Cause when you be raised up in a family where don't nobody help each other then you be like—why don't you never help each other? Then you say, "Well, I ain't gonna be like that." And then you try not to be like this, so you go out and help somebody else. Not only do I help. I help other peoples too. I guess that the heart that I have . . .

INSOO: And you didn't learn that from your mother.

GLADYS: No. Oh no, because mom was never there. She was an alcoholic, and then she would play cards all the time like gambling . . .

INSOO: [*returning to goal formulation*] Suppose that, after you stop coming here, you say: "We got help from that lady." [to Gladys] What will be going on differ-ent with your family so you can say, "We don't have to go see that lady anymore"?

GLADYS: They won't be doing the things that they do now, like . . .

INSOO: [*asking for the presence of something*] What will they do instead of that?

GLADYS: They will learn how to control their hands and mouths and keep them to themselves, and I could let them go over to other people's houses and spend the night and don't worry about, like, is they off over there sassing, and fight-ing, and showing somebody's else child bad habits. That I would be able to trust them to go away and stay by themselves at somebody's else house.

INSOO: [*asking for concrete, behavioral, measurable description*] And what would they do at somebody else's house that you can trust them?

GLADYS: The same thing that they will show me that they would do at my house. Like, if Marcus go to his friend's house, he might fight with the little boy and sass his mama. He'll go over there and be sassing and fighting. Where, instead of him doing that, he'll go over there just so he could play with the lit-tle boy and have a good time and come home.

INSOO: OK. So he will not be doing things that he's not supposed to be doing. He will be perfectly well behaved. OK. Like a gentleman.

GLADYS: Right.

INSOO: Good. All right. What about Offion? What would Offion be doing different that it would tell you that "we don't have to go see that lady anymore"?

GLADYS: Offion got this attitude where, if he tell you to do something he want, he expect for you to do it. Or, like, if you're talking and you're not listening to him and he trying to tell you something, he gets real upset and sometime he'll hit you, and sometime he do violent things to you.

INSOO: [*searching for the presence of desirable, positive behaviors*] So he will stop that. So what would he be like instead of being violent?

GLADYS: If he was talking to you and you didn't want to listen to him, he'd say forget it. You know, go on about his business. Maybe come back to you later and talk to you about what he wanted to talk to you about. He see you busy. It's not like he gonna get upset and wanna hit you 'cause . . .

INSOO: OK. So he can come back and talk to you calmer.

GLADYS: Right.

INSOO: Yeah. That's what he'll be doing. OK. So when he does, both Marcus and Offion can do all this, OK? [turning to the boys; *inviting goal description in interactional terms*] Let's suppose you can do all this. You learn to do all this. How would mom be different?

OFFION: There'd be less things that she had to do.

MARCUS: She won't have they heart pains.

INSOO: She won't have a heart pain. What will she be like when she doesn't have a heart pain?

MARCUS: We can go on picnics and, like, go different places without being all stressed out.

INSOO: Uh huh. I guess you would like to see mom do that. No stress and able to go on picnics and stuff like that. And you too. Uh huh. [*complimenting client strengths*] You must care about your mom very much? Huh? Yeah? Does mom know that?

MARCUS: I don't know.

INSOO: You don't know? Does mom know how much you care about her? What do you think, Marcus?

MARCUS: No; she don't know.

INSOO: She don't know? She don't know how much you care. How about for you, Offion? What do you think? Mom knows?

OFFION: I don't know.

INSOO: You don't know.

GLADYS: Do you know how much I love you?

OLAYINKA: Yes, mama.

GLADYS: I don't even think you know. [*her voice rising*] I don't think you know 'cause if you did you wouldn't so do the things you did.

INSOO: [*refocusing on possible strengths in the mother-child relationship*] Wait a minute. What do you think, Offion? Do you know?

GLADYS: Do you know?

OFFION: Yes.

INSOO: Yeah? How can you tell that mom cares about you?

MARCUS: Because if she didn't care about us—she's a single parent; if she didn't care about us, we would know.

INSOO: Right. She's a single parent and she takes care of you. That's how you know she cares about you. How about for you, Offion?

OFFION: 'Cause we have things that other kids don't have.

INSOO: Like what?

OFFION: Everything a kid would want.

INSOO: Yeah, really? You mean, like a Nintendo and that kind of stuff?

OFFION: Yeah.

INSOO: Yeah. Wow. [*complimenting client strengths*] You must be trying very hard with these kids.

GLADYS: I'm trying. I try my best; that's all I can do. And pray that they grow up the right way.

INSOO: Well, it's sounds like they know that you're trying very hard.

GLADYS: I would hope they do.

INSOO: Well, it sounds like they know it.

ALBERT: They know, but that ain't doing it.

INSOO: [*inviting the family to think even more broadly about an alternative future*] Now let me ask you some strange questions that I'm gonna ask all of you. OK? Let's say I have a special wand. You know about magic wands? [to the children, who have taken on skeptical expressions] You don't believe it. That's OK. Let's say I have a secret magic wand, and I'm going to sort of wave my magic wand, OK? Today. And, uh, after we talk like this, you guys are all gonna go home, and obviously you're gonna go home and go to bed tonight.

GLADYS: OK.

INSOO: And everybody's sleeping. The whole household is sleeping and, with this magic wand, I just wave a magic wand and just gold dust comes down, and the problem that brought you here today is all gone, just like that, through this magic. But you don't know. Nobody knows because everybody's sleeping.

GLADYS: OK.

INSOO: OK. Everybody. Everyone of you will be sleeping. Except when you wake up the next morning, how will you know that there was magic overnight while you were sleeping?

For many young children, the word *miracle* is too abstract and may not stir their imagination. However, the Williams children, like many others, were able to work with ideas like magic wand, gold dust, and magic:

OLAYINKA: There will be a change.

INSOO: [*emphasizing that a miracle future is a different future*] There will be a change? How can you tell there is a change? What would be different?

OLAYINKA: We . . . would do what mama wants, clean the house . . .

INSOO: [*asking for amplification to clients' interactional context*] So you automatically start to clean the house and do what you're supposed to do. Every one of you. Uh huh. OK. All right. So when you do that, what will mom do when mom sees all of you doing things that you're automatically supposed to do?

MARCUS: She'll think and scratch her head and wonder what happened. [laughter]

INSOO: What about for you? How will you know that's there's been magic overnight?

OFFION: Because when all my brothers and sisters are helping clean house and everything it's gonna be like: "Why are you guys being so nice? What do you want?"

INSOO: That's what mom would say?

OFFION: That's what I would say.

INSOO: [to Albert] How will you be able to tell? How could you tell that there's been a miracle overnight? That magic happened?

ALBERT: I wouldn't know a heck of a lot.

INSOO: How come? How come you wouldn't know?

ALBERT: Because, I told you already, that's the type of mind I got. It just ain't . . . Sometimes it function right, and sometimes it don't.

INSOO: [*giving Albert another chance to participate in developing a joint miracle picture*] OK. Suppose it did function right [laughter amongst family] and there's been magic, and the problem is solved.

ALBERT: Well see, even if I was in the problem and you put your wand over me, I'll probably wake up and probably be like, well, maybe I just changed. I mean I don't know.

INSOO: [*persisting*] OK. Suppose you changed.

ALBERT: But for 23 years, I mean, I ain't changed. I don't think it's gonna change that quick.

INSOO: Well, that's why it takes magic to do that.

ALBERT: Yeah.

INSOO: [*inviting him to think about the possibilities one more time*] That's why it takes magic to do that. So suppose it does. How will you be different?

ALBERT: If it does, I don't know. I'll probably stop drinking. Stop having sex with so many different women. Stop doing drugs.

INSOO: Yeah?

ALBERT: And have my own place and get a nice woman and settle down and have kids, I guess.

GLADYS: That sounds nice.

ALBERT: But, see, that's 23 years I still been trying to stop and make it happen, and it ain't happened yet, so I guess it gonna take a magic wand. So where's it at?

INSOO: [*encouraging Albert to think about what would be different before worry-ing about how to make it happen*] Wait a minute. So that's what you will do?

ALBERT: Yeah.

INSOO: So you will settle down with a nice woman and you will . . .

ALBERT: Get a job, have kids, get married.

INSOO: Like everybody else.

ALBERT: Right.

INSOO: [*inviting him to expand the possibilities by viewing himself through the eyes of a significant other*] Uh huh. So when you do that, what do you sup-pose your sister will notice different about you that will tell her something happened with Albert?

ALBERT: Well, she probably be like, "Well, he must have got his own and started back selling drugs" or something; I don't know.

INSOO: That's what she would think?

ALBERT: Yeah.

INSOO: But she will know that you were having a normal life, have a job?

ALBERT: [*to Gladys*] How would you know I changed?

INSOO: [*creating an opportunity for Albert to look at himself through the eyes of a significant other*] Yeah, how could you tell that he changed?

GLADYS: I'd be saying, "God musta came while I was sleep and cleaned that man life up and he left me."

INSOO: [*persisting, inviting future possibilities by picking up on the client's words*] So suppose he does that. Suppose God comes during the night while you're sleeping. How would Albert be different?

GLADYS: How would he be different?

INSOO: Yeah.

GLADYS: He wouldn't play Nintendo no more.

INSOO: [*continuing to work toward a joint miracle picture with the family*] How would he be different with you?

GLADYS: With me? If I said, if I told him to let the kids go to bed at a certain time, he wouldn't say, "Let 'em stay up five more minutes" or ten more minutes. When I say, "Let 'em go to bed at a certain time," he'll say OK. That's what your mom wants you to do, so he'll let 'em do it.

INSOO: So he will help you out with the kids?

GLADYS: Yeah.

INSOO: What about you? [*attempting to focus her on a small beginning step*] So when you wake up tomorrow morning and God's been there overnight and somehow God performed a very small miracle, how will you know? What will be a sign to you that, wow, God must be here?

GLADYS: When I tell my children . . . like, if I tell Offion, I said, "Offion go in there and wash our tub," he won't say, "I didn't do it" or, "I washed it out yesterday." I didn't ask you that, I said go wash the tub. Or if I say, "Go downstairs and . . ."

INSOO: [*asking for the presence of something, not the absence*] So when you say, "Go wash the tub," what will he do?

GLADYS: He go do it.

INSOO: He'd go do it. OK.

GLADYS: He won't tell me whose turn it is or who's supposed to do it.

INSOO: So what about Marcus? What will Marcus do different?

GLADYS: He quit thinking he more than everybody. He thinks he more than the other childrens. He, like, think of himself as Godlike and, to me, he don't know half as much as they do, but then he go around and talk about them and down them. Like, Offion got a friend . . .

INSOO: How would he change? What would he do instead of that?

GLADYS: He would try to be his brother's best friend. He would try to let his little brother look up to him and not say, "I don't want you around me" and treat him like dirt.

INSOO: So he would act like an older brother?

GLADYS: Right.

INSOO: OK. What about Olayinka? How would she be different?

GLADYS: She'll quit lying. When she stop—if God can perform a miracle, she would never lie again. You do not believe nothing she says.

INSOO: [*asking for a small sign of the presence of truthfulness*] So how will you know that she stopped lying tomorrow?

GLADYS: God would have to come to me himself and say, "Gladys, Yinka is not gonna lie to you no more for the rest of her life." I'm serious. 'Cause just, just looking at her and listening to her, it ain't gonna happen.

INSOO: [*encouraging her toward something more realistic*] Well, God's not likely to do that.

GLADYS: That's right, so I won't believe it.

INSOO: OK. So what would be the first sign to you then that, hmm, I think Yinka is starting to tell the truth?

GLADYS: Then she'll come to me and sit around me and she'll want to be around me.

INSOO: She'll want to be around you?

GLADYS: Yeah.

INSOO: How will she show you this? She wants to be around you.

GLADYS: Like she, she'll come in. Like when we all in a room watching a video, she'll come. She won't say, "I don't wanna come. I wanna go in my room and play." Or, "I want to go in the basement and play." That's where all the toys are at. Or if she, uh, like, don't wet the bed no more. Ever. Ever. I'd say, "Wow, God really touched that child. And maybe he touched her for lying. Let me check her out." But that would be a hard one.

INSOO: So she would not wet the bed anymore, and she would start to be honest. How could you tell that she started to be honest with you?

GLADYS: I don't know. I ain't figured that one out yet.

Insoo went on to ask more questions about how various family members would be different after the miracle happened and about the consequences of these differences for family interactions. In the course of these efforts, Gladys revealed more about her strengths and how much she wanted things to be different in her family:

GLADYS: They think they get away with things 'cause they smart. They go to private school.

INSOO: [*focusing on a possible success*] They do?

GLADYS: Yeah. Nonsectarian. No religion. Just private.

INSOO: [*exploring a possible success*] How did you manage to get them into a private school?

GLADYS: 'Cause when I called [sigh] . . . I called, like, three schools before I called Crestview, and these people was real rude to me on the phone and it's like, "Well, if you want to come in and fill out an application, I guess you can, but I can't give you any more information." They would hang up. And I called Crestview, and the secretary answered the phone and I, you know, I hesitated for a while, and she took they names, asked me they names, and then she told me some days that they can come in and we can look at the school, and she said we could come in and talk to the principal and that she would try to do everything that she could to help me, and she told me about some of the programs—they take up speech; they know French. And then she was nice to me. It wasn't like the other two peoples I had talked to before; they hung up in my face, so I didn't want them. I wouldn't want to treat nobody the way they treated me, and I wouldn't want to go to they school.

INSOO: [*affirming client perceptions*] Absolutely. Wow. You care about your children very much, huh?

GLADYS: Yeah, I try to. Didn't nobody care about me when I was little like them, so I told my mom, I said, "I'm not gonna do my childrens the way that I was done when I was little coming up." And she look at me now, and you know I ain't lying. The things I do for my kids, she do not like it. She look at me, . . . something like—if I gave them $100 for Christmas, which I did one year. It took me a long, it took me like the whole year to save $400, 'cause I'm just on one income, but I struggled and I saved $100 a piece for them and put it in they stocking, and she got very upset and told them to give her $50 a piece. She demanded $50. And I told 'em no. It took me a long time to save 50, $100 a piece for them.

INSOO: [*recognizing, complimenting, and exploring client strength*] Wow. So where did you learn to be such a good mother?

GLADYS: By being abused.

INSOO: Yeah?

GLADYS: If somebody keep treating you like a dog all your life, you'll say, "I don't wanna do that. I don't wanna treat nobody like that." At least that was my mind. I thought peoples, like, would think that way but everybody don't. My husband, he was abused, but he didn't think like that. He wanted to go and abuse other people.

INSOO: Right. So how did you learn to be such a good mother?

GLADYS: By being abused. I was sexually molested when I was little. And then my mother was never there to listen to me. Then when she was, it was like, "So what? Get out of my face." And I got to the point where I said, "Naw, that ain't right. If I had kids, I wouldn't wanna treat my kids like that."

INSOO: [complimenting] How did you know that ain't right?

GLADYS: 'Cause the things they did to me wasn't right.

INSOO: Oh, you knew that already.

GLADYS: Yeah.

INSOO: When you were a child.

GLADYS: Yeah.

The Art of Interviewing for Well-Formed Goals

The preceding dialogue includes examples of all of the solution-focused interviewing procedures that we have discussed so far in this book. Insoo made artful use of everything from complimenting and affirming the clients' perceptions to the miracle question and its follow-up questions. All of this work centered on helping the clients to develop well-formed goals, within their respective frames of reference. Insoo's task was to explore an alternative future, affirm those helpful things that the clients were already doing, and invite them to amplify their successes. The clients' part was to struggle to conceptualize answers to her questions from their points of view and past experiences.

If you are new to solution-focused interviewing, one aspect of Insoo's goal-formulation work with the Williams family might be especially useful to you. Beginners often have difficulty in sustaining a conversation around well-formed goals and feel awkward asking the miracle question, even though clients may find it intriguing. Insoo's work with the Williams family offers a way to address both concerns.

Let's return to the dialogue and study its development. We see that Insoo chose not to begin the goal-formulation work by asking the miracle question. Instead, she opted to shift the Williams' focus from problem description to goal-formulation work less abruptly, by asking some other questions. She started by asking what would have to happen for the clients to feel that it had been a good idea to see Insoo. Using the Williams' answers as a starting point, she asked follow-up questions to elicit the characteristics of well-formed goals. Thereafter, she asked variations of her first question: What would be different when the family's problem was solved? What would be different when the family was doing better? What would be different when the family didn't have to visit Insoo anymore? She gave the family members many opportunities to expand and clarify their answers, with appropriate follow-up questions. Only then, after the family members had spent several minutes describing various future possibilities, did she ask the miracle question and its follow-ups. Thus, by using other goal-formulation questions to build up to the miracle question, Insoo sustained the conversation for much of the first session and, at the same time, eased the conversation from less unusual questions to the more intriguing miracle question.

Avoiding Premature Closure

This lengthy dialogue, which represents considerable effort for both practitioner and clients, is only the beginning of a process in which the Williams family thinks about, and settles on, a more attractive future. As we know from experience, the Williams family, individually and together, will most likely continue to ponder Insoo's questions after they leave the office. You should not expect to reach closure with clients when amplifying the miracle picture. In fact, it is preferable to leave the dialogue open-ended, so that clients have the freedom to explore further possibilities.

Nevertheless, we know how difficult it can be to let clients explore for themselves the possibilities that might exist for them. We, too, have been tempted to push clients toward closure and offer them suggestions from our point of view, in an attempt to relieve their confusion and frustration. However, over time, we have found it increasingly easy to persist in our questioning and to avoid pushing for immediate closure on goals. Experience has taught us that clients are competent. Given the chance, they not only are able to formulate and aspire to more satisfying futures but also, in the process, they reveal many of their strengths and past successes. Insoo certainly found this to be the case with the Williams family.

Exploring for Exceptions: Building on Client Strengths and Successes

When I focus on what's good today, I have a good day, and when I focus on what is bad, I have a bad day. If I focus on a problem, the problem increases; if I focus on the answer, the answer increases.

(Alcoholics Anonymous, 1976, p. 451)

We began Chapter 5 by discussing the process of planning a trip as a metaphor for the solution-building process. As we saw, both processes involve two main steps. First, both the would-be traveler and the client must decide on a destination. To do so, the traveler gathers more information about what is there at each of several possible destinations, whereas the client generates ever more concrete and detailed descriptions of what will be different in his or her life when the miracle happens. Second, once a sense of destination begins to develop, both traveler and client must think about how best to get there. The traveler considers the pros and cons of different modes of transportation, whereas the solution-building client does so by exploring exceptions, the subject of this chapter.

Exceptions

Definition

As noted in Chapter 3, we find that, when we first meet with our clients, they tend to be very problem-focused. They have done a whole lot of thinking about those things in their lives that they wish were not happening and can usually describe them in great detail. For example, suppose that you have a client called Joy, whose problem is her disobedient children. Joy can describe what her children do when they are disobedient ("they sass me and refuse to do what I ask"); can indicate when those times happen ("whenever I ask them to do their chores"); is able to state who is involved ("all three of them do it, but my oldest, Ken, is the worst"); can describe where the problem happens ("anyplace we happen to be together"); and is able to indicate when the problem is most severe ("it's worst when they want to watch TV or a friend is over"). Such problem descriptions can be helpful, because they allow clients to vent their frustrations and unhappiness, thereby offering some relief. They can also provide a preliminary idea of how dangerous a situation might be for the participants involved. However, we have not found that problem descriptions are a useful resource for building solutions. Descriptions of exceptions are more useful for that purpose.

Exceptions are those past experiences in a client's life when the problem might reasonably have been expected to occur but somehow did not (de Shazer, 1985). For example, returning to Joy, an exception would be anytime Ken obeyed her order and did the dishes without sassing.

Exceptions may be a matter of lesser degree. Ken may never have done all the dishes without any sassing, but there might have been a time in the recent past when, after 5 minutes of talking back to his mother, he did some of them.

Interviewing for Exceptions

As a solution-focused interviewer, you will quickly learn that there are several identifiable parts to the exploration of exceptions. The first is to find out from your client whether he or she is aware of any exceptions. You might ask: "Have there been times in the last couple of weeks when the problem did not happen or, at least, was less severe?" If the client cannot answer that question, you could ask: "I'd like to ask your best friend whether you had any better days recently. What do you suppose your best friend would say?"

Notice that these questions ask for exceptions in the recent past. Experience has taught us that recent exceptions are most useful to clients. We think that this is because clients can remember recent experiences in greater detail and, since they just happened, it is all the more plausible that they could happen again.

Once your client has identified an exception, you should ask for details. In doing so, pay special attention to the ways in which this exception time was different from the problem times. Whereas a problem-focused interviewer would explore the who, what, when, and where of client problems, you should be interested in exploring the who, what, when, and where of exception times.

As with questions designed to elicit well-formed goals, clients may struggle to answer exception questions, but will find them intriguing and do their best to answer them.

Remember that, in listening to a client's answers to exception questions, you would be listening for what is different between the exception and problem times. It's a good idea to paraphrase and summarize such differences for clients, because they are part of the raw material for solution building.

Deliberate and Random Exceptions

When your clients have done what they can to describe their exceptions, you can proceed to explore how the exceptions may have happened. To find out about the how of an exception, you inquire who did what to make the exception happen. Sometimes a client is able to describe how an exception happened. For instance, Joy, when asked how it happened that Ken did the dishes once last week without sassing her, might tell you that she had decided to wait until after he had eaten supper and was in a better mood before reminding him it was his turn to do the dishes. If she were to agree that this shift in her behavior may have made the difference, you would have uncovered what de Shazer (1985) calls a *deliberate exception.* If, on the other hand, Joy had responded to your questions about Ken's behavior by shrugging her shoulders and saying, "I don't know; lightning must have struck him," you would regard Ken's doing the dishes as a *random exception* from Joy's point of view.

As an interviewer, it is important to develop a keen awareness of whether a client is describing deliberate or random exceptions. This distinction plays a key role in determining what feedback is given to the client at the end of a solution-building session, as we'll see in the next chapter.

Ah Yan's Exceptions

Let's return to the case of Ah Yan and see how Peter explored exceptions with her. If you recall, Ah Yan wanted help with her panicky feelings. When Peter asked the miracle question, she was able to begin describing some things that she, her husband, and her children might be doing differently after her problem had been solved. At that point, Peter turned to some exception exploration:

PETER: Ah Yan, are there times, in the last month or so, which are something like the miracle picture you just described?

AH YAN: Yeah, there are times when I feel real good. I'm OK, like everything is gone.

PETER: When was the last time you felt real good?

AH YAN: I don't know . . . maybe one day three weeks ago.

PETER: What was different about that day?

AH YAN: I felt real good. It's like—I can breathe better, no shakes, no worry. . . . I'm happy.

PETER: Really, you were happy, no shakes! That must have felt great! How did that happen?

AH YAN: [pause] I don't know.

PETER: If your husband were here and I were to ask him what he noticed you doing different that day, what would he say?

AH YAN: He tells me to sit down, stop doing housework, to eat right.

PETER: Is he right? Do those things help?

AH YAN: I can't just sit there and watch my kids make a mess. I have to . . . people come and the house is a mess.

PETER: What about eating right?

AH YAN: Yeah, I have to do that—fruit instead of cookies and candy. My sister-in-law says the same.

PETER: What else does she say?

AH YAN: To eat right every morning. Mostly I don't and my stomach is upset. She says to walk and exercise and take a deep breath when it's bad.

PETER: And do those things help? Do you do more of those things on a real good day?

AH YAN: Ah . . . maybe . . . I don't know. . . . I can't figure it out—what's wrong with me. I don't know what to do. . . . I got all these feelings. . . . I gotta figure out what's wrong with me.

This dialogue gives some useful information about how far Ah Yan has come with her solution building. She is clear that there are exception times in her life; she calls these days when she feels real good. She can also give some description about how they are different than her problem days: "I can breathe better, no shakes, no worry. . . . I'm happier." However, when Peter followed up, she could not give a more detailed description of these exception days. Nor was she able to answer when he asked about how they happened. Therefore, at this point in their conversation, she was experiencing random exceptions rather than deliberate exceptions. Because she was unable to describe step by step how her real good days happen—much less what she might have done to make them happen—she didn't have a sense of control over her panicky feelings. In her frustration, at the end of this interchange, she returned to her original frame of having to "figure out what's wrong with me."

In this first session with Ah Yan, Peter chose to explore exceptions after he had asked the miracle question and its follow-up questions. As an interviewer, you don't have to do it this way, but there are some good reasons for following his example. First, clients beginning work with practitioners are rarely aware of their exceptions, because they are focused on describing their problems. Asking exception-finding questions at that point can seem jarring. However, once a client has been able to give a concrete description of what life will be like when the miracle happens, as Ah Yan did, it is very natural for the practitioner to move on to exception exploration. Second, this sequence makes it more probable that the client will give exceptions directly related to the miracle—that is, to the amplified version of what the client might like to have different in his or her life. These are the most useful exceptions for solution building, because they are most closely related to what the client wants.

Client Successes and Strengths

By exploring exceptions you can help clients to become more aware of their current and past successes in relation to their goals (De Jong & Miller, 1995). In a sense, whenever you and a client bring an exception to light, both of you become aware that some good things are happening in the client's life and, consequently, you can both feel more hopeful about the client's future. For example, when Peter and Ah Yan became aware that Ah Yan had recently had a day during which she felt real good—that is, something of a successful day— they sensed that Ah Yan, indeed, might have possibilities for a more satisfying future. Correspondingly, we have noticed that clients' interest in solution building often picks up when they are able to identify exceptions. They frequently sit up straighter, smile more, and seem more willing to work hard.

Specific client strengths are also often uncovered during exception exploration. If a client is able to describe what he or she did to help make an exception happen, the practitioner can readily paraphrase that description and compliment some strength of the client. Let's return to our example of Joy and the night that Ken did the dishes. When Joy tells you that her contribution to that exception was that she decided to wait until after he had eaten supper and was in a better mood before reminding him to do them, you could then point out and compliment some of her strengths in a variety of ways. You might ask, "Was that new for you—waiting until after he had eaten and was in a better mood?" or, "How did you know that waiting might be helpful?" Or you might comment, "You seem to know your son very well" or, "You must be a mother who cares; you realize how important it is for a son to do his chores."

Respecting the Client's Words and Frame of Reference

Exception exploration is similar to other aspects of solution-focused interviewing in that, when it is done well, it respects the client's frame of reference. In exploring exceptions, an interviewer listens for a client's words and then demonstrates respect for these words by asking the client to clarify them. When Ah Yan told Peter that she had had a real good day, he asked her what was different about that day that made it real good. As in other solution-focused interviews, Ah Yan's words were used as the doorway to her experiences and frame of reference. Ah Yan was treated as the expert about these and their meaning, while Peter's role was to ask the questions that would allow him to learn more about Ah Yan's view of her world.

Scaling Questions

By means of scaling questions, a practitioner can help clients to express complex, intuitive observations about their past experiences and estimates of future possibilities (Berg, 1994; Berg & de Shazer, 1993; Berg & Miller, 1992; de Shazer, 1988). Scaling questions invite clients to put their observations, impressions, and predictions on a scale from 0 to 10. For example, you might ask Joy: "On a scale of 0 to 10, where 0 means no chance and 10 means every chance, what do you think the chances are that, sometime in the next week, Ken will do the dishes again?" When asking scaling questions, the practitioner cites a specific time in the client's life, such as "today" or "the day you made the appointment to see me" or "sometime in the next week." Scaling is a useful technique for making complex aspects of the client's life more concrete and accessible to both practitioner and client.

Scaling questions have great versatility. They can be used to access the client's perception of almost anything, including "self-esteem, pre-session change, self-confidence, investment in change, willingness to work hard to bring about desired changes, prioritizing of problems to be solved, perception of hopefulness, and evaluation of progress" (Berg, 1994, pp. 102–103).

At this point, we are going to present scaling questions that are often used during the first meeting with clients. The first of these represents another way to uncover exceptions in clients' lives.

Presession-Change Scaling

In the past, it was a common assumption that clients begin to change when the practitioner starts to help them with their problems. Practitioners would talk about clients as "stuck" or "overwhelmed" before they came for services. We now know, to the contrary, that change is regularly happening in most clients' lives; when asked, two-thirds of clients will report positive change between the time they made the appointment for services and their first meeting with practitioners; this is called *presession change* (Weiner-Davis, de Shazer, & Gingerich, 1987).

In solution-focused interviewing, you can call your client's attention to the existence of presession change by using a scaling question. Then, by exploring any change that you discover, you can further sharpen the client's awareness of exceptions. In fact, some clients who were not able to identify exceptions when asked exception-finding questions do acknowledge presession change if the practitioner employs scaling questions. With follow-up questioning, these clients are usually able to begin identifying exceptions.

In his first meeting with Ah Yan, Peter asked her to scale any presession change:

PETER: Here is a different kind of question, Ah Yan, one which puts things on a scale from 0 to 10. Let's say that 0 equals how bad the panicky feelings were at the time you made the appointment to see me and 10 is the miracle you described to me earlier. Where are you on that scale today?

AH YAN: Umm, about a 6.

PETER: A 6, no kidding. That's pretty high. What's different about being at 6 than at 0?

AH YAN: I can't just sit; I have to do somethin'. . . . Try and do things, like come here and figure out what's wrong with me.

PETER: Besides coming here, what else makes you a 6.

AH YAN: Talking to my sister-in-law. She says: "If there's something you want to talk about, let's talk." And try to talk and go out more.

PETER: So you've been going out more lately?

AH YAN: Yeah, with my husband and the kids on weekends, like to the lake.

PETER: And anything else?

AH YAN: Yeah, pray. I've been praying more.

You might notice three things about this sequence. First, Ah Yan paused after Peter asked her the presession scaling question. It was as though she had an intuitive sense that things were better today than when she made the appointment, but she had to think for a moment before she could put a number to her intuitive sense.

Second, by asking the scaling question, Peter offered Ah Yan an efficient and even satisfyingly accurate way to express that sense. Suppose that, instead, Peter had asked: "How are things today compared to the day you made the appointment to see me?" This question might have been more difficult for Ah Yan; she might have found herself struggling to decide what parts of her experience to report and in what words. The scaling question, however, gave her a way to represent her perception in a straightforward and accurate manner.

Third, when Ah Yan surprised Peter by choosing a 6, he had a meaningful way to explore for exceptions that may have happened just before their first meeting: He asked Ah Yan what was different about being at 6 rather than 0. He expected her to say something about feeling better and to more fully describe some exceptions, but she skipped right over that. Instead, she started identifying some of the things that might account for her being at a 6. Peter found this very interesting because she had seemed perplexed earlier in the session when he had asked how her exceptions were happening. Asking the presession-change question, however, not only confirmed the existence of Ah

Yan's exceptions for both of them, but also began to build their awareness of who might be doing what to make them happen.

That presession-change exploration can reveal new information should not seem surprising. As we have already seen, solution-focused interviewing tends to build on itself in the direction of a solution; it does not work by hitting upon the only possible solution to some complex puzzle. This is another reason why we prefer the language of solution building to that of problem solving.

Scaling Motivation and Confidence

It will be useful for both you and your clients to know how motivated they are to work on building solutions. Clients' answers to a scaling question about how hard they are willing to work will help you in formulating end-of-session feedback. Clients who indicate a high motivation to work are generally more likely to continue what has worked for them in the past and to try new strategies.

Scaling motivation to work hard is a simple matter. Here is how Peter did it with Ah Yan:

PETER: I want to ask another scaling question, this time about how hard you are willing to work on the problem which brought you in. Let's say that 10 means you are willing to do anything to find a solution, and 0 means that you are willing to do nothing—just sit and wait for something better to happen. How hard, from 0 to 10, are you willing to work?

AH YAN: Ten. I've gotta.

PETER: A 10—that's top of the scale. Where does all that willingness to work come from?

AH YAN: I gotta, for me and my family.

Notice that Peter did not stop when Ah Yan indicated a 10 on willingness to work. By asking where her motivation came from, he gave Ah Yan an opportunity to say that her willingness to work was "for me and my family." As most clients do, Ah Yan tied her motivation to her values. This observation confirms once again the critical importance of finding out what is important to the client and what the client might want.

Early on in your relationships with clients, you will also find it useful to regularly scale the clients' perceived confidence that they will find a solution to their problems. Peter almost always does this in first sessions with clients, after goal formulation and exception exploration. By that stage of the session, clients have had lots of opportunity to do solution talk and their confidence is more likely to be up:

PETER: If 0 means you have no confidence that you will find a solution and 10 means you have every confidence, how confident would you say that you are right now that you will find a solution to the panicky feelings?

AH YAN: Ten. I'm not gonna stop until I'm all the way.

PETER: Are you that kind of person—once you decide to do something you're confident that you can make it happen?

AH YAN: I have to, I want to, I can't sit there the rest of my life. I want the answers . . .

PETER: OK, so where does all your confidence come from that you'll find a solution?

AH YAN: Well, my mom, she told me to finish school and I didn't. She was right, and I learned my lesson. I want it, and I have to.

PETER: You seem very determined.

AH YAN: Yeah.

Scaling questions offer clients opportunities to define themselves in particular ways. Notice that each time Peter offers Ah Yan a chance to state her determination or her confidence, she has an additional opportunity to convince herself that she is a determined and confident person.

Similarly, by scaling motivation and confidence, you can explore and reinforce client strengths. Peter learned that Ah Yan is a determined person who cares about her family, who can learn from past experiences, who has long-range personal goals, and who can prioritize her goals. He was especially impressed by Ah Yan's self-description as a very determined person who learned from her mistake of not listening to her mom.

Finally, when responding to scaling questions about their levels of motivation and confidence, clients will frequently identify more exceptions, which the interviewer can then pursue.

Exceptions: The Williams Family

In her first meeting with the Williams family, Insoo mainly worked on developing well-formed goals. In the rest of that interview, she focused on exceptions; she did not ask any scaling questions.

If you recall, the Williams family consisted of Gladys, her four children, and her brother Albert, who came to live with her from time to time. Gladys had been struggling with stress-related chest pains, which her doctors could not tie to physiological causes. Insoo helped the family begin to develop a joint picture of what they wanted. In the goal-formulation work, family members were able to suggest several things that might be different in their family life when the problem that brought them in was solved: Albert would be doing more dishes; the children would be better behaved when they visited their friends' homes; the children would be more obedient and helpful to Gladys and one another; Albert would have his own place and get a nice woman and settle down and have kids; Olayinka would want to be around her mother more because she was telling the truth; and so on. Once several possibilities had been identified, Insoo began to explore exceptions:

INSOO: [*asking for the perception of exceptions*] Now, let me ask you. Are there times when little bits of these miracle pictures, little bits—not all of it, little bits of it—happen? Even now?

GLADYS: Yeah. Like Yesh stopped peeing in the bed for two weeks.

INSOO: [*acknowledging an important exception, Insoo responds with excitement in her voice*] She did?

GLADYS: And last night she peed in the bed. So I didn't say nothing 'cause she stopped for two weeks.

INSOO: [*very interested and asking about how the exception happened*] Two weeks? How'd you do that?

AYESH: I didn't drink as much and . . .

INSOO: Yeah? So when you don't drink as much you have a dry bed? Wow. So, two weeks. OK. [*asking for more exceptions*] What else happened? Other little pieces.

GLADYS: Offion got a friend.

INSOO: Got a friend? A good friend?

GLADYS: Yeah.

INSOO: [to Offion] Do you have a good friend? [he indicates two] Yeah? Two friends?

GLADYS: Who, Antowan? And Brian.

INSOO: And they are good kids?

GLADYS: They are. They are good kids. I don't mind them coming around me. They can even spend the night.

INSOO: [*asking about how the exception happened and indirectly complimenting*] How'd you do that? How'd you get two good friends?

OFFION: Going to summer school and going to Crestview.

INSOO: Yeah? Huh. [*complimenting*] They must think that you're a pretty good kid, too, then. Is that right?

OFFION: I don't know.

INSOO: They must. Right? Uh huh. [Offion agrees] That's great. That's fantastic. What else?

GLADYS: I forgot now. I don't know what else.

INSOO: Little bits of miracle picture that we were talking about . . .

GLADYS: Sometime, sometime, like, I don't have to tell Marcus to clean up; I don't have to tell Offion to pick his clothes up from over behind the bed. See, Marcus' side of the room stay clean.

INSOO: [*complimenting an apparent strength*] He's very neat.

GLADYS: Yeah. But then you look at Offion's side, you say, "Is this the same room?" He like . . .

INSOO: But sometimes he picks it up?

GLADYS: Every blue moon I hear Marcus in there saying, "Offion, you have to pick up them clothes. You know mama gonna come in here." The majority of the time he says, "So what?" and he won't pick 'em up.

INSOO: [*focusing on the exception times*] But sometimes he listens to Marcus?

GLADYS: Yeah. And sometimes he'll say, "Yeah, I better go and pick 'em up" and he'll do it.

INSOO: [*complimenting*] Is that right? So sometimes you're being a big brother? Wow, it's a good start. What else? Little pieces.

GLADYS: [*indicating Ayesh*] When she take and, uh, don't bring food in the room and leave it for the roaches. See, they go to private school so I have to fix lunch. She bring the lunch home 'cause she don't eat and then she say, "Forget it" and hide it in the room. Why hide it in the room? If you don't want it, throw it in the garbage. Not her.

INSOO: OK. Now I'm wondering about the little pieces—pieces like the miracle?

GLADYS: I mean I see her pick her clothes up, her new clothes, and hang 'em up. Yeah. I don't have to tell her to do it. She'll pick 'em up and hang 'em up.

INSOO: Really? She knows how to do that?

GLADYS: Yeah. She knows how to clean up her bed, she know how to sweep the floor, she wash dishes. She 7 years old. She do all that stuff.

INSOO: [*indirectly complimenting and asking how the exception happens*] Where did you learn that?

AYESH: Offion, Yinka, and Marcus.

INSOO: Oh. They taught you? They taught you how to do that? Oh. Fantastic.

GLADYS: [*proudly*] And she match her own clothes. She put this on. She went and got that and put it on. Everybody get they own clothes. So they wear what they wanna wear.

INSOO: [*complimenting by pointing to how the children are dressed*] They did a very good job!

GLADYS: If they put on something that's for winter, I say, "You gotta take that off; that's for winter." Then they go get something else. They say, "How 'bout this?"

INSOO: [*acknowledging exceptions and a strength in the children*] So they do listen to you sometimes?

GLADYS: Sometimes. On some things. Not all the time, though.

Several aspects of exploring for exceptions are demonstrated here. Insoo asked about the perception of exceptions. She also asked questions to clarify how the exception times are different from the problem times. She highlighted and indirectly complimented client strengths by paraphrasing the implications of exceptions for what the various family members can do. For example, the fact that sometimes Offion listens to Marcus' appeals to pick up his own clothes indicates that, even though he is inconsistent, Offion does know how to pick up his side of the bedroom. And, when an exception emerged, Insoo asked about how it happened, thereby beginning to gather information about whether the exceptions are random or deliberate.

In working with exceptions, as in goal formulation, clients tend to minimize or dismiss the importance of their perceptions. In minimizing their exceptions, they return to problem talk; they indicate how frustrating and serious the problem seems. This is to be expected because, at first, client exceptions may not appear to be of much value to either the client or the practitioner, in the face of seemingly overwhelming problems. Even so, we have found that clients can start to build some momentum by gaining an increased awareness of moves in the right direction. Success tends to feed on itself—even when successes are small. Consequently, when family members left exception description for more problem talk, Insoo listened for a short while and then returned her clients to solution talk by paraphrasing the hopeful signs and small beginnings that had already emerged.

In summary, as a practitioner, you should follow the following guidelines:

- Get accustomed to regularly asking your clients exception-finding questions.
- Tune your ears so as to hear exceptions even when the client minimizes their importance.
- Ask about how exception times are different from (or better than) problem times.
- Find out who is doing what to make the exception happen.
- Paraphrase and affirm client strengths and successes embodied in the exceptions.

Building Toward a Difference That Makes a Difference

In exception exploration, as in goal formulation, practitioners new to solution-focused work tend to push for closure too quickly. As soon as a client mentions an exception, they want to turn this difference into the solution. For example, a couple seeking help to reduce the conflict in their relationship may say, "We fight less when we go out together for dinner." The novice at this point will often be tempted to say, "Well, do you think it would help if you started going out to dinner more often, say, once a week?"

For most clients, such a move for closure will be premature. Exception-finding questions are new for most of them; they are more accustomed to problem-focused questions. When asked about exceptions, they may be noticing them for the first time. They may also doubt whether those that they noticed are indeed exceptions. Certainly, they are not yet ready to decide whether an identified exception represents a solution to their problem. Consequently, rather than pushing for closure, the practitioner should give clients opportunity to dialogue about the meaning and significance of their exceptions on the basis of our guidelines.

Another of de Shazer's (1988, 1991) observations is helpful in this context. Influenced by Bateson (1972), he characterizes what occurs in exception dialogues as working toward a difference that makes a difference. He emphasizes that solutions are often built from formerly unrecognized differences, that is, exceptions (de Shazer, 1988, p. 10). Having heard and explored these exceptions, the practitioner needs to incorporate information about them, together with information about client goals and strengths, into session-ending feedback for clients. This feedback is designed to give clients every chance of both repeating past exceptions and producing new exceptions that come ever closer to solutions—closer, that is, to differences that make a difference. In our next chapter, we look at how to formulate feedback.

Formulating Feedback for Clients

Each of you pick two days over the next week, secretly, and on those days, we want you to pretend that that miracle we talked about has already happened.

(de Shazer, 1991, p. 144)

In previous chapters, we have discussed several components of a solution-focused way of interviewing clients: how to form productive working relationships with clients; how to respect what clients want; how to interview for well-formed goals; and how to explore for exceptions. By now, you may be wondering how all of this can be pulled together for the benefit of clients. In this chapter, we examine how you can take the information you gather in interviews and organize it into feedback that will be useful to clients in their solution building.

End-of-session feedback in solution building is not the same thing as intervention in the problem-solving approach. In the latter case, the practitioner uses assessment information about the nature and severity of client problems to decide on what actions would best benefit the client. The practitioner then takes those actions or encourages the client to do so. These actions—the interventions—are thought to produce the positive changes for the client. Because interventions are designed by practitioners on the basis of expert assessment information and professional theory, the practitioner is the primary change agent in the problem-solving approach (Pincus & Minahan, 1973).

In solution building, by contrast, we do not regard session-ending feedback as any more important than any other component of the process. Instead, as we have been emphasizing all along, we think that solutions are built by clients through the hard work of applying their strengths in the direction of goals that they value. Clients, not practitioners, are the primary agents of change. In the course of the interview, clients disclose information about themselves and their circumstances; session-ending feedback merely organizes and highlights the aspects of that information that might be useful to clients as they strive to build solutions.

In this chapter, we first indicate at what point of the session we go about formulating feedback. Second, we discuss the structure of feedback messages to clients. Third, we explain just how you can go about formulating feedback on the basis of interview information; we illustrate that process by returning to the cases of Ah Yan and the Williams family. Fourth, we present several common messages used in feedback by solution-focused interviewers. Finally, we offer a protocol for a complete first meeting with clients that identifies and sequences the several interviewing activities presented so far.

Taking a Break

When interviewing clients in a solution-focused manner, practitioners generally take a break of 5–10 minutes before giving clients feedback. Although you might find this strange at first, it will have definite benefits for you and your clients.

At the beginning of your first meeting with new clients, as we stated in Chapter 4, you can clarify how you like to organize work sessions. Mention your wish to take a break and explain the purpose of the break: It gives you time to think about all that they have told you and to formulate some feedback that you hope will be helpful to them. We have noticed that clients readily accept this rationale for a break. We also find that the break increases clients' anticipation about what we have to say when we return; they listen very carefully. Taking a break seems to put an exclamation mark behind any concluding observations that we might have.

Sometimes we work with a team; team members monitor our sessions from behind a one-way mirror. In that case, we meet with the team during the break, and they offer their suggestions for the feedback. Mostly, however, we work alone and use the break for quiet reflection.

When we take a break, we get up and leave; the client remains in the interviewing room or, if it is a home visit, in the living room or kitchen. Usually, the client sits and reflects on what we have been talking about; sometimes, the client may pick up a magazine and begin looking through it or go outside for a cigarette. If, now or in the future, you interview clients in your office, you might want to ask your clients to return to a waiting room. After you have formulated your feedback, you can invite them back into your office.

As an experiment, some practitioners are giving clients an assignment during the break. For example, when working with a team, Andersen (1987, 1991) has clients listen in on the team's ideas. Scott Miller has reported to Peter that he now asks clients to think during the break about a task for themselves that might be useful. When he returns, he asks the clients if they have come up with anything. If they have, he blends it with his own feedback. Both Andersen and Miller view their experiments as efforts to make their work with clients more collaborative.

The Structure of Feedback

In formulating feedback for clients, we recommend that you adopt the structure developed by de Shazer and his colleagues (de Shazer et al., 1986). There are three basic parts to this structure: compliments, a bridge, and usually a task. All are designed to convey to clients that you have been listening carefully and agree with their views about their problems, about what they want to have different in their lives, and about the steps they might take to make their lives more satisfying.

Compliments

As noted earlier, compliments are affirmations of the client. First, compliments affirm what is important to the client. For example, it is clear that Ah Yan cares very much about the well-being of her husband and children. She said that she wanted to figure out what was wrong with her for the good of her family, as well as herself. She can be complimented, therefore, as a real family person who wants to be the best she can for the good of her children and husband.

Second, compliments affirm client successes and the strengths that these successes suggest. In Ah Yan's case, when she and Peter were exploring exceptions and presession changes, she stated that there were times when the panicky feelings were not as bad, that she was doing better at the time of the first session with Peter than she had been several days earlier, and that she had tried several strategies to control her panic. Consequently, Ah Yan could rightly be complimented for her persistence, hard work, and creativity in trying several different ways to build a solution.

Beginning the feedback with a list of compliments can have a surprising and dramatic effect on clients. Most clients, struggling under the weight of their problems, are not expecting to hear a series of affirmations about what they want and what they are already doing that is useful to them. More often, they are feeling discouraged about their past choices and prospects for the future. When the practitioner returns from the break, many clients are thinking negatively and nervously ask, "Well, how bad is it?" or, "Do you think there is hope for us?" Beginning feedback with compliments not only creates hope, but also implicitly communicates to clients that solutions are built around client goals by drawing mainly on client successes (exceptions) and strengths.

If you choose to offer compliments to clients, be sure to watch their reactions to the affirmations. Their reactions will give you important clues about whether the compliments make sense to them. If your observations connect, they usually will shake their heads in agreement or smile. If they do not, you can reevaluate your thinking about the information you have gathered before you see them again. We have found that, at minimum, clients tend to be intrigued by the compliments we give; more often, they seem demonstrably pleased with them.

The Bridge

The bridge is the part of the feedback that links the initial compliments to the concluding suggestions or tasks. As with compliments, any suggestions that the practitioner might offer must make sense to clients, or else they will be ignored. The bridge provides the rationale for the suggestions.

The content of the bridge is usually drawn from client goals, exceptions, strengths, or perceptions. Commonly, the practitioner will begin the bridging statement by saying, "I agree with you that . . ." When possible, it is also a good idea to incorporate client words and phrases. For example, in feedback to Ah Yan, Peter might offer the following bridging statement: "I agree with you, Ah Yan, that trying to figure out your panicky feelings is an important goal; it would not be good for you or your family for you to sit there with those feelings for the rest of your life. Therefore, I suggest that . . ."

Tasks

The third component of feedback is to give tasks to clients. Although there are important exceptions, tasks are usually given in solution-focused work. These tasks fall into two main categories: observation tasks and behavioral tasks (de Shazer, 1988). In an observation task, the practitioner suggests—on the basis of information gathered in the interview—that the client pay attention to a particular aspect of his or her life that is likely to prove useful in solution building. For example, Peter might instruct Ah Yan to pay attention to those days when she is feeling less panicky—especially to the ways in which they differ from her bad days. He would also suggest that she keep track of those differences—when the better days happen, what she was doing then, who she was with, and so on—and report them to him the next time they met.

Behavioral tasks require the client to actually do something—to take certain actions that the practitioner believes will be useful to the client in constructing a solution. As with observation tasks, behavioral tasks are based on information gathered during the interview and should therefore make sense to the client within his or her frame of reference. Because Ah Yan has implied that talking to her sister-in-law is somehow helpful to her, Peter can assign her the behavioral task of continuing to do so.

As you begin to formulate solution-focused feedback for clients, you will soon discover that deciding whether to give a task and what type of task to give will be the most difficult part of feedback. Workshop participants and students consistently tell us that summarizing client successes and strengths in a list of compliments is easy and enjoyable and that figuring out a bridging statement is feasible once they have settled on a task. However, coming up with a task often leaves them feeling confused and ambivalent. We expect that you will experience the same feelings. Formulating tasks requires you to review the content of each of the dialogues that you have had with the client—dialogues about problems, well-formed goals, exceptions, motivation, and confidence. Let's look at how you can best process those bodies of information in order to formulate client tasks.

Deciding on a Task

Are There Well-Formed Goals?

In Chapter 5, we described the characteristics of well-formed goals and the interviewing questions that you can use to sustain a dialogue with clients around goals. We also emphasized that developing well-formed goals is a demanding process for most clients and that you can be most useful to clients here by not pushing for closure too soon.

When you formulate feedback, it is important to reflect on how far along your clients are in developing well-formed goals. Have the clients specified what differences they might want in their lives? Can the clients define those differences in concrete, behavioral terms? Can the clients define them as the presence of something desirable rather than the absence of problems and as a beginning step rather than the final result? Can the clients describe them in interactional and situational terms? Clearly, clients will vary in their capacities to describe accurately what they want. In general, as their descriptions correspond more closely to the characteristics of well-formed goals, you can be more confident that a behavioral task based on their goal descriptions will make sense to them and will aid them in solution building. Therefore, when formulating feedback, begin by asking yourself: "To what extent has my client developed well-formed goals?"

When you are working simultaneously with more than one client, as in our example of the Williams family, you must ask yourself the same question about well-formed goals for each of the clients present at the interview. If one client has well-formed goals and the others do not, you probably will not give the same suggestions to all the clients.

What Is the Client-Practitioner Relationship?

In Chapter 4, we discussed three possible relationships that can develop between practitioners and clients as they talk about what differences the clients may want in their lives. In the customer-type relationship, clients and practitioners are able to jointly define goals, and the clients see that they will have to do something different if a solution is to emerge. In the complainant-type relationship, clients and practitioners are able to jointly identify a client concern or problem, but the clients do not yet see any steps they might take toward a solution. In the visitor-type relationship, practitioners and clients are unable even to jointly identify a client concern on which to work.

We also indicated how you could proceed in interviews for each type of relationship. We want to emphasize again our belief that it is not helpful to think of clients in visitor or complainant relationships as resistant. It is more fruitful, in such circumstances, to acknowledge that you and the clients still have work to do on defining what differences the clients might want in their lives. And, in giving feedback, you should maintain the posture of not knowing that you employed during the interview.

During the break, if you perceive that a customer-type relationship exists between a client and yourself, you should think about suggesting a behavioral task. Certainly, the behavioral task that you suggest for a client who can describe well-formed goals and related exceptions will differ from the task that you suggest for a client who is not able to give such descriptions. Nonetheless, as a general rule, if a customer-type relationship exists, a behavioral task is in order.

If you sense that a complainant-type relationship has developed, you should contemplate some sort of observational task. Clients who do not perceive themselves as part of any solution will not be willing to change their behavior. No matter how well intentioned and sympathetic the practitioner might be, a behavioral recommendation here would not fit the clients' frame of reference and might lead them to suspect that the practitioner had not listened carefully. It is far preferable to point such clients toward those parts of their experience that could provide keys and clues to their eventual solutions (de Shazer, 1985, 1988).

Lastly, if you find yourself in a visitor-type relationship with a client, it makes little sense to assign any task. The two of you have not jointly defined a problem to work on and so—within the client's frame of reference, anyway—there is no need for a solution. As we saw in Chapter 4, clients with whom you form a visitor-type relationship have often been coerced into services. In these situations, you should limit your feedback to compliments: Simply state what the clients are doing that is useful for them in their current circumstances. For example, you might point out that seeing you makes sense because it will increase the chance of a positive relationship with whomever directed the client to consult you in the first place.

Are There Exceptions?

The next step when formulating feedback is to review exceptions. Was the client able to identify exceptions related to what he or she wanted to be different? If so, you can assign the client an observation task focused on the exception. If the client could not identify any exceptions but the two of you had jointly defined a problem on which to work, you might still assign an observational task, but it would be more general; you might ask the client to pay attention to what is happening in his or her life that indicates that the problem is solvable.

If you and the client could identify an exception related to what the client wants to be different, you must ask yourself whether the exception is random or deliberate. If random, you might suggest an observational task—to pay attention to similar exception times that occur in the future and especially to how they happen. If the exception is deliberate and the client is able to specify his or her contribution to making the exception happen, the client has already defined the appropriate behavioral task—to do more of the same (de Shazer, 1988).

Feedback for Ah Yan

After Peter had spent 30–40 minutes interviewing Ah Yan, he announced that he would like to take a break, so as to think about what she had told him. His thoughts first turned to what tasks the interview information indicated because, as we have seen, tasks are the bottom line in formulating feedback. Once an interviewer has settled on the task, it is relatively easy to formulate the compliments and a bridge.

Peter first thought about the type of relationship he and Ah Yan had formed. It seemed to him that a customer-type relationship had developed. They had been able to jointly identify a problem (the panicky feelings). They had also jointly identified some general goals (to reduce her fear and sense of being trapped and to do what is good "for me and my family"). Lastly, Ah Yan indicated that she saw herself as part of the problem and any eventual solution. (When asked about how motivated she was to work hard for a solution, she scaled her motivation as a 10 and said, "I gotta, for me and my family.") All of this information suggested to Peter that he and Ah Yan were in a customer-type relationship.

Next, Peter thought about how well formed Ah Yan's goals seemed to be. He decided that their conversation around the miracle question indicated that Ah Yan was developing well-formed goals. He recalled that she had said that, when the miracle happened, several things would be different: She would smile more. Her husband would see her doing more around the house. She and her husband would make things look better around the house together and hug and kiss more and maybe go out together. Noticing that she was doing better, her 6-year-old son, Di Jia, would feel more free to go outside, play on the swingset, and go around on his bike.

And, thirdly, Peter reflected on the exceptions Ah Yan had identified. He remembered that Ah Yan had said that she did have some real good days. Upon exploration, these days proved to be random exceptions because, as yet, she could not describe who did what to make them happen. Peter also recalled that, later in the interview, Ah Yan indicated that there had been presession change. When he had asked her how she was feeling, on a scale from 0 to 10, where 0 described the panicky feelings at the time she made the appointment and 10 described the miracle, she responded that she was a 6; in other words, she was doing considerably better than ten days earlier. Moreover, she was able to identify some things that she was doing to move toward her miracle picture: talking to a professional and her sister-in-law, going out more with her family, and praying.

In summary, Peter concluded that: (1) a customer-type relationship existed; (2) Ah Yan's real good days were random exceptions; (3) her improvement since making the appointment could be traced to deliberate exceptions. Then, on the basis of the interview information, he developed three tasks that reflected these conclusions. Next, drawing again on the information from the interview, he formulated compliments and a bridge. He wrote the feedback down, so that he could deliver it to Ah Yan accurately and with confidence. He felt he could deliver it with conviction because he believed in its truthfulness and usefulness. When he returned to the interviewing room, this is what he said:

PETER: Ah Yan, I have thought about the many things you have told me about yourself and your situation. I have some thoughts and suggestions for you. I have written them down because I did not want to forget any of them. [Ah Yan nods, to indicate that she is listening and understands]

[*compliments*] First, I want to tell you that there are several things about you which impress me: For one thing, I can see that you care very much about your family. You want to talk more with your husband and see him happier; you want your kids, like Di Jia, to go out and play on the swing set without worrying about you. You are a person whose family is important to her, so you want to figure out about your panicky times.

I'm also impressed by how clear your miracle picture is. You can tell me specifically about what will be different around your house and about how you will be different when you figure things out.

I'm struck, too, by how hard you are willing to work and how confident you are of finding solutions.

And, finally, I can see you are already doing things which make a difference—things like coming here, praying, and trying to talk to others and go out more. And when others, like your sister-in-law, make a good suggestion, you have the good sense to give it a try and see if it works for you. Sometimes you come up with a good idea—like praying—and you have the courage and strength to try it. I am really impressed with all you have tried and how hard you've worked. With all this, I am not surprised that you are a 6 today.

[*bridge*] Ah Yan, at this time, I'm like you: I haven't figured out yet either what's wrong. But, while we both continue to think about it, I suggest the following:

[*tasks*] First, continue to do the things that got you to 6.

Next, pay attention for when you have a good day and what's different about it—all kinds of information about when it happens, what's different around your house that tells you it's happening, who is doing what, and so forth. Then, come back and tell me about it.

And, the last thing, pick one day between now and the next time we meet and pretend the miracle—that is, just live that day like the miracle has happened. But don't tell anyone; just do it and come back and tell me what's better.

Peter delivered this feedback deliberately, and carefully watched Ah Yan's reactions to each point. He felt he was connecting, because she was consistently nodding her head in agreement. At times, she smiled and said "Yeah" or "Uh huh."

Feedback for the Williams Family

Following the same solution-focused format for her session with the Williams family, Insoo took a break after she had interviewed the family about their concerns, goals, and exceptions. As it happened, Insoo was working with a team on the Williams case. So, when she took her break, she went behind the one-way mirror to the viewing room to confer with her team members. Because several members of the family were present at the interview, the team discussed each family member separately before settling on the final content of the feedback. They began with Gladys. (At this point, you should review the Williams' interview information from Chapters 5 and 6.)

The team quickly concluded that it was Gladys' idea to come. Not only had she set up the appointment but Gladys was the one who identified the problem when Insoo asked how she could be helpful to the family. Together, she and Insoo identified a problem (Gladys' stress and chest pains and the need to shout at the children and to "put 'em on punishments" to control them) and some general goals (to get the children to listen more; and to learn ways to say yes and no to her relatives so that they would hear her). However, the interview information also suggested that Gladys tended not to see herself as part of the problem; she viewed it more as children who would not listen and a brother who did aggravating things. Nor did the information suggest that, at this time, she viewed herself as part of the solution; her answers to the miracle question and its follow-up questions were mainly in terms of what others would do differently when the miracle happened. (Albert would not be playing Nintendo and would leave; her husband wouldn't want to do the things that put him in jail; Marcus would be a friend to his brother; Olayinka would quit lying; and so on.) Finally, Gladys did acknowledge the existence of exceptions; she mentioned times when she did not have to tell Marcus to clean up, when Olayinka picked up her clothes, and when Offion played with friends who were good kids. The team noted that these were random exceptions, because there was no information yet about what Gladys and the other family members might be doing to make the exceptions happen.

The team concluded that Gladys and Insoo had developed a complainant-type relationship. In addition, although Gladys seemed motivated and had general goals, her goals were not yet well formed, nor did she clearly perceive a role for herself in any solution. Consequently, the team decided it would be most helpful to suggest an observational task around the random exceptions that she had identified.

The team soon came to the conclusion that the children all stood in the same relationship to services—somewhere between a visitor-type and complainant-type relationship. The children acknowledged the stress on their mother and a general goal of learning to share and all getting along. When Insoo asked, they made some contributions to the family miracle picture, but their answers were consistently in terms of what the other children would be doing differently. For example, Offion stated that, when the miracle is happening, "all my brothers and sisters are helping clean house." Further, the children did not identify exceptions or say anything to indicate that they were motivated to work hard for a solution. In the end, the team decided to treat the children as being in a visitor-type relationship and to provide compliments but no tasks.

The team's thoughts about Albert were similar to those about the children. Albert's responses to Insoo's questions only tacitly acknowledged a problem for the family, if one existed at all. He certainly did not define himself as part of the problem, as did Gladys and the children. When asked to contribute to the family's goal formulation, he had little to offer. (He couldn't answer the miracle question, he said, "because . . . that's the type of mind I got . . . . Sometimes it function right and sometimes it don't.") Albert did describe an individual miracle picture for himself ("have my own place and get a nice woman and settle down and have kids, I guess"), but he expressed no hopefulness or motivation about making any parts of it a reality. In addition, he did not identify any exceptions, whether random or deliberate. Consequently, the team thought that he, like the children, came closest to being in a visitor-type relationship with Insoo. As a result, they prepared feedback for him that contained compliments but no tasks.

The team's response to Albert and the four Williams children illustrates another rule of thumb about preparing feedback: Lean in the conservative direction. Often, when thinking about the interview information, you will find that the case falls between categories. In such situations, base your feedback on the more conservative estimate of the relationship. (Thus, on concluding that the Williams children stood somewhere between a visitor-type and a complainant-type relationship to services, the team decided to give only compliments, thus adopting the more conservative estimate of a visitor-type relationship.) By leaning in the conservative direction, you reduce the risk that you might misinterpret the interview data and suggest a task that makes little sense to the clients. The conservative attitude also protects clients from later having to save face for not carrying out a task that you've suggested. Finally, we regularly find that clients stretch themselves far beyond the suggestions in the feedback. By erring on the conservative side, you will be in a position to authentically compliment clients for the often insightful, dramatic, and unforeseen steps that they have taken to build solutions.

Now that we have reviewed the team's observations and conclusions, here is the feedback that they developed for the Williams family. Notice how simple and straightforward it is, despite the thoroughness of the thought upon which it rests. You'll also observe that family members chose to interject comments and offer more information as Insoo delivered the feedback. These comments demonstrate that the feedback fit the family's current frame of reference.

INSOO: OK, I have something to tell you. I have lots of things to tell you.

ALBERT: OK.

INSOO: [*compliments*] To all of you. First of all, Gladys. We want to tell you how impressed we are that, considering what you've been through, and considering that your life has not been easy . . .

GLADYS: I know.

INSOO: No, it has not been easy. And, in spite of that, you have a very good idea of what kind of a good mother you want to be for your children. You have done a very good job.

GLADYS: I take parenting class, too.

INSOO: [*indirectly complimenting a possible success and an indication of strength and motivation*] You do?

GLADYS: Yeah. Over at the center. I got a certificate—well, I can go pick it up. You go once a week, every week.

INSOO: So it's very important to you to be a good mother.

GLADYS: Yeah.

INSOO: You've done a good job with these kids.

GLADYS: [*identifying another exception*] Yeah, like, this lady down from me—I don't know her that good but she, like, beat her kids all the time. And I told her, I said, well, when I want something from my kids and I done called 'em like five times and they don't wanna come, then I start counting 1-2-3-4 up to 10. When I get to 10, then they in trouble, but they always come before I get to 10.

INSOO: You figured that out, too. Great. It's like, even with your very difficult circumstances, you have real nice kids. [*directly complimenting Gladys and indirectly complimenting the children*] The team noticed they have been very well behaved here.

GLADYS: Yeah. [*identifying more exception times*] They like that anywhere.

INSOO: Is that right?

GLADYS: All except when I'm not around. When I'm not around they do anything. If I'm there then they be halfway civilized.

INSOO: Wow! They're very well behaved here. They are very attractive, very well mannered, you know; nice kids you have. And obviously it's because you work so hard being a single parent. It sounds like you raised them properly by yourself.

GLADYS: [*beaming*] Yep.

INSOO: So we just have to give you a lot of credit for that.

GLADYS: [*smiling*] Thanks.

INSOO: [*beginning to build a bridge*] And I guess what's amazing to us is that, because of what you've been through, you want to give your children a better life than you had.

GLADYS: Yeah.

INSOO: You want them to have a good life.

GLADYS: Yeah, like him. [*points to Marcus*] He don't want to go to private school no more 'cause a boy told him that public school is better. But, to me, he can go to private school 'cause I never went, and he can get something that I never had and that little boy, the same little boy that told him that public school was better, now he want to go to the same school that he go to.

INSOO: I'm just really impressed by how you kept at it and made sure that you got them into private school.

GLADYS: Yeah. It took a lots of work.

INSOO: [*complimenting Gladys' strengths*] You want them to get a good education. I mean you went through a lot of trouble to find a school that would be good for them. You figured it out that, if the school people are not so friendly with you, they're not gonna be friendly with the kids. You figured out what's good for the kids, what kind of education you want for them.

GLADYS: Yeah.

INSOO: Yeah. And sometimes they even do things . . . on their own, trying to help out.

GLADYS: Sometimes

INSOO: It's a good start, right?

GLADYS: Yeah.

INSOO: The fact that they know how to do that sometimes?

GLADYS: Yeah. I know they know how. It's just getting 'em to do it.

INSOO: Right. Absolutely. Absolutely. So you taught them all the right things.

GLADYS: Yeah, I try to.

INSOO: You're doing a good job. We can see that.

GLADYS: Yeah, and two weeks and I'll be in the nut house.

INSOO: Now, Albert. We really like your miracle picture.

ALBERT: My who?

INSOO: Your picture of a miracle. When [quoting Gladys] "God comes" and takes care of all your problems, how you like things to be. And, I guess the good thing is that sometimes you are very helpful to your sister and you come over and she can count on you to help out.

[more compliments] And we are also very impressed that all of you, all of you, all six of you want a better life for everybody. That you want to get along better, you want to be a good family, and you want to have fun together.

[turning to Gladys] Little kids like this, they all know that's what they want. So I guess we have to give you a lot of credit for that.

GLADYS: Thanks.

INSOO: [making a bridging statement] So you've done a very good job. OK, so we know that you want your kids to have a good life and to be good kids who listen. And we know that, at times, they can be well behaved and very well mannered, and that you are working hard, doing a lot. What we don't know much about is how you are doing all this. So, we want to meet with you again.

GLADYS: OK.

INSOO: [giving an observation task to Gladys] OK. And we want you to pay attention—between now and when we meet again—so that you can tell us how it is that you manage to do all this good work for this family.

GLADYS: OK.

INSOO: OK. So let's go set up another time for us to get together.

ALBERT: Me too?

INSOO: Sure, you are welcome to come back.

GLADYS: No. He can't come back again.

INSOO: He can't come back?

GLADYS: No. He got to go home.

Gladys' assertion at the end of the feedback that Albert can't come back again is striking in that, at the very beginning of the session, Gladys had said that one of the things that she wanted to be different was to learn how to say yes or no to her relatives so that they would hear her. It may prove to be another example of the wisdom of thinking conservatively when formulating feedback. Given the information from the interview, Insoo and the team chose to give Gladys an observational and not a behavioral task. Still, before she left the first session, Gladys seemed to be moving her solution building beyond the limits of the feedback—to be taking action rather than simply observing. In doing less, the team may paradoxically have been doing more.

Feedback Guidelines

In solution building, as we have seen, the feedback that you give to clients at the end of a session is intended: (1) to aid them in their development of well-formed goals; (2) to focus them on those exceptions in their lives that are related to their goals; and (3) to encourage them to notice who is doing what to make these exceptions happen—especially what they themselves might be doing. To summarize what we have said so far, here are several useful guidelines for formulating and delivering feedback to clients:

- Find the bottom line first: What tasks do the interview data indicate?
- Develop tasks by assessing the type of relationship between client and practitioner, the extent to which well-formed goals exist, and the existence and type of exceptions.
- When unsure about the bottom line, favor the more conservative option.
- Agree with what is important to the client and what the client wants.
- Compliment the client for what the client is doing that is useful for solution building.
- Provide a bridging statement so that any tasks seem reasonable.
- Use the client's words to stay within the client's frame of reference.
- Keep the feedback simple and straightforward.
- Deliver feedback deliberately and authentically; observe the client's reactions.

Common Messages

As you gain experience in formulating feedback for clients, you will soon discover that certain situations come up again. There are some basic statements—called *common messages*—around which you can build your feedback in these recurring situations. Originally developed by de Shazer (1985, 1988) and his colleagues, they have spread throughout the solution-focused literature (Berg,

1994; Berg & Miller, 1992; Dolan, 1991; Furman & Ahola, 1992; O'Hanlon & Weiner-Davis, 1989; Weiner-Davis, 1993; Walter & Peller, 1992). Here, we will present the most widely applicable common messages in their simplest forms. With experience and practice, you will be able to adapt one of these messages to most feedback situations that you encounter.

These common messages are intended to focus clients on those aspects of their experiences and contexts that will be most useful in building solutions. As we noted in the guidelines, where you decide to point a client will depend on your assessment of: (1) the type of relationship in which your client stands to your services; (2) the degree to which the client has developed well-formed goals; and (3) the presence or absence of random and deliberate exceptions related to what your client wants. Let's consider the most common situations that you will encounter.

Client in a Visitor Relationship

If you judge that a client stands in a visitor relationship to your services, then by definition there is nothing at the moment that the client wants to work on with you. There is no joint definition of a problem, much less of any goals or related exceptions. Consequently, the bottom line is to give the client compliments and say that you would be happy to meet with him or her again. For example, Insoo gave the following feedback to such a client who had been sent to her for substance abuse services (Berg & Miller, 1992, p. 99):

> Curtis, we are very impressed that you are here today even though this is not your idea. You certainly had the option of taking the easy way out by not coming. . . . It has not been easy for you to be here today; having to give up your personal time, talking about things you really don't want to talk about, having to take the bus, and so on. . . .
>
> I realize that you are an independent minded person who does not want to be told what to do, and I agree with you that you should be left alone. But you also realize that doing what you are told will help you get these people out of your life and you will be left alone sooner. Therefore, I would like to meet with you again to figure out further what will be good for you to do. So let's meet next week at the same time.

If Insoo had given this client a task, it would have made no sense. It would only have indicated that she was not listening carefully. By giving only compliments at the end of the session, however, she ensured that, when he left, the client knew his perceptions had been heard and respected. Our experience is that this approach increases the chances that the client will return and will be willing to develop a complainant-type or customer-type relationship with us.

Client in a Complainant Relationship

No Exceptions and No Goal

In this very common situation, your interview information at the time of the break indicates that you and your client have jointly defined a problem, but the client cannot identify exceptions or so minimizes them that you believe the client doubts their existence. Such clients tend to focus on detailed descriptions of the severity of their problems, which they believe to be caused by sources outside of themselves, such as other persons or organizations. With no sense of any role in the problem, they also do not see anything they might do to solve the problem; they tend to feel powerless. Generally, they have little sense of what they might want to be different, except that they want others to be somehow different. As we saw in Chapter 4, it is very easy to become impatient with such clients and to start offering them advice about what they could do differently to solve their problems.

There are two common messages you can choose from in this situation. The first simply repeats as an observational task an interviewing question that we frequently use in interviews with such clients. In this case, you first set a positive, respectful tone by authentically complimenting the client for carefully observing this problem and its effects on his or her life and for thinking so hard about it. You then create a bridge by agreeing that this is a serious and stubborn problem and suggest this task:

> Between now and the next time that we meet, pay attention to what's happening in your life that tells you that this problem can be solved.

As we know, such clients have little sense of what they might want. Consequently, the second option in such cases is to assign a task that directs the client toward those parts of his or her experience and context from which some sense of direction might emerge. This task—called the *formula first-session task,* because it was originally given in the first session to all clients, to assist them in goal development (de Shazer, 1985)—focuses the client on that part of his or her life where the problem is located, but suggests that the client look for anything attractive there, instead of the aspects that are painful and problematic. In this case, you begin by complimenting the client for whatever useful work and thought that he or she has invested and for expending the effort and time that meeting with you may have required. Then, after agreeing with the severity of the problem, you can suggest this task (de Shazer, 1985, p. 137):

> Between now and the next time we meet, I would like you to observe, so that you can describe to me next time, what happens in your (pick one: family, life, marriage, relationship) that you want to continue to have happen.

Exceptions but No Goals

In this situation, you and the client have developed a joint definition of the problem and the client can identify exceptions. However, this is a complainant-type relationship; the client views the problem as existing in the outside world and does not yet perceive anything he or she might do differently to create a solution. (Insoo and her team faced this situation when formulating feedback for Gladys.) In such situations, the bottom line should be an observational task around the identified exceptions:

> Between now and the next time we meet, pay attention to those times that are better, so that you can describe them to me next time in detail. Try to notice what is different about them and how they happen. Who does what to make them happen?

This sort of observation task does two things: First, it implies to the client that exception times will happen again—in a sense, that better times are inevitable—and, thus, creates hope. Second, it suggests that the useful information lies, in large part, in the client's own experience.

A slight variation on this task may be useful when a client has been able to tell you something about how the exceptions happened, but the client's description is framed completely in terms of someone else (often a significant other) somehow having decided to do something differently. In other words, though the exceptions may have resulted from deliberate actions, the client implies that they were someone else's actions. For example, Peter once had a client, Alice, who was very discouraged about her relationship with her boss; she described him as "overbearing, demanding, and uncommunicative." However, she described some occasions when her boss was more polite, reasonable, and open toward her—"when he acted like a real human being." Peter asked how those times happened, but Alice couldn't identify anything that she might have done differently; instead, she said that the exceptions "happen because of him; sometimes he tries harder." Not perceiving a role for herself in the exception, she seemed to feel powerless and clueless about possibilities for solution. Peter offered her an observational task that respected her perception of the exceptions but, at the same time, suggested a possible place to begin looking for clues to a solution:

> Alice, pay attention for those times when your boss is more reasonable and open—the times when he acts like more of a human being. Besides paying attention to what's different about those times, pay attention to—so you can describe to me next time—what he might notice you doing that helps him to be more polite, reasonable, and open toward you. Keep track of those things and come back and tell me what's better.

When clients view the problem as existing outside of themselves but are able to identify random exceptions, you can modify the basic observational task by adding an element of prediction (de Shazer, 1988). For example, Peter could have described the task to Alice in these terms:

> Alice, I agree with you; there clearly seem to be days when your boss is more reasonable and open and acts like more of a human being and days when he doesn't. So, between now and the next time that we meet, I suggest the following: Each night before you go to bed, predict whether or not tomorrow will be a day when he acts more reasonable and open and polite to you. Then, at the end of the day, before you make your prediction for the next day, think about whether or not your prediction came true. Account for any differences between your prediction and the way the day went and keep track of your observations so that you can come back and tell me about them.

De Shazer (1988, pp. 183–184) notes that adding an element of prediction might be useful in this situation. He admits, of course, that he really does not know why these tasks work and that "at first glance having someone predict anything about the next day prior to going to bed seems rather absurd." On the other hand, experience suggests that prediction tasks are useful. Why?

According to de Shazer, the usefulness of a prediction task probably lies in the power of suggestion it contains. The client has already admitted that exceptions do occur. By giving the prediction task, the practitioner suggests that they will occur again, probably within the next week. Moreover, having accepted this task and predicted a better day, the client is likely to have higher expectations for a better day and thus, unknowingly, to set in motion the processes involved in having a better day. Expecting a better day, the client may also be more inclined to look for signs of it and thus more likely to perceive such signs. In other words, according to de Shazer, a prediction task includes several elements that increase the probability of setting a self-fulfilling prophecy in motion.

When contemplating whether to frame an observational task in a prediction format, you should be guided by how confident the client seemed that the random exception did in fact happen. Sometimes, as we have seen, clients suggest that exceptions may be happening but minimize their significance or even waffle on their existence; Gladys would be an example. At other times, clients are more definite. "Yes," they say, "there are times that are better." When you ask, "When was the last time a better time happened?" they describe the time and place of the exception. And when you ask, "What was different about that time?" they give concrete details.

Recognizing these differences among clients' descriptions of random exceptions, we think that, when the random exceptions seem more clearly defined, it makes good sense to frame the observational task in the prediction format. After all, the wording of this task implies a fairly distinct demarcation in the client's mind between good and bad days. When, on the other hand, the client's random exceptions seem less clearly defined, we suggest that you use the other wording of the task, as Insoo did with Gladys. That wording only requires the client to look for any exceptions between the current session and the next, no matter how vague they might seem.

Client in a Customer Relationship

A Clear Miracle Picture but No Exceptions

Here you and your client have developed a joint definition of the problem, the client accepts that he or she will have some role in the solution and seems motivated to work, and the client has been able to describe a concrete miracle picture that includes changes made by the client. However, the client cannot identify exceptions—certainly not deliberate exceptions. In such situations, you can compliment the client for the clarity of the miracle picture and suggest that the client pretend the miracle has happened (Shazer, 1991). For example, this is what Peter said to a client named Ann:

> Ann, I can see that you have been through a lot. Things are very tense at home, what with Al [her husband] and Tina [her teenage daughter] always yelling at each other. I think it makes good sense for you to be here; it shows that you care a lot about your family and about yourself. Like you said, it's getting to where you just can't take it anymore.
>
> Ann, what also stands out for me from what we talked about is what a clear miracle picture you have. You described several things that will be different around your house when the miracle happens, and several things that you would be doing differently with Al and Tina. [she nods in agreement]
>
> I agree with you that something has to be done. But I'm like you; I'm not sure yet what the solution is going to be. So, for now, what I suggest is this:
>
> Pick one day over the next week and without telling anyone—including Al and Tina—pretend that the miracle has happened. And, as you live that day, pay attention to what's different around your house, so that you can tell me about it when we meet next time.

By asking clients to pretend that the miracle has happened, the practitioner gives these clients permission to try the various possibilities that they have been able to generate. Asking them to do it once (or perhaps twice) rather than every day is recommended, because that is a smaller step toward a solution and thus requires less effort. In addition, doing it once sets the miracle day off from other days and makes it more likely that clients will notice any difference that might occur.

Remember, too, that pretending the miracle has happened is a behavioral task; it requires the client to *do* something different. As such, it is more demanding than an observational task and the stakes are higher: Success may be sweeter, but failure can be more bitter. Therefore, before suggesting this task, you should be convinced that the client is motivated to carry it out.

High Motivation but No Well-Formed Goals

In this situation, you are faced with finding the bottom line for a client who says, "Something has got to change" and, "I'd do anything to find a solution." You may find yourself strongly impressed with such clients, and your heart will go out to them, because, almost always, they have tried several things to find a solution, but without success. Also, they can describe to you in detail what they have tried; their high motivation to work hard is obvious. However, they are unable to identify exceptions, particularly deliberate exceptions. As you formulate feedback, you may find yourself straining to come up with something—anything—that will offer some hope of improvement.

In such situations, it is a mistake to think that, from your frame of reference, you could ever come up with anything specific that will be the difference that makes a difference for the client. We have learned over and over from our clients that, as a rule, it is wiser to trust their perceptions of their resources and their intuitive understandings of what might be helpful.[1] De Shazer (1985) and his colleagues have designed a task that will allow you, when formulating feedback in this situation, to put the focus squarely on the client and his or her resources. It is called the do-something-different task:

> I am so impressed with how hard you have worked on your problem and with how clearly you can describe to me the things you have tried so far to make things better. I can understand why you would be discouraged and frustrated right now.
>
> I also agree with you that this is a very stubborn problem.
>
> Because this is such a stubborn problem, I suggest that, between now and the next time we meet, when the problem happens, you do something different—no matter how strange or weird or off-the-wall what you do might seem. The only important thing is that, whatever you decide to do, you need to do something different.

This task gives the client permission to be spontaneous and creative at those times when it is most needed. Clients who successfully use this task come up with solution-building strategies that surprise themselves—strategies that their practitioners could never have foreseen or designed for them ahead of time. For example, Peter once gave this task to a couple who complained of deteriorating marital and family relationships. Their problems had begun sev-

---

[1] We realize, of course, that there are circumstances in which we would move to connect certain clients with community resources. We will address such circumstances in later chapters.

eral years earlier, when the husband, formerly a carpenter, had suffered a severe back injury. The husband had been forced to go on disability; with this significant reduction in family income, it was all but impossible to make ends meet in their family of five. The couple had grown isolated and estranged from each other and also from their children; family members did not talk to each other except to criticize and no one smiled anymore. They had tried several things, such as making sure to have one meal a day together and setting aside one evening a week for a family activity, like going to a game or a movie. Nothing seemed to help. Peter, convinced they were motivated to work toward a solution, gave them the do-something-different task. When they returned, he asked what was going better. The two shrugged their shoulders and said they were not sure, but both were smiling about something. With further questioning, they told of a really "bizarre evening." Earlier in the week, when the family was at the start of supper, with dad and the children around the table and mom getting the spaghetti sauce from the stove, one of the children made a cynical comment to his father. Feeling "angry and down," the father stuck his fork in the noodles and "flicked them at my son across the table. I hit him right in the face." The other kids laughed cautiously and looked up to their mother, who was carrying the sauce to the table. Thinking back, she recalled: "I was so mad, I was so ready to start in on my husband about 'that's no way to handle a child.' But all I could remember to do . . . was that you had said whatever I did I should do something different . . . so I stuck the spoon in the sauce and flipped it at my husband and we got into this 5-minute food fight with noodles and sauce flying all over the kitchen." The couple knew that something unforeseen but important had happened, and further discussion revealed that the family had spent "two hours cleaning up the mess we made in five minutes, but talking and laughing like we hadn't done in three years." Peter spent the rest of that session exploring with them what they had done during the clean-up to make such family communication happen and what they thought they would have to do to keep it going.

Well-Formed Goals and Deliberate Exceptions

In this situation, the client has described times that are better and told you step by step the sorts of things he or she has done to make them happen. In addition, the client has told you, in so many words, that these deliberate exceptions, although not yet a complete solution, are moves in the right direction; that is, they represent satisfactory strategies for bringing about what the client wants. Often, such clients seem more hopeful and confident at the time of the break than at the beginning of the interview. In this situation, which Peter encountered with Ah Yan, formulating feedback for clients is easy to do. Here's an example of such feedback:

> Ralph, I am impressed with you in several ways: First, how much you want to make things go better between you and your children. Second, that there are

already several better times happening like [give examples]. And third, that you can describe to me so clearly and in such detail what you do to do your part in making those times happen, things like [give examples]. With all that you are doing, I can see why you say things are at a 5 already.

I agree that these are the things you have to do to have the kind of relationships with the children that you want.

So, between now and when we meet again, I suggest that you continue to do what works. Also, pay attention to what else you might be doing—but haven't noticed yet—that makes things better, and come back and tell me about it.

The task here is to do more of the same, with an added observational task that suggests the client is probably doing more than he or she realizes and should pay attention to those extra strategies. It is a concrete and meaningful way to compliment a client for successes and encourage the client to build on them.

When you encounter clients who identify deliberate exceptions, it is important to make sure that what they do to make those exceptions happen represents aspects of potential solutions that are acceptable to them. Deliberate exceptions don't always represent solutions for clients, even when they are related to the difference the clients want to bring about. For example, Peter once interviewed a young mother who was discouraged about how early-morning piano practices were going with her 8-year-old daughter. The practice sessions were tense; at the end of the sessions, both she and her daughter were in tears "80% of the time." The mother described two deliberate exceptions: There were no problems whenever she paid her daughter to practice and whenever she permitted her daughter to practice after the daughter's normal bedtime. Although Peter was impressed with the exceptions, the mother was not: "Somehow doing it that way just doesn't sit right with me." Peter knew then that, as things stood at that point, payment and delayed bedtimes did not represent solutions.

Other Useful Messages

Solution-focused practitioners have developed several other useful messages (Berg, 1994, Berg & Miller, 1992; de Shazer, 1985, 1991; Weiner-Davis, 1993). However, most of these are either more specialized than those we already presented or variations on those messages, and we won't discuss them here. Instead, let's look at two more tasks that are widely applicable in basic practice.

The Overcoming-the-Urge Task

This task, developed by de Shazer (1985) and his colleagues, is useful when clients define their problem as an inner tendency to feel or act in some way that they want to see changed (for example, a tendency to feel scared, or angry, or discouraged; or to engage in certain behaviors such as yelling at others, hitting them, or using alcohol or drugs). If you interview such persons, you will find that some stand in a complainant relationship and others in a customer relationship. But, regardless of whether you think an observational or behavioral task is indicated, you will usually be able to give some variation of the overcoming-the-urge task as the bottom line. Here we state it as an observational task for clients who have been able to describe random exceptions. Let's say the client tends to get panicky:

> Pay attention for those times when you overcome the urge to get panicky. Pay attention to what's different about those times—especially to what you are doing to overcome the urge.

This task, like the others we have been describing, encourages solution building by pointing clients toward episodes of success in their lives and the strengths they are using to make them happen.

Addressing Competing Views of the Solution

When you interview couples or families about their concerns, they will often argue with each other about what is the best solution to their problem. Of course, it is a mistake to take sides. By doing so, you will lose credibility with the person whose view you are ignoring or rejecting. To handle this often tense and difficult feedback situation, you need to formulate a task that affirms the different participants and their multiple perspectives. Here is an example of how Insoo, working with a team, used this approach with two parents who were arguing about how to solve a serious problem with their son. The parents had said they could see their different family backgrounds at work in their conflicting views:

> We are impressed by how much both of you want to help your son not to steal. The team is also impressed by what different ideas the two of you have about how to help your child through this difficult time. We can see that you were brought up in different families and have learned different ways to do things.
>
> The team is split on which way to go: One half feels like you ought to go with John's ideas, and the other half feels like Mary's might work best. Therefore, we suggest that each morning, right after you get up, you flip a coin. Heads means that Mary is in charge, and you do things her way with Billy, while John stays in the background. Tails means John is in charge that day. And also—on those days when each of you is not busy being in charge—pay careful attention to what the other does with Billy that is useful or makes a difference, so that you can report it to us when we meet again.

This task is noteworthy in at least three regards. First, it affirms the views of both parents and encourages each, at least to a degree, to do what he or she thinks is best for Billy. Second, it undermines the categorical either/or thinking of two people who are caught up, as so many clients are, in the idea that there must be a right answer to their problem (de Shazer, 1985). Such thinking leads to win/lose impasses, where each person is privately thinking, "Either I'm right and my spouse is wrong, or it's the other way around." The task offers them a face-saving replacement for the impasse, by suggesting that both of their approaches likely have elements of value and that a way to build a solution is to discover and use the best of both. Third, the coin flip is a clever way to remove the opportunity for yet another argument between two seemingly independent, determined people.

When you assign this task, most clients build a solution by combining elements from both possibilities. You can then explore the contributions of each client and compliment them for these. However, emerging solutions do not necessarily have to be both/and constructions; sometimes clients build a solution that incorporates only one of the two original possibilities. Theoretically at least, when John and Mary return to see Insoo, they may both be convinced that Mary's way worked best. In that case, Insoo, respecting client expertise and maintaining the stance of not knowing, would explore with them why they had concluded that Mary's way was the most helpful for Billy. Once the exploration was completed, Insoo might compliment Mary for having a mother's deep understanding of a son and the ability to act on it and compliment John for having the wisdom and flexibility to see the value of Mary's way of handling their child.

You can use the same sort of task with individual clients who cannot decide among options. In such situations, it can be important to compliment your client for moving deliberately and carefully, because clients struggling among clearly defined possibilities often feel very anxious or discouraged about not yet having made a choice. As an example, here is what Peter said to a client who was trying to decide whether or not to break up with a verbally abusive boyfriend:

> Karen, I first want to say that I think taking your time to decide what to do about your relationship to Bill is the right thing to do. A lot of people would not have had the strength to think it through the way you are doing. Bill is important to you; at times he is wonderful and the two of you like to do a lot of the same things. On the other hand, he does put you down and that really hurts, and you don't know if he can change. Second, I'm impressed by what you have already done to get him to understand. You've talked to him straight out and told him things have to change or you can't stay in the relationship. I can see that telling him those things was difficult for you; it took a lot of courage. [she agrees]

I'm like you. I'm not sure about whether it would be best for you to stay in the relationship with Bill or leave him and begin a new life. I agree that this is a tough decision, and figuring it out is going to take more hard work. And, as you continue to work on it, I have a suggestion for you:

I suggest that each night before you go to bed, you flip a coin. If it comes up heads, live the next day as much as possible as though Bill is no longer a part of your life: Don't contact him, start to take the first steps toward the things you said you would do differently if you were on your own like spending more time with your friends and family and so forth. If it comes up tails, live the next day as though he is still a part of your life—all those things you described to me about what that means for you. Then, as you do these things, keep paying attention to what's happening that tells you that you are becoming more clear about whether to leave him or stay in the relationship, realizing, of course, that usually a person cannot be 100% sure. And come back and tell me what's better.

An alternative approach to individual clients who are confused about different options is to suggest an observational task: Ask them to pay attention to what is happening that tells them it is a good thing to be confused about their problem at this time. You can suggest that the client keep a ledger sheet and record both the good and the bad things for her about being confused. Unlike the previous task, this one does not suggest that a solution probably lies in becoming more clear about a particular option. Like the previous one, however, it does suggest that it is acceptable and even an asset to be confused sometimes.

Decisions about the Next Session

You will have noticed that the messages in this chapter consistently end with a statement that assumes the client will come back and describe progress that has occurred between sessions. It is important to understand that these messages, although easily adaptable for use in later sessions, are formulated for use at the end of the initial meeting. Unless clients have made it quite clear that they do not need to return, we end our feedback in first sessions with a suggestion that they come back. If they were to balk at the suggestion, we would certainly explore their concern, but they usually do not. In second meetings and beyond, we ask clients whether they think it will be useful to continue meeting and, if so, what interval should elapse before they return. In later chapters, you will see how we go about getting client perceptions on this matter.

It is our experience that, during first sessions, clients are taking the measure of us and the context in which we offer our services; that is, they are beginning to build a sense of whether they can trust us and whether they want to work seriously on anything with us. In addition, we think that most clients who come for services expect that it will take more than one session to solve their problems. In that case, if we ask clients at the end of the first session whether they think it makes sense to come back, the clients may perceive that somehow we do not want to work with them—that we lack confidence in our abilities to be useful or, worse yet, that we lack confidence in their capacities to build solutions. Consequently, at the end of the first meeting, we tell clients that we want to see them again and that, when they come back, we'd like to hear about what is going better. We believe this approach best fosters client trust and confidence in us and, at the same time, has the added benefit of fostering an expectation of positive change in the client. On occasion, at the end of our feedback in the first session, we will ask the client: "So, when do you think it would be most useful for you to return?" Such questions begin to send a message that we believe clients are competent to decide what is best for themselves, while at the same time letting the clients know that we think it would be useful to see them again. In later sessions, after clients have become more confident in both our and their own capacities, we begin asking whether they think they need to meet with us again.

Cribsheets, Protocols, and Notetaking

We know from our own experience that formulating feedback for clients can be difficult and confusing. During the session, clients give a great deal of information, which must be organized in a short period according to the criteria summarized earlier. If you are new to solution-focused interviewing and developing feedback, it is easy to get lost or overwhelmed during the break and end up responding to the client according to a paradigm with which you are more familiar. Doing so may leave you disappointed and wondering whether you will ever be able to stay consistent in offering clients feedback that is focused on solutions of their own making.

Many of our workshop participants and students have found that cribsheets and protocols help them stay on track. They can be especially helpful for those who are just beginning to learn the procedures. Once students are more familiar with the techniques, the cribsheets and protocols may be used periodically as refreshers. At the end of Chapter 5, we directed you to a cribsheet in the Appendix consisting of questions for developing well-formed goals. That cribsheet summarizes in two pages the interviewing questions discussed in Chapter 5 and provides several examples. Two more items the Appendix relate to material covered in this chapter. First, you will find a protocol for formulating feedback to clients. You can use this form during the break. If, with your client's permission, other practitioners or students are observing your session, they could use the protocol to record ideas for the bottom line and compliments that occur to them during the interview. Second, you will find a summary of the common messages presented in this chapter.

We have now presented all of the basic interviewing and feedback procedures necessary for you to conduct a first solution-building meeting with your clients. We have described these in a sequence that you can follow during your first meeting with clients. This sequence began in Chapter 4, where we suggested that, after some preliminaries, you begin by asking your clients: "How can I be helpful?" It ends with your giving feedback and scheduling a next meeting, if you and your clients so decide. The protocol in the Appendix, which lists the various parts of this sequence, may be used as a map in your first meeting with clients.

When we offer this protocol to workshop participants and students, they often ask how we use it; in particular, they wonder whether it is advisable to take session notes on this protocol. Although both of us take notes during sessions, Insoo does not use the protocol, whereas Peter does. Insoo prefers to trust her sense of which solution-focused procedures to pursue and in what order, while Peter appreciates having the structure of a protocol to fall back upon. We both take notes on the clients' words for their problems, miracle pictures, exceptions, scaling responses, and so forth. Insoo writes these on a blank piece of paper; Peter records them on a copy of the appropriate protocol form. Writing down clients' words sensitizes us to their shifting perceptions in the solution-building process and gives us the information we need to formulate end-of-session feedback. We both include these notes in our clients' files and use them as the basic resource for completing any other necessary client paperwork. Like Benjamin (1987), we have noticed that clients consistently accept our notetaking after we explain that we are doing it to better remember what they tell us about themselves and their circumstances.

Later Sessions: Finding, Amplifying, and Measuring Client Progress

Always there and listening to me. Always made time for me. Encouraged me to get on with what I have to do; he had confidence in me and that helped me get on with what I knew I had to do.

(BFTC client, describing her practitioner)

Throughout this book, we have been emphasizing that clients build solutions more by drawing on their successes and strengths than by analyzing their problems. All of the interviewing procedures presented here reflect this emphasis. It should come as no surprise, then, that the purpose and structure of all later solution-focused sessions is no different. In this chapter, we will describe how to interview clients in later sessions in ways that encourage them to build on their strengths.

The purpose of all later meetings is the same—to open and sustain a dialogue around what's better for the client. In other words, the purpose is for the interviewer to engage the client in a search for exceptions that have occurred since the last time they met. These exceptions are the building blocks for a solution.

The structure of later sessions reflects their purpose. As the exceptions emerge from the interaction between practitioner and client, the practitioner, using solution-focused interviewing procedures, invites the client to amplify the exceptions. This work takes up most of the later sessions. Thereafter, the practitioner uses scaling procedures to get the client's estimate of progress to date and to do some additional goal-formulation work. The goal-formulation work includes figuring out what the next steps are for the client and thinking some more about what will have to be different in the client's life for the client to feel ready to terminate services. Then, as in first sessions, the practitioner takes a break, develops feedback, and returns to deliver the feedback.

In this chapter, we review each of the components of a later session. These components are summarized in the protocol for later sessions included in the Appendix. We have organized our discussion here to correspond broadly to that protocol. By doing so, we hope to clarify the nature and flow of interviewing in later sessions. Once again, we will present segments of dialogue with Ah Yan and the Williams family as illustrations.

What's Better?

We begin later sessions with clients by asking, "What's better?" Many workshop participants and students have told us that, at first, this seems strange. "Wouldn't it be more logical," they ask, "to begin by asking whether the client completed the task assigned at the last session?" Or they ask: "Why not be more cautious and inquire, 'Is anything better since we last met'?" We have reasons for doing neither.

We do not explicitly ask if clients have done their tasks for at least three reasons. First, as we indicated in Chapter 7, we do not view our suggestions and tasks as the solutions to clients' problems. Instead, we offer them as an extension of the information that emerges from the interaction between us and our clients. We believe it is important to maintain our view of the client as the expert with regard to the tasks we suggest; experience has taught us that clients, not practitioners, can best decide whether or not completing a particular task would be useful to them in building solutions. Second, by not explicitly asking about the task, we avoid putting both our clients and ourselves into an awkward position: If our clients have not done the task, they might feel obliged to explain why they did not do so; for our part, we might have to explain why we now imply that the client should have done what we had only offered as a suggestion at the previous meeting. Third, as we mentioned at the end of the last chapter, clients often go beyond the limits of tasks suggested. Alternatively, something may have happened in the client's life soon after the previous session to make the task less relevant; in that case, the client would understandably take solution building off in another direction. (In such cases, the client may even forget the task.) Therefore, it makes good sense to begin later sessions with a question that is sufficiently broad to cover a range of possibilities.

Nor do we begin later sessions by asking, "Is anything better since we last met?" As Insoo has written elsewhere (Berg, 1994, p. 150), to ask this question would be to imply that we are somewhat doubtful about improvements and thereby feed any client ambivalence about progress. Consequently, following the suggestion of de Shazer and his colleagues (de Shazer et al., 1986), we prefer to begin later sessions by simply asking: "What's better?" This question better reflects our confidence that clients are competent to have taken steps—no matter how small—in the direction of what they have said they wanted.

The most fundamental reason for beginning later sessions by asking this question is that it once again reflects the conviction that solutions are primarily built from the perception of exceptions. Given that both problem times and exception times will most likely have happened in any client's life since the previous session, why not begin later sessions by asking about what will be most useful to the client—any perceived exceptions that have occurred.

You should expect different responses when you ask clients, "What's better?" Berg (1994) identifies three different groups of clients on the basis of their responses. The first group, easily the majority, will be able to identify experiences that are better since the last session. Some are able to identify these exceptions right away; others need encouragement and probing from the interviewer. A second group will say, "I'm really not sure" or "I think that things are about the same." A third group, a small minority, will say that things are worse.

When you encounter clients who fall into the second and even the third group, it is a good idea to stay with the same line of questioning for a while. In our experience, with probing and encouragement, many clients who are at first unsure about any improvement are able to identify exceptions that turn out later to be valuable. A useful technique is to ask the client to think about whether particular days went better than others. For example, if a client is unsure whether anything was better, you could ask, "OK, let me see. The last time I saw you was last Thursday morning. So, was last Friday any better than, say, Thursday afternoon?" Then you might ask, "Was the weekend any better than Friday?" Ask about the past week one day at a time. Usually, under this more specific questioning, even ambivalent clients and those who start out by saying things are worse are able to identify some exceptions.

Thus, with some persistence on the interviewer's part, by far the majority of clients will be able to identify exceptions. Then the interviewer's task is to open and sustain a conversation with clients around their exceptions and to move in the direction of solutions. Because the majority of interviewing work in later sessions will involve such conversations, we now look at solution-focused procedures that you can use in that work. In the next chapter, we will address the much less common situation in which, despite the interviewer's best efforts, the client cannot identify exceptions and may be feeling deeply discouraged.

EARS

Once a client of yours identifies an exception, however vaguely or unconvincingly, it is your role to explore it in detail. Insoo and her colleagues at BFTC have spent many years working out new and more effective ways to do this. They have developed the acronym EARS to capture the interviewer's activities in this work. *E* stands for *eliciting* the exception. *A* refers to *amplifying* it, first by asking the client to describe what is different between this exception time and problem times and second by exploring how the exception happened, especially the role that the client might have played in making it happen. *R* involves *reinforcing* the successes and strengths that the exception represents, largely by noticing exceptions and taking the time to explore them carefully and, of course, through complimenting. Lastly, the *S* reminds interviewers to *start again*, by asking, "And what else is better?"[1]

Ah Yan

As you develop a solution-focused way of interviewing, you can expect to devote an increasing share of your later sessions to EARS activities. To illustrate this process, let's look at Peter's second session with Ah Yan. Here's how it began:

PETER: What's happening that's better, Ah Yan?

AH YAN: Umm. Well, umm . . .

PETER: Well, what have you noticed that tells you that things are better?

AH YAN: I'm back to work. I didn't go to work all week last week.

PETER: [*wondering if returning to work might somehow represent an exception*] Oh, you went back to work this week?

AH YAN: Yeah, this week I went back to work.

PETER: [*noticing that she seemed pleased with herself and complimenting her apparent success*] Well, good for you!

AH YAN: Thanks.

PETER: So did you work today?

AH YAN: We worked till seven. I just got out.

PETER: Oh, wow! You must be very busy?

AH YAN: Uh, yeah, this week we are; working 12 hours.

PETER: Twelve hours a day?

AH YAN: Yeah. And I work Saturday too.

PETER: And Saturday?

AH YAN: Yeah.

PETER: Are you working 12 hours each day, six days a week?

AH YAN: Yeah.

PETER: You're working 72 hours a week?

AH YAN: Yeah. Well, I didn't work last week, so it's kind of OK.

PETER: It's OK this week. Are you going to work that much next week too?

---

[1] By now you can see that asking what's better is another way of finding exceptions. For a summary of the various different ways to ask clients about exceptions and the various points at which to do so, see the cribsheet of exception-finding questions in the Appendix.

AH YAN: No, I don't think so. I think it's just this week because he [her employer] got a big order in, and so he wants to try to get it all in.

PETER: So, sometimes you have a lot of work, and then it falls off.

AH YAN: Yeah.

PETER: How did it happen that you went back to work?

AH YAN: I felt better. Like, um, I told him I was ready to work.

PETER: [*now more convinced an exception has been elicited and beginning to explore it*] And, ah, when did you wake up feeling better, knowing that you could go back to work?

AH YAN: Monday.

PETER: Monday morning?

AH YAN: Yesterday. Sunday it was like, um, I don't know, all weekend it was like . . . bad, like I was going to get the shakes. It would make me feel, you know, . . . that way, and I just get these feelings that I just can't really fight. And I just want to lay down, just . . . I don't know. It puts me down.

PETER: [*affirming her perception and asking Ah Yan to begin amplifying the exception*] Yeah, it sounds very difficult. But sometime during the weekend, you said, you felt better?

AH YAN: Yeah, and this weekend, I fought it. Me and my husband went to a dance. We went to a wedding dance Saturday, and I got kind of sick there in the middle of the dance. And he, my husband, asked me "Are you OK?" And I says, "No, I don't think so. I want to get out." You know. And he says, "Well, let's go outside." And we went outside for a walk, you know. We went walking like 10 minutes. And he says, "Are you OK? Do you want to go home?" And I says, "*No!* We're not going to go home."

PETER: [*exploring for what was different about the exception and indirectly complimenting*] Really? Was that different for you—saying no to leaving like you did?

AH YAN: Yeah, it was and I said, you know: "We're not going to stop." You know, I just—I have to keep going.

PETER: [*reinforcing with an indirect compliment and asking for more description*] How did you know that what you needed at that time was to listen to your husband and leave the dance and go for a walk with him?

AH YAN: [*amplifying her description of both the exception and how it happened*] I don't know, I feel like, 'cause we were—well, there was a lot of people, OK? I don't know if it's me or, I don't know, I can't say, because I feel like it's too stuffy, it's too . . . you know, and I felt like I couldn't breathe. I don't know, I just—I don't know if I was nervous or what, I don't know; I just told him I was going to have to get out. "I want to be alone right now." You know. "Let's get out." You know, so we just went outside for a while, you know, and we hiked, and then we were just talking and, you know, and he said, "Are you OK?" And I said, "Yeah, let's go back in."

Clients usually have to struggle to conceptualize their exceptions, their roles in bringing them about, and thus the significance of these exceptions for their lives. Ah Yan's work here is a good example of that process. Peter's task was to keep her focused on such solution talk. To do so, he picked out successes and strengths that could be reinforced through compliments and then asked for more amplification. In the next segment, pay special attention to how Ah Yan seemed to develop a clearer and more complete sense of her role in building a solution to her problem:

PETER: That's amazing! [*indirectly complimenting*] Did you know that would work?

AH YAN: Huh? No, but I just walked out, you know, just not going to let it stop me. There were too many people in there, and it was real crowded, and I had to get out. You know, I just walked outside, you know, to cool off. It was better for me.

PETER: Yeah. And then you went back to the dance, and did it come back?

AH YAN: Like it wanted to. But I'd just ignore it, and it wanted, you know—I just kept talking, and, you know, just ignored it. Something like . . .

PETER: [*amplifying by explicitly asking for her role in making the exception happen*] How do you do that—ignore it?

AH YAN: Because it's like, when it starts, and my mind goes to what's happening to me, it gets worse. It gets worse. And if I just, like, brush it off, you know, like they say, brush it off, just forget it, I, like, start talking, you know, paying attention to the people that are talking to me and just . . . I forget about it. You know.

PETER: And when you brush it off, what do you do differently? You said, talking to other people?

AH YAN: Just talking to them, yeah, or laughing, and dancing.

PETER: You like to dance?

AH YAN: Yeah.

PETER: Is dancing something you are good at?

AH YAN: Yeah, real good.

PETER: Yeah? Great, not everyone is; that's for sure. OK. And I know that you like to talk with people. You were telling me last time that you liked to talk to your sister-in-law. [*asking for more amplification of how she makes the exception happen*] So, what else do you do when you brush it off?

AH YAN: I don't know. Pay attention to something else, you know, 'cause, I don't know, I'm trying to figure it out myself, too.

PETER: I can tell you're working pretty hard at figuring yourself out.

When Ah Yan talked about figuring it out, Peter recalled that she had used the same phrase several times in the first session. It occurred to him that these words seemed to be taking on a different meaning for her. In their first session, she spoke of figuring out what was causing her shakes and her shortness of breath and her hair falling out, as though she had to uncover some underlying cause in order to stop these symptoms and get better. (She wondered aloud whether her heart or her personality might be the cause.) Now, figuring it out seems to mean discovering strategies that she can use to keep it (presumably, the shakes) under control. As she develops a clearer sense of her exception times and what she has been doing to make them happen, any concern she might have had about underlying causes seems to have been set aside or forgotten.

Ah Yan's changing use of this phrase is an instance of something we witness regularly in solution-building work: Client perceptions and meanings shift over time, sometimes dramatically so. As those working with a solution focus have become more aware of this, their interviewing procedures have evolved toward ever greater openness and flexibility, so as to track the client's shifting perceptions and meanings.

As you to read the remainder of the dialogue, notice the continuing shift in Ah Yan's sense of what it will take to solve her problem and even of the problem itself:

AH YAN: I guess, too, after I left from here last week, I went to the library, and I found a book of—what was that, anxiety panic or anxiety attacks?

PETER: Anxiety attacks.

AH YAN: And I was reading through it, and a lot of the symptoms is what I'm going through. I feel like those are the symptoms, you know, and it says, "The less you worry, the healthier you are," and it says, "Who's in charge: you or your brain?" or something like that. You know, I'm trying to read, and maybe that's what it is, just worry too much, you know, and what really got me was, "The less you worry, the healthier you are." I don't know, those words meant a lot to me.

PETER: That was in the book?

AH YAN: Yeah. I'm still reading it.

PETER: And those words are: "The less you worry, the healthier you are." And those words are real meaningful to you?

AH YAN: Yeah, they are. And it says, "Who is in charge?"

PETER: [echoing] "Who is in charge?"

AH YAN: "You or your mind" or "your brain." I don't remember which it said: mind or brain. It's like, you got to control your thought. Your brain controls you, or you control it. You know. Seems like maybe that's what's wrong with me. 'Cause it's—I don't know, I'm reading all these symptoms they have on it, and it's what I'm going through. And it's like—I couldn't explain it to nobody, but I don't know—when there's so many feelings I'm going through, all these symptoms I go through, and all these thoughts I have, and you know, it's hard to explain. It's hard to explain to somebody, so I got the book and I'm reading it. I'm not done with it, but I just started it.

PETER: Wow, you're learning a lot. So, you have the book at home.

AH YAN: Yeah.

PETER: OK, and it's really helpful.

AH YAN: Yeah. And I'm trying to learn it.

PETER: [*asking once again for amplification*] I can see that you are. Seems like you've already learned a lot. OK. Is there anything else you do differently to put yourself in charge?

Although Ah Yan had already indicated several things she had done to account for feeling better and had clarified—for both Peter and herself—how she was doing them, Peter kept asking for more details about how she made the exception happen. It is clear from the dialogue that she identified herself as having the major role in making the exception happen, and it seemed to Peter during the interview that her confidence about her own capabilities was building. Consequently, he wanted to get as much detail as possible about her deliberate exceptions around feeling better. She had more to tell him:

AH YAN: Faith. I got to have faith in myself before I do anything. And deep breathe saying, "OK, you know, stop thinking about what's wrong," you know, 'cause I'm that type. I get a little panicky, "Oh no, what's wrong with me?" You know. Now I says, "No, that's the way I was before," and then, you know, I think back to the way I used to get, really bad. I'm thinking, "At the time that was happening, what was I thinking then?" I was thinking to myself, I would think more things wrong—you know, "This is going to happen to me, what if this, or what if . . . ?" It just—my mind was going and going and going, you know, and it's like . . .

PETER: So instead of that, now you're doing what?

AH YAN: I'm trying to, you know—how do you say this? [she takes an exaggerated breath]

PETER: You take a deep breath?

AH YAN: Yeah, and say: "OK, do what you have to do, or keep doing what you're doing. Don't stop." You know, 'cause I used to stop and just, like, start thinking, "Oh no, what's wrong with me?" You know. Now it's like I say: "No, just keep going," you know; do what I have to do, you know. Or it's like, I'm going to take control.

PETER: Yeah, yeah. Is this new for you—what you're doing differently?

AH YAN: Yeah! Yeah, it's new . . .

PETER: Does that surprise you that you're able to do that?

AH YAN: Yeah. It's just like every day that's going by, I'm trying to figure, you know, something, you know, and I feel like, any stuff that I can take, I'll take it. I can, and, like, I read that book. "Who's in charge: you or your mind?" Or—well, you know. Like, *I am!* I am going to do it, you know, and if you really think about it, I don't know, I am really—if I really put my head to it, you know, I will.

PETER: Ah Yan, that's amazing; congratulations!

AH YAN: Yeah, thanks. And I see it does help. You know, it's not all on you, but I have to learn how to control myself too, you know. That's what I think, you know. It takes time.

PETER: Yes, it takes time. It takes practice.

AH YAN: Yeah, practice, yeah.

PETER: [*continuing to reinforce and compliment her success and strengths, focusing especially on the role that she played in the exceptions*] Yeah, and you're working. Seems like you're working very hard at this. Very hard. So, you told me that the way you've been putting yourself in charge is by deep breathing, by keeping going with whatever it was you were doing at that time, and sometimes, um, you take charge by leaving the situation—like leaving the dance for a while when you knew that it was too crowded.

AH YAN: It was too many people. People were smoking, and it's like, "No, I just have to walk out," you know.

PETER: Is that different for you, to figure out what's a good situation for you, what you need in a situation?

AH YAN: I guess it depends where I'm at. Like Sunday, I was kind of, you know, kind of getting like the way I get when we were in the car. You know, and it was like, you know—I try, I guess, when it's happening to me, I figure, "OK, I'm here, what am I going to do here?" You know, there's no way I'm going to get out of the car, you know; it's going, you know. So I just roll the window down . . .

PETER: So, you had that to work with—the window.

AH YAN: Yeah, I roll the window down. Anything where I feel comfortable, that's what I do. We were at my Grandma's Sunday till—no Saturday—and all my relatives were there. We were talking, and I guess I started getting these symptoms again, and I just got out the paper. It's like, you know, we're all laughing, and just gradually, you know, I calm down. It's like, I'm trying to do it where people don't realize, you know, and I don't think that they realize that anything is even wrong with me, you know.

PETER: So, usually you don't even tell the other people around you.

AH YAN: No, I don't. No.

Ah Yan continued to describe exceptions—times when she felt better—over the previous week and what she was doing to take control. Peter then went on to the fourth letter of the EARS acronym, the *S* for starting over. He asked: "What else is better?" In the resulting conversation, Ah Yan was able to describe that she was learning to distinguish between times when it was good for her to tell others that her anxiety was coming on and times when it was not. Besides the exception with her husband at the dance, she described another involving her sister-in-law, in which she discovered that her sister-in-law had her own fears. Ah Yan found opening up to her sister-in-law helpful. She concluded that "I'm not the only one who gets panicky" and "It's OK to show that you're human."

At a certain point, as Peter continued to ask her what was better, Ah Yan began to say, "I don't know." Then Peter turned to relationship questions as a way of sustaining Ah Yan's solution talk. He asked: "So when you're feeling better, what do you suppose your husband notices different about you that tells him you're feeling that way?" He asked similar questions about Ah Yan's mother and her children. Sometimes new exceptions emerge through relationship questioning; sometimes not. In either case, such questions help clients to view the consequences of any progress they might be making from a contextual or systemic perspective. Here is a brief illustration:

PETER: How about the kids? What do you imagine the kids might notice that's different about you that would tell them that their mom is feeling better?

AH YAN: I don't know. They're always all over me. They're all over me. I don't know, um. I don't know. They still play. I don't know, I guess they're just themselves —the way they're supposed to be. They don't even have to look at mommy, you know. I'm OK, you know; they're playing. But when I don't feel good they're like . . .

PETER: You mean they're worried too?

AH YAN: Yeah, you know, they're playing, but they're kind of quiet . . . watching me . . .

PETER: Now they don't need to watch as much?

AH YAN: Yeah, when I'm better, they don't even remember mommy when she's OK.

PETER: When they remember mommy but go ahead and are little children, how is that for you? What's different for you?

AH YAN: It's good. It's real good. It's what I want. [tearfully] You know, they have to not worry about me. Let them be them. They're kids. They're not supposed to worry.

PETER: "Real good." Yes, I can see, "real good." [pause] So, is there anything else that's better that we haven't talked about yet?

AH YAN: No, we took care of everything.

Doing More of the Same

When clients can identify exceptions, it is useful to inquire about what it would take for the exceptions to happen again. This can be especially helpful when clients seem unclear about how the exception happened, but it's important even when clients can state what they have been doing to make the exceptions happen. For example, Peter might ask: "What will it take for you to keep on with what you've been doing to make yourself feel better?" Or he could ask: "What's most important for you to do to keep all this going?" He did not ask either of these questions. Instead, he asked for similar information, as you will see shortly, by scaling confidence.

Scaling

Peter and Ah Yan talked for approximately 25 minutes about what was better. It seemed to Peter that she was developing a clear sense both of the several exceptions to her anxiety and of the steps she was taking to make these happen. Judging that she was ready to move on to something else, Peter turned to scaling, in accordance with the protocol for later sessions. After scaling Ah Yan's perception of her current level of progress and her level of confidence, he used her scaling responses for further goal formulation. In the dialogues that follow, notice how scaling helps Ah Yan and Peter to get a sharper awareness of Ah Yan's progress and what she needs to do next.

Scaling Progress

When Ah Yan told Peter that they had covered everything that was better since their last session, he began scaling:

PETER: OK, great. So, let me ask you a question using my numbers again, OK? Let's say that 10 equals the miracle and 0 was where you were at when you decided that you were going to come in and talk with me about this. Where would you say you are at this week?

AH YAN: Now?

PETER: Yeah, now.

AH YAN: 7, maybe 8.

PETER: Oh, wow! 7 or 8. OK. Sure, that makes sense. You've been telling me about feeling better and all the things you do to make that happen: Like you're back to work and you're smiling more and, even when it comes on, you come up with ways in which to handle it . . .

AH YAN: Yeah, yeah, that's right. I'm doing that.

The number that Ah Yan chose made sense to Peter; because she had so many deliberate exceptions, Peter expected her to select a high number. Had she chosen a low number, he would have explored the apparent discrepancy. Such exploration often uncovers important new information.

Scaling Confidence

Peter went on to scale Ah Yan's level of confidence that she could maintain her gains:

PETER: OK. So you're at a 7 or an 8 . . . umm, and I've been asking you about all the things that you do to keep them at a 7 or an 8. . . . Now, if I were to ask you, "On a scale from 1 to 10—where 1 means that you have no confidence and 10 means you have every confidence—how confident are you that you can keep them at a 7 or an 8?" what would you say?

AH YAN: I think a 9.

PETER: Is that right?

AH YAN: Yeah, and I can tell because some things just . . . I don't know . . .

PETER: Where does that confidence come from? What tells you that you can be that confident, that sure?

AH YAN: I want to be that way . . . to repeat it.

PETER: [*complimenting an apparent strength*] So you're determined.

AH YAN: Yeah, I am. I want to be . . .

PETER: So where does that determination come from?

AH YAN: I don't know. You know, it's just the way I feel right now. It just feels good to feel like this. I just want to keep quiet, so it doesn't come back anymore. I just want to keep going. I know how positive if feels, you know; it's very good.

Ah Yan seemed to have an intuitive sense that she could continue her recent gains, but could not articulate its source beyond saying emphatically that this was how she felt. Other clients will more fully describe the source of their confidence; they will describe past experiences that reveal their strengths. Ah Yan did not. To follow up, Peter could have asked her, for instance, whether there were times in the past when she had similar feelings and, if so, whether they had been similarly helpful. However, he chose not to.

Next Steps

Up to this point in the second session, everything had centered on Ah Yan's exceptions and their implications for building a solution. It is important in every later session to also address goals, mainly because clients' perceptions of their goals may shift, just as their perceptions of problems and possible solutions do. For example, after considering what's better since the last session and finding little, clients may decide that their original goals are unrealistic and revise them so that they seem more achievable. Or, because they make more gains in the solution-building process than they had expected, clients may develop additional goals.

Goal formulation in later sessions does not involve repeating the miracle question. As a solution-focused interviewer, you can shift relatively easily and effectively into goal formulation on the basis of the client's answer to the scaling question about progress. For example, when Ah Yan said she was at 7 or 8, Peter could have asked her, "What will be different when you're a 9?" Asking her to think about what will be happening in her life when she moves up the scale is an invitation to explore her present perceptions of what she wants next, given her awareness of what's been better since the previous session. By moving up the scale in small gradations, Peter encourages her to work toward smaller, more realistic goals.

In later sessions, goal formulation begins later than in the first session, because it depends on thorough exploration of what's been better. About 30 minutes into their second session, Peter initiated a dialogue on goals with Ah Yan:

PETER: Let's talk just a little bit about the next step. When you move up to say an 8½, what will be different that will tell you that you're at an 8½, instead of a 7 or an 8?

AH YAN: I think I wouldn't be so scared to even think like . . . wherever I'm going to go—I mean, I get these symptoms and—and, you know, I don't think I would even—it's like forgetting about it. I think I would beat the level of training.

PETER: So when you forget about it, what would you be thinking about instead?

AH YAN: Healthier and happier and . . . I don't know.

PETER: How about when you move all the way up to a 9?

AH YAN: Nine? More healthier and happier thoughts like now, I guess. I don't know.

PETER: So it sounds like it'll be more of the same thing of what's happening right now.

AH YAN: Yeah.

Aside from the miracle question, all of the goal-formulation questions in Chapter 5 may be used in later sessions. How far you want to go with the goal-formulation dialogue depends on the interviewing situation. You will do more goal formulation with clients who have unclear or seemingly unrealistic goals and with clients for whom little has gone better over the past week. When you work with clients like Ah Yan, who spend some 25 minutes describing progress and how they produced it, you will have less time and, sensing their confidence, less need to work on goal development, because such clients have a greater sense of direction.

When Peter asked Ah Yan about possible next steps, she gave a fairly vague answer: She would be having happy and healthy thoughts more of the time. Peter could have followed up by seeking greater clarification and specificity. Instead, he chose to invite Ah Yan to work at goals by asking relationship questions involving her husband, mother, and children. Let's look at the relationship question he asked with regard to her children. Notice how, in working on goals here, Ah Yan mentioned a new exception. This illustrates again how asking relationship questions can clarify—and perhaps enhance—what is happening in the client's solution building:

PETER: So, when you move up to 8½, what will your children notice that will tell them that you are doing just that much better?

AH YAN: With my kids, I have to be more—I have to let them go a little bit. I see other kids, and I have to like . . . My little boy, I never wanted him far from me. I was scared something's going to happen to him or hurt my girls. And it's like, "You stay in front of the house. *Don't* leave the front of the house.

Don't." All these kids his age are on their bikes, going around the blocks, you know. And it's like—let him go, let him go, just give him a certain length, you know. And I tell him, "Now, OK, five houses this way and three houses this way; you cross the street just make sure you watch for cars." And I don't know, I saw him Saturday, I let him go. I saw him.

PETER: [*noticing an elicited exception*] Was that different for you?

AH YAN: And it felt like, like, ah, relief. OK, it's a big step, you know. I'm still kind of like, "Don't cross the street."

PETER: [*exploring the exception*] You did that on Saturday.

AH YAN: Yeah.

PETER: [*echoing her words*] Really? You let him go?

AH YAN: Yeah. He crossed the street.

PETER: So that's another thing that you did differently?

AH YAN: Yeah, he crossed the street. I don't know, it's still scary, but he has to grow up too.

PETER: How old is he?

AH YAN: Di Jia, he's 6.

PETER: He's 6? Is this the first time you let him go across the street like that?

AH YAN: Yeah, yeah.

PETER: [*indirect compliment, a single word to punctuate the exception*] Wow!

AH YAN: And it's like, I kind of—I wanted to cry, and I wanted to laugh. I don't know. It's something that I did let him go, you know, but it's hard, 'cause I'm scared something's going to happen.

PETER: Yeah, it really is something.

AH YAN: I just can't . . . I hear all these things that kids get hit, you know. I just think that's what bothers me. I'm scared to lose somebody.

PETER: Yeah. Sure. Of course.

AH YAN: When I saw him, I kind of laughed, you know, and I wanted to cry, you know, at the same time. He's so big, and it's like, I want him by me. It's like, I can't do that. I just can't.

PETER: It's not easy, is it?

AH YAN: My little girl got stitches. She was running, of course, like kids do. And she got a stick and it went in her hip. And I see at times that I can be happy, and then something goes wrong. It makes me think wrong, you know, or think bad, like what happened to my little girl. OK, but my little boy, he was playing OK, and it made me feel good because I let him go, you know—kind of like he's got to have confidence . . .

PETER: Wow, I'm impressed. That was so tough for you to do. How did you get yourself to do that?

AH YAN: People tell me, "You don't let your kids do anything. Let them go, you know. Let them go. You're too close to your kids," they tell me.

PETER: [*refocusing on Ah Yan's success*] What told you on Saturday that these people were right, that what you needed to do was to let him go?

AH YAN: Because I see all these little kids. They're playing, and he's looking at them.

PETER: Sure. Of course.

AH YAN: He feels left out. I don't know. I think I would feel left out if I was in his place, so I have to. I have to. He's got a bike, the kids got a bike, and they're his age. Why can they go, and he can't? He's going to be left out.

PETER: So you're paying attention to him and figuring out what's right and good for him?

AH YAN: Yeah, and I says, "OK, you're going to go this many houses, and that's your part, and that's how far mom is going to let you go. And you can't go around the block because I can't see you." And I think he still kind of answers to that. And I said, "You can cross the street. Be careful. Please. You know, and this part, you can't go too close because there's more traffic out this way, you know." I saw him, and it felt good 'cause he looked happy. He looked like, "I'm on the street," you know, and it's like—I don't know, it feels good. My little girl got hurt, you know. She was running and running; there was sticks, and she got it, and she got stitches. And it's like, why, why did I let her do that? You know, but I can't think that way. My sister-in-law says, "My little girl's had a broken leg, a da-da-da, a finger's broken, arm broken, you know, all of it." And it's like she goes, "Things happen. It don't matter if they're in the same place. Things happen." And like . . .

PETER: Things happen.

AH YAN: It's hard to—I don't know—just kind of scared any—something else is going to happen. You know, I have to because, if I don't, they're not going to grow up, you know. They're not going to learn how to do things by themselves. They're going to want me there 'cause I'm going to show them that way. But I want them to have confidence in themselves. I'm trying. I'm trying.

PETER: [*amplifying and complimenting her determination to do what is best for her children*] Yes, I can see that; I can see that you want to let them go more, so that they can have confidence. You care very much about them.

AH YAN: Yeah, I love them.

In this dialogue, Peter made it possible for Ah Yan to arrive at her own conclusion: "I love them." Rather than praising Ah Yan for loving her children, Peter asked questions that helped Ah Yan to make her own assessment of her strengths. We believe that this is true empowerment; in this process, clients make their own claims about what kind of good and competent people they are.

Termination

In solution-building interviews, we think about—and work at—termination with clients from the first session. The initial goal-formulation question asked of clients in the first session reflects that attitude: "What needs to be different in your life as a result of coming here for you to say that meeting with me was worthwhile?" The same attitude continues in later meetings.

You can address termination efficiently and naturally in later sessions by working from clients' responses to the scaling question about progress. After working on additional goals, you can begin a conversation about termination by asking, "What number do you need to be in order not to come and talk to me anymore?"

Here is what happened when Peter did this with Ah Yan:

PETER: OK, let me ask you this. Right now, you're at a 7 or 8. What do you need to be in order not to come back here and see me anymore?

AH YAN: To learn not to worry and, I don't know, to just stop thinking wrong, you know, like the opposite of good. And I just want to feel good about myself.

PETER: What does that mean in terms of a number? You're at a 7 or an 8 now. Is that good enough for you? Can you live with a 7 or an 8?

AH YAN: Yeah, yeah, 'cause I have confidence right now. I don't know, when I'm lower, it's just like I'm not sure. I'm kind of scared, more scared than positive. I'm trying to fight the scared away. The book, you know, it helps, and the talking about it, the talking and opening up . . .

PETER: That helps too.

AH YAN: I think, when I talk to people, I don't know, I don't feel so like—like, when I didn't talk to anybody, it was like nobody's listening to me, nobody.

PETER: You felt alone.

AH YAN: Yeah, I felt alone. I felt trapped. I don't know. I just felt so lonely, and now that I'm talking—like, my sister goes, "I heard that you didn't feel good," and she says, "I told mom you worry too much. You think too much." You know, now that I talk to people, it's like I can talk to anybody, you know. Someone can be there. It's not—I guess it's me that wouldn't talk so no one would be there. And now I talk, and it's like, we both share each other's problems or . . .

PETER: Is that different for you that sometimes now you're the one that's taking the first step?

AH YAN: [*seemingly broadening her concept of her problem*] Yeah, it's different. I'm always listening and never talking; maybe that's my problem too: I never talk, always keeping everything inside. And, now, I'm starting . . . and it kind of makes me, "Oh, someone's listening to me." It makes me feel better.

PETER: That makes a lot of sense. That makes a lot of sense. You've been doing a lot of thinking about this, haven't you?

AH YAN: I just want to get better. I just want everything better.

PETER: Yeah, I can see that you're working very hard to do that. OK, so right now, I was asking you what number you needed to be in order not to come back again. I'm still not clear on that.

AH YAN: The symptoms, I just want them to go away. They're like, I don't know. I go to my husband—I feel like they're little attacks, like seizures or something, but I mean, like, I have a brother that has epilepsy. You know, he gets attacks. He doesn't remember anything. He blacks out, and I don't. I know what's going on, and it feels like a dream to me. It feels like a dream to me, and the more I put my head to what's going on with me, that now it's worse, and when I feel like that, I just forget about it and it just goes away. You know, it's like I'm trying to figure out if I can control it, if it's just me. It's me that's letting myself be like this, you know, and—I don't know. It's so weird . . .

PETER: And now you're doing some of the things you need to do to control it.

AH YAN: Yeah, and now I'm noticing I can control it if I want.

PETER: What's the most important thing that you need to, ah, to do to make sure that you keep things at a 7 or an 8, to keep your confidence?

AH YAN: What I feel like—I don't know. I'm trying, you know, I'm trying to get everything together. I feel like it's really me that's making myself feel like this. I feel it's me. I'm trying to figure out things, and—I don't know. People can tell you, OK, they tell you you get exhausted, you know, you're tired, and you just want to bum around. They tell you that, but, I don't know, I realize that I think I do put too much on myself. I think that's my problem, and I think—I'm not positive about it, but I think I need help for them to show me, I don't know, like how to . . . I don't know. I don't know; I can't explain it.

PETER: OK. Listen, I'm going to take a break and think about what you told me. OK? [she nods] Is there anything else we should talk about first?

AH YAN: No; I said it all.

Although Ah Yan never gave Peter a number, she did begin to ponder what would have to be different for her to feel comfortable and confident about terminating services. She said that she would like the symptoms to disappear, but she also seemed to be developing the idea that the severity of the symptoms had a lot to do with her ("it's really me that's making myself feel like this") and that she had some control over them ("now I'm noticing I can control it if I want"). Realizing that Ah Yan was not ready yet to define a scale score for termination, Peter decided to take a break and formulate feedback, instead of pushing her to come up with a number. His decision here illustrates an important point: When clients have done their best to put words to their perceptions and cannot for the moment, the interviewer must accept that situation and respond respectfully. As always, the question plants the seed, and the client may do some more thinking later.

The Break

At this point, you may wish to turn to the Appendix and review the protocol for formulating feedback. As an exercise, complete this protocol for Ah Yan, on the basis of information from the second session. Write down a bottom line, compliments, and a bridge for Ah Yan. You may even want to read it aloud, as if you were delivering it to her. As you follow our account of Peter's reflections during the break, compare your conclusions with his.

The second session with Ah Yan reminded Peter forcefully how much clients' perceptions can shift during solution building. In their first session, Ah Yan had talked as though the problem troubling her life was some unknown cause that was producing frightening symptoms like hair loss, shakiness, and hyperventilation. By the end of the second session, however, she seemed to be shifting toward a different definition, in which the problem was Ah Yan herself and the way she made certain choices ("I think I do put too much on myself"). Her perceptions, definitions, and meanings seemed to be changing over time and through interaction with others—her husband, mother, sister-in-law, children, and Peter.

During the break, Peter did not need very long to figure out a bottom line. He felt, as he did after the first session, that the two of them stood in a customer-type relationship. The problem (feeling panicky) and the general goal (to reduce her fear) still stood. At that point, near the end of their second meeting, Ah Yan seemed even more aware of herself as part of the problem and any eventual solution. Peter also noted that several exceptions had occurred since the first session; Ah Yan's description of them indicated that they were deliberate exceptions. Finally, she seemed to have well formed goals: She perceived that her deliberate exceptions had been successful ("I'm noticing that I can control it [the panic] if I want") and she seemed to have every intention of repeating just what she had been doing to make the exceptions happen. Therefore, Peter decided that the obvious bottom line was to suggest that she do more of the same. He formulated compliments and a bridge, and he decided to give Ah Yan more responsibility for deciding about a next session. Then he was ready to deliver his feedback.

Feedback

Compliments

PETER: OK, Ah Yan, I thought about all that you told me and, as I'm sure you can imagine, I am very impressed with what's been happening and what those things suggest about your strengths: First, you seem to be a very *creative* person. Just in this last week there have been so many different ways in which you have been able to brush it off and things you have done to put yourself in charge, things like leaving the dance when it came on, to take a break and get some air; like rolling down the window and breathing deep; like talking more and opening up with your sister-in-law; and so forth.

AH YAN: [smiling and nodding] Yeah, thanks.

PETER: And, uh, I'm also impressed that you want to educate yourself about these panicky feelings, that you took the time and made the effort to get that book, and that's another way in which you're taking charge. You know, you're getting more knowledge about it, and you found some real meaningful ideas in that book—like "who's in charge" here? And "the less you worry, the healthier you are."

AH YAN: Yeah, OK.

PETER: You also are a person with *courage*. After being away from work, you got your courage back up, and you went back to work. That's really something because, even though you felt better, you didn't know how it would turn out when you went back to work. Umm, I also think that it takes a lot of courage to decide that you're going to put yourself in charge. And it takes courage to then take the risks to try new things—such as talking more to get out of the trap of loneliness. Or deciding that you have to do things differently with Di Jia and then taking the risk of letting him cross the street. That was a big step for you to take; that took courage and strength.

AH YAN: Yeah, it did.

PETER: Right; no wonder that you're at a 7 or an 8! [pause] And it's also impressive that you not only are doing things but that you are paying such careful attention to exactly how you do it. That makes it two times impressive.

Bridge

PETER: Ah Yan, I agree with you when you say the words, "it's me which makes me feel this way," and I agree that a big part of the solution for you lies in your taking charge.

Task

PETER: So what I suggest you do is that you continue to do those things that you've figured out for yourself that have been working, and as you continue to get better, I suggest that you pay attention to what else you might be doing that's helpful, things that you haven't noticed yet.

AH YAN: [nodding] Yeah, yeah.

PETER: OK. And now I'm thinking about, what next? Do you think it's a good idea to come back and talk more?

AH YAN: Yeah, I want to try not coming , but I don't know yet. . . . I want to have confidence. You know, what if it happens again?

PETER: Right. OK, I thought so from what you said. So, when? One, two, three weeks, or what?

AH YAN: I think two weeks.

PETER: OK, that sounds good; let's set it up.

AH YAN: Thanks, I think that's good.

The Second Session with the Williams Family

The second meeting with the Williams family provides an example of working simultaneously with several family members in a later session. You'll see how Insoo works with the perceptions of individual family members but, at the same time, uncovers and works with the strengths of the family as a unit.

What's Better?

Gladys returned with her four children for the second session. As she had indicated that she would at the end of the first session, Gladys had sent her brother Albert away and did not invite him to the second session. Insoo began the session by asking, "What's been better since the last time we met?" Gladys answered that she had sent her mother home too and that she and her children had spent a week at the Salvation Army Family Camp, where they went swimming and fishing and enjoyed other recreational activities. Gladys and the children indicated that they had a good time there and got along well. Insoo then shifted the focus to family interactions at home:

INSOO: [*exploring for exceptions*] Yeah. So when the kids are getting along better, what are they like?

GLADYS: To me they like sisters and brothers should be. They play together and they're not fighting each other. It's not like I gotta sit there and constantly watch 'em. But that's only when they outside. If they in the house then I still have to watch him.

INSOO: [*asking about exceptions again, by refocusing on the original question*] OK. So tell me about—what are they like when they get along?

GLADYS: It's peaceful.

INSOO: You said they're like brothers and sisters. What's that mean?

GLADYS: They're not fighting; they not fussing and arguing at each other. Like Marcus. He argues all the time.

INSOO: What's he like when he doesn't argue with them?

GLADYS: I don't know yet, because it's, like, he got this Nintendo and he feel like he's the only one that should play it, and he always arguing with them because they're in his room and they want to play it too. I could put it in the living room and use his TV but he wouldn't like that. So I said, "Well, I'll put it in your room and you can play," 'cause the kids, they don't be there in the daytime, so he have all day to play it. Then, when they get home, they can play it but he don't want them to play it.

INSOO: Uh huh. So you want him to share. [*to Marcus, asking for an exception*] What are you like? You must get along with somebody sometime, right?

MARCUS: Yeah.

INSOO: Yeah. Who do you get along well with?

MARCUS: I get along with my friends and sometimes I get along with Offion.

INSOO: How do you do that?

MARCUS: When, like . . . me and my friends, we, like, well like, we go to birthday parties and everything. We go bowling and basketball games and baseball games. And, like, over at the Center, that's, like, a place where I can go, like, and Offion and them, they're not allowed. It's just for teenagers. I can just go and have fun.

INSOO: [*indirectly complimenting*] Is that right? And you don't hear complaints from where he goes?

GLADYS: No. I get complaints in my house around the clock. I don't understand how he can go and play with somebody else, but he have to live with us and he can't play with the ones that in the house. I don't understand that.

INSOO: [*affirming her perception*] Yeah. This must be baffling for you.

GLADYS: [*returning to problem talk*] Yeah. It's like these are your brothers and sisters. You got to stay with these people. You got to live with these people. Then when you get grown, you might need them one day. And then he say he don't want to be around them. He said they—uh, he always say he wants to go somewheres where peoples are his age but Offion is 10 an' he's 12. That's his age.

INSOO: Now, so you're concerned that they may be—what? Fighting too much? You want them to love each other?

GLADYS: Yeah, that's a big concern.

INSOO: Uh. OK. Now do you think that these two fight more than most 12-year-old and 10-year-old brothers?

GLADYS: I don't know. . . . I'm not gonna say the two of 'em; I'm gonna say Marcus. He be fighting too much and don't listen.

INSOO: What do you make of this? How come he listens to other people and he doesn't listen to you?

GLADYS: Rebellion. Yeah. It's like, "Hey, let me test her. Let me see how far I can get with her." To me, that's what I see in him.

INSOO: That's what you think. OK. [*continuing to explore for exceptions*; asking about Offion] Now, are there times when he is nice to his sisters?

GLADYS: It's a lots of times when he's nice to them.

INSOO: Yeah? Tell me about this. Tell me about the times you're nice to your sisters.

OFFION: When they want me to play with them, I'll play with them.

INSOO: You do? Really? Huh. Is that right? He plays with you? [to Olayinka and Ayesh] Do you like to play with him? [they nod]

OFFION: And it's like more funner 'cause Marcus, he's always in the room playing Nintendo, not bugging us.

INSOO: [*exploring for an exception around Marcus' behavior*] OK. Now. What happens when you and Marcus are home alone? Without these three?

GLADYS: Then I go to sleep, and he stay in his room or he go where he wanna go in the house, because no one's there but me and him.

INSOO: So then he's no trouble.

GLADYS: No. He'll go outside and ride his bike or he goes to the Center, but I would have to tell him sometimes to turn the TV down.

INSOO: [*asking for what's different about the exception times*] How come you're no trouble then?

MARCUS: Because it's like I have the whole house to myself. Mom's usually not really telling me to do anything and, like, if I know it's my turn to do dishes or something, I probably will do dishes, and then I'll ask her, "Can I go ride my bike?" because I can't just leave out the house, 'cause she'll wonder where I'm at. But I ask her and then I go.

INSOO: [*complimenting*] Is that right? You do dishes sometimes?

MARCUS: Well, we all have to do dishes. We take turns.

INSOO: Oh, you all have to do dishes. Not you. Not you. You do too? My goodness. Honest?

OFFION: All of us do dishes.

OLAYINKA: We take turns.

INSOO: [*complimenting Gladys*] You trained them well.

GLADYS: They hate dishes—to wash dishes.

INSOO: [*persisting in her complimenting*] But they do it, though.

GLADYS: Yeah.

INSOO: [*emphasizing Gladys' success with her children*] Even though they hate it; they still do them.

GLADYS: Yeah, but they don't always get 'em clean.

INSOO: Of course. Wow. You did a very good job of training them.

GLADYS: Wow. Thanks.

INSOO: Not many kids this age can do that.

GLADYS: Really?

INSOO: [*asking for exceptions around what the family had identified as the toughest problem; to Marcus and Offion*] So tell me about what you two are like when you get along?

MARCUS: Well, like, sometimes, this, like, really never happens, but sometimes we're outside playing and then I—me and Tony, we're, like, playing a game, and then we go, "Well, I'm tired of this game." Why don't we play another game." And then we toss the football back and forth.

INSOO: No kidding. You do that?

MARCUS: Sometimes we can play Nintendo together. Sometimes.

At this point, well into the session, it was clear to Insoo that the Williams family perceived that it had successes and strengths. They described that they had been to family camp together; three of the children had enjoyed each other's company; Gladys indicated that she had set more boundaries on extended family members whom she felt to be unsupportive of her; and Gladys demonstrated that she cared very much about rearing responsible and caring children who could participate in family chores and get along with her and with one another. It was also clear to Insoo that Gladys was the leader of this family and the person primarily responsible for holding the family together. Consequently, although the most worrisome difficulty to Gladys at the moment was Marcus' rebellion, Insoo decided to set that matter aside for the time being and to focus on Gladys' strengths and successes:

INSOO: [*complimenting and asking about how she makes good things happen in her family*] Now Mrs. Williams, how did you get this idea that you wanted to be such a good mother?

GLADYS: I didn't. It was . . . like, after I started having kids, I knew I didn't want to treat my kids like I was treated, so I had to do something about that. I chose not to abuse them. That's where it came from, I guess. But it wasn't, like, planned that way, 'cause I didn't want any kids.

INSOO: So somehow you turned out to be real conscientious about you being a good mother.

GLADYS: Yeah.

INSOO: You try very hard to be a good mother.

GLADYS: I guess after what happened to 'em too, with the abuse from their father, that, like, made me more aware of watching 'em closer and taking 'em with me everywhere I go now. 'Cause I used to leave 'em with him, by him being the father, and felt I didn't have to take and drag them everywhere I went. Even in the wintertime, I would go and cash my check and pay my bills and come back home, and I felt like why take the childrens out and it really wasn't necessary. He could stay at home and keep 'em, and I didn't have a car. They had to go on the bus and go everywhere I walked. And he was doing these cruel things to 'em, and I just wasn't aware that he was doing these things to 'em, or they would have been with me then.

INSOO: [*quickly recognizing the need for confidentiality*] Umm, let me ask the four of you to go out in the waiting room and wait, because I want to talk with your mom. OK?

GLADYS: Good-bye. Au revoir.

MARCUS: Bonjour.

GLADYS: Bonjour, bonjour.

MARCUS: Bonjour.

INSOO: "Bonjour"? My goodness.

GLADYS: Oh yeah, they learning French.

INSOO: Great. [*returning focus to Marcus*] Marcus is a pretty bright kid, isn't he?

GLADYS: Yeah. To me, he is. As, that's the highest he can go; he do get Bs, but the top grade is As and he got more As than Bs.

INSOO: Wow. You must be very proud of him.

GLADYS: [*indicating another success and more strengths*] Yeah. I like the work. He just keep doing the work. I help him with his work if I can. I went back to school and they put me on a level that he's on now and I was able to teach him some of the things that they was teaching me.

INSOO: And he talks very nice. Did you notice that? He can explain himself very well.

GLADYS: Hopefully, because going to that school, you know, because they teach him the correct way to talk and I do too at home. If they say, like, he keep saying "can't" and "ain't." [giggle] I told him, I say it's not a word and he get mad. He goes get the dictionary. He say it's a word. But at least I don't feel he should use it.

INSOO: He goes to get the dictionary and show you that it's a word?

GLADYS: Yeah, to show me it's a word.

INSOO: Is that right? You have very bright kids.

GLADYS: Yeah. Tell me!

INSOO: Yeah. And that's hard to raise bright kids. Don't you know that?

GLADYS: Well, thank God, I can do it.

INSOO: Yeah, really. Thank God, you can do it, and it seems like you're wanting to keep up with that.

GLADYS: Yeah. 'Cause I want them to go to college, too. Umm, Marcus, he's, like, into art. He really don't want to go to college if he can avoid it. He wants to go to art school.

INSOO: Oh, he does?

GLADYS: Yeah. Offion is fascinated with limousines and Cadillacs. He'd be more reluctant to go to college.

INSOO: At this age, he is. He would be.

GLADYS: I said, "In order to get those things you have to go to college," and he's like, "Yeah, OK. If that's what I have to do." But Olayinka and Ayesh, I don't know yet.

INSOO: Yeah, well they're too young yet. You have to wait a while. [*complimenting*] Wow. So you have a lot of ambition for your children.

GLADYS: Yeah.

INSOO: [*indirectly complimenting and asking about the source of her strength*] Where did you learn to do that?

GLADYS: I don't think it's—it was like learning. It was the things that I went through if I had learned anything. It was the things that I went through that taught me. Like, when I had Marcus, I was 15 and I wanted to go to school. I continued to go. And then I got afraid that when Offion and my mom . . . I was paying her $100 a month for rent and $50 a month to see to Marcus while I went to school. And she got my food stamps. All of my stamps. And when I got pregnant with Offion, she didn't want to see to him anymore. Even though I hadn't had the baby, I was just pregnant with 'im. Wasn't even showing. I was about a month, if she even knew. And I said, you know, I found out I was pregnant and I was gonna continue to go to school, and she said, no, she's not gonna keep him anymore. So . . .

INSOO: So even then you were pretty ambitious.

GLADYS: Yeah. If I could've went to school, I would have continued going but she didn't want to help me out, so I say forget it and then she started, like, you have to find your own place and get out. So.

INSOO: So you've been independent ever since.

GLADYS: Well, I couldn't leave. When I did leave, she called the police on me and came and got me, so I didn't leave anymore until I made 18. And when I made 18, I had three. So, I had moved out. I had two and was on my way with my third one.

INSOO: So life has been pretty tough for you. You've been through a lot.

GLADYS: Yeah. And I don't want to see my kids have to go through nothing that I had went through. And if I can keep them from going through it, I will.

INSOO: Yeah.

GLADYS: My mom. I sit down and try and talk to her like I'm talking to you, and she tell me she don't want to hear it.

INSOO: [*exploring for how Gladys makes her successes happen*] So, you know it seems like, in spite of all those things that happened with your mother, somehow you decided not to listen to all that. How come?

GLADYS: Yeah. Because I know what I went through with her, and it's like, if I sit and listen to her, my life would be like hers.

INSOO: [*emphasizing her determination to break the cycle and assert her independence*] And you want your life to be different than your mother's.

GLADYS: Yeah.

INSOO: How successful are you, that your life is different already from hers?

GLADYS: I have my own home. I don't have a man over me, controlling me. I have my childrens to myself. If I tell one of them to do something, more than likely they will do it. Sometimes I have to threaten them to do it, but more than likely when I tell them to do something they'll do it. Umm, I don't have—I have a small savings account. Forty dollars I found out today, but it's mine. I can—I have clothes that I can wear. I don't have to borrow other people's clothes. When I get ready to take a bath, I have deodorant and soap and shampoo.

INSOO: So you already, at your age, you have done better than your mother has done. [*inviting Gladys to amplify her perception of her strengths*] Where'd you get this kind of ambition?

GLADYS: I—to me, I wanted to get out the house so bad. I had been molested by my father. My mother wouldn't believe it, and he would beat me, because he didn't want me to tell her. She would beat me, because she said I was lying on him by him being her husband, and I wanted to get away from that. And I kept saying, "If I can get out, I know I will make it." And after I got here in this city, me and my husband, he didn't get paid for three weeks and I started to going around, and peoples started telling me where food pantries were and how I could get my kids some clothes and, you know, how to do volunteer work and get things. And if you tell me how to do something—I might can't read that good or spell that good, but if you can show me or tell me then I can help me and my family out from there. And that's what happened here. And my mother, she came to me when she was here last week, before she left, and she wanted to move in with me, and I said no.

INSOO: [*indirectly complimenting and asking about the how of the exception*] So how did you know that you don't want to do that? How were you able to say no to your mother when she wanted to move in with you?

GLADYS: [Sigh] My husband is in a halfway house right now, and he's . . .

INSOO: Yeah? Oh, he's in a halfway house.

GLADYS: Yeah. He's—he went. He turned himself in, for what he did to the kids. To me, that was a start. Better than my father, you know. And I said, well, maybe it help him after all. Who knows? But if I did want to wait until my childrens get grown and go back to my husband or somewhere down the line before they get grown—get to be big enough where they can really handle themselves, and I want to go back to my husband, I don't want her staying in my house telling me that I couldn't. And right now, that's what she's telling me, and she's not in my house. But she's still with my father, and he hasn't served a day of sentence. He done abused me, her sister, and my little sister, and you still with this guy? And you gonna tell me that I can't be with my husband, and he the one that served time for what he did? I don't understand that. So I told her, I told her. I said, "Well, my husband might come back" and I know she don't like him and, to keep down confusion, I am still his wife. And I said, "To keep down confusion, you get your own house, then you won't have to see him."

INSOO: Good. Good. So I guess this is something you will talk about, your husband coming back.

GLADYS: Yeah.

INSOO: OK. We could do that next time then.

GLADYS: OK.

INSOO: OK. All right. So I want to take some time and talk to my team, and I'll come back in about 5 minutes. OK?

GLADYS: OK.

Break

Insoo chose not to scale progress and do additional goal formulation using the results in this session with Gladys. However, Insoo's questions about exceptions and the strengths that Gladys was using to make them happen had provided clear evidence that, despite difficult circumstances, Gladys was making impressive things happen, both with her children and in her extended family. Further complicating Gladys' life was the prospect of her husband's release. He had abused the children and now, it seemed, was in a halfway house awaiting release.

At this point, as an exercise, take some time to write out what you would say if the Williams were your clients. On the basis of the guidelines in Chapter 7, organize your feedback into compliments, a bridge, and a task (if warranted).

Now let's look at how Insoo presented the feedback that she and the team developed.

Feedback

Compliments

INSOO: OK. The team wanted me to tell you kids that we're absolutely astounded about how well you behaved here. All four of you. It's sort of boring to sit here and talk about things, right? When adults sit around and talk, it's boring, but you really handled it very well. And also, they said they could tell that there's a lot of love and affection going on underneath. Under there, underneath it all. And this is what especially they wanted me to mention about Marcus, about how well he speaks and how smart he is. [turning to Gladys] And we think that what's important is that you know that each child has its own good points.

GLADYS: Mm hmm.

INSOO: You can see that. Each one of them. And they are different, and you can see that.

GLADYS: Yep.

INSOO: So we again wanted to tell you what a wonderful job you have done all by yourself.

GLADYS: Thanks.

INSOO: And it has not been easy.

GLADYS: No, it hasn't. It's still not easy.

INSOO: Still is not easy; you have a long way to go.

GLADYS: Yeah.

INSOO: But, so far, you have done a very good job.

GLADYS: Thanks.

INSOO: And uh, they are just nice kids. Just nice kids. And uh, it's because, I think, that you raise them with love and you want them to be successful.

GLADYS: Thanks.

INSOO: OK. So. Well, you guys, we want you to keep it up, OK? And if you want to go wait outside again, I want to talk with your mom a couple more minutes. OK?

GLADYS: Au revoir. Bonjour.

AYESH: Bonjour.

OLAYINKA: Bonjour, turkey.

GLADYS: [laughing] I'm getting you for that one. Did you hear? She called me a turkey! I'll get her.

INSOO: [laughs] Umm, again, I can tell, you've been through so much. Yet in spite of that, here you are. You have a very good idea what you want to do with your children—how you want to raise your children. You want them to do better than what you have done. And you want them to not go through what you have gone through, and already you are a good mother. Already. You have a long way to go, but you're amazing because, in spite of the fact that your mother didn't praise you, still you can see that each child has good points.

GLADYS: Yeah.

INSOO: And you're trying to figure out . . . "How can I help each child bring out his good points?"

GLADYS: [*pointing to still another success*] Yeah. I can do that when I sit down and look at each one of them. Like Offion, he need lots of help in reading and math and, when he's learning, it make him feel better. And I ordered some books for him.

INSOO: Yeah. And you're doing that. And it's amazing, because your mother has never done that with you. And still you figured it out how to do that.

GLADYS: Yeah.

INSOO: Yeah. Umm, the other thing is that you are using your life experience to not only help yourself but also help your children.

GLADYS: Yeah.

INSOO: You are learning from yourself.

GLADYS: I didn't understand with my husband why he did what he did, because he said that it was done to him, but it was done to me too and it didn't make me want to do it.

INSOO: And you didn't. That's right.

GLADYS: And I didn't understand that. But that's his reason.

INSOO: That's right. Yeah. We can talk about that next time. [pause] You are very resourceful, you know, coming here at a young age to a strange city. You figured it out—what you had to do. And you figured out how to get food and how to get clothes for your kids and how to take care of your children. You did it all by yourself. There was nobody helping you.

GLADYS: Yeah.

INSOO: And so I think that you are a real good role model for your children.

GLADYS: I keep telling—you know, I don't know how to read and spell that good but it don't—if you want to do something then you'll find a way.

INSOO: Yeah, and you were doing it. And again I think that you figured it out—what you need to do with your mother—and, you know, you want to be different. So you have figured out what is best for you and best for your children. That's a lot you've figured out.

GLADYS: Yeah. I'm trying to leave the church I'm at. Because the childrens, they, like, go because I make 'em go. [*indicating her thoughtful use of another community resource*] But I took 'em to other churches and they—they want to go back. They have children programs.

INSOO: And you said you've done the same thing about figuring out about school.

GLADYS: Yeah.

INSOO: So you're using the same ideas.

GLADYS: Yeah. They like the school they at.

Bridge

INSOO: Good. Good. Right. So the team—we are all amazed at what you are doing for yourself and your children, and we agree that it's important and worthwhile for you to do it.

GLADYS: Yeah. Thanks.

Task

INSOO: So we think you should keep right on doing what you're doing, continuing to figure out what's best for you and for your children.

GLADYS: OK.

INSOO: And also, about all this stuff about what to do with your husband. Do you know when he's going to be released?

GLADYS: No. I don't know when, but he just moved where he is, and I do go see him and the kids can too. And they seem to be comfortable with him.

INSOO: OK. So he came out of prison and he's in a halfway house now.

GLADYS: It's not—to me, it's not like a halfway house. It's still a correctional facility, because a halfway house he can get out and go back at a certain time. He can't go on the streets.

INSOO: So he can't come out; he can't come home for now?

GLADYS: No. Not this place. He can't come out for weeks.

INSOO: OK. So, let's go set up a time for us to get together. OK?

GLADYS: OK.

Insoo's work with Gladys toward the end of their second session demonstrates how keeping the focus on successes and strengths helps clients to sharpen their sense of what they are doing that is useful for solution building. By directing and redirecting the dialogue toward solution talk, Insoo kept giving Gladys opportunities to remember and verbalize her past successes. Gladys did just that. As she related those successes, she increased her confidence that she could respond successfully to the challenges facing her family.

Setbacks, Relapses, and Times When Nothing Is Better

Life is full of ups and downs. Sometimes, when you ask what's better, you must expect your clients to respond with a description of how things have taken a turn for the worse. They may tell you that their teenager who was making such good progress was caught breaking and entering last week. Or they may say that they have started drinking again, or that they are more depressed than ever. You may find these reports discouraging, especially when you and your clients have already worked hard at solution building. Clients, too, will be discouraged; they may feel embarrassed or even ashamed at having to report setbacks and relapses. In these situations, it is easy for the practitioner to feel like nothing seems to work, and for clients to wonder what use it is to try so hard.

We view setbacks and relapses differently. Without change, how would we recognize stability? Without stability, how would we recognize change? Similarly, we cannot know successes without failures; they are two sides of the same coin. Most people tend to focus on one side of the coin; they forget its opposite. For example, most people will tell you how the fight started and how it continued, but forget that the fight stopped somehow. Or they will be keen to tell you that they fell back into drinking last week for three days but will fail to mention that somehow they have not had a drink in the last two days.

When clients are intent on relating their failures and do not respond to your attempts to explore what is better, we think it is important to respectfully listen to these accounts and to accept and normalize their disappointment. After they feel heard, you can move on to ask them about how the fight stopped or how they managed not to take the next drink. We believe that clients have the capacity to control their own behavior. Therefore, it is logical, for example, to ask a client who drank 12 beers, as Insoo once did, how the client knew not to take a 13th. Similarly, if a young mother was tempted to hit her sassing child, ask how she managed to walk out of the room instead. When clients become more aware of their ability to stop themselves, instead of following their usual patterns, the instances in which they stop themselves become perceived exceptions and something to build on.

Rarely, a client may respond consistently to your questions about what's better by saying, "Nothing, nothing is better; in fact, things are horrible and getting worse." In addition, the client's manner may suggest that he or she is deeply discouraged and is having trouble in completing simple daily activities.

In such circumstances, you can turn to coping questions, which we discuss in the next chapter.

Conclusion

At this point, we have presented all the skills and procedures normally used in first and later sessions of solution building, with both individual clients and families. By now, you may have lost sight of the big picture—the flow of the whole process. Therefore, we suggest that you go back to Chapter 5 and find the point at which the case of Ah Yan begins. Follow her case through from start to finish, by reading the dialogues between her and Peter in Chapters 5–8. Once you have finished, go back and do the same for the Williams family. As you read, note how consistently Insoo and Peter maintain the posture of not knowing, and thus invite their clients to be experts about their own lives. Notice, too, how solution-focused interviewing keeps the focus on clients' perceptions of their own successes and strengths; as a result, practitioners can conclude sessions by giving feedback that draws attention to client competencies.

Interviewing
in Crisis Situations

Great emergencies and crises show us how much greater our vital resources are than we had supposed.
(James, 1920, p. 254)

At the very least, the strengths perspective obligates workers to understand that, however downtrodden or sick, individuals have survived (and in some cases even thrived). They have taken steps, summoned up resources, and coped. We need to know what they have done, how they have done it, what they have learned from doing it, what resources (inner and outer) were available in their struggle to surmount their troubles.
(Saleebey, 1992, pp. 171–172)

In the helping professions, a crisis may be any of various events or circumstances that provoke strong reactions in people. Roberts (1990, p. 4) lists the following examples: "the aftermath of a violent crime, a suicide attempt, a drug overdose, a natural disaster, a divorce, a broken romance, sexual impotence, or an automobile crash." Others include reactions to sexual assault, military combat, a diagnosis of terminal illness, and the death of a family member or cherished friend. Such events disrupt people's lives and often leave them feeling disorganized, disoriented, vulnerable, frightened, and alone. Victims may also experience flashbacks to the traumatic event, have nightmares, or lose their ability to concentrate on daily activities.

After a crisis, people need immediate support to stabilize their reactions and to begin the process of adapting to the disruption in their lives. The recognition of this need has spawned crisis services in hospitals, as well as the rapid growth of crisis hotlines, rape crisis programs, shelters for abused women and children, crisis centers for youths, and home-based crisis intervention programs. In addition, support groups and individual counseling services have expanded to provide ongoing support and therapy for victims.

Gilliland and James (1993) have reviewed several different definitions of a crisis. Like earlier theorists in the field (Parad, 1971; Carkhuff & Berenson, 1977), they share the view that a crisis is characterized not so much by any particular situation as by the individual's perception and response to that situation. They write that a "crisis is a perception of an event or situation as an intolerable difficulty that exceeds the resources and coping mechanisms of the person" (Gilliland & James, 1993, p. 3). This approach acknowledges differences in individual reactions to the same traumatic event and different rates at which people adapt.

We are comfortable with this approach. Our experience with clients confirms that a crisis is a matter of perception. We would add that clients' perceptions of crisis events can and do shift, sometimes remarkably so. These shifts are further evidence of clients' strengths. And, once again, we have found that solution-focused interviewing fosters these positive shifts.

Solution Focus versus Problem Focus

When you meet with a client who has just experienced a traumatic event or is contemplating suicide or injury to others, your tendency will probably be to dwell on the details of the trauma. You will be tempted to make a problem assessment of just how deeply in crisis the client really is. Once you have gathered that information, you will feel more confident about what services to recommend. This problem-focused response represents a return to a problem-solving approach. Its appeal in this situation is obvious. Clients who have just experienced a trauma will most likely have been caught off guard by events and will have lost a sense of control over their lives. They will either be withdrawn and uncommunicative, or else they will say, "I can't handle this; I think I'm going crazy." These responses seem to indicate a client's lack of resources, and so you will find yourself reluctant to begin any solution building.

Students and workshop participants have often told us that they find it particularly difficult to be solution-focused when working with clients in crisis. They ask, "Shouldn't I just supportively and empathically explore the client's crisis symptoms and then suggest ways in which the client can become more stable? Shouldn't I leave the work of solution building for a later meeting, when the client is more together?"

In our experience, most clients in crisis situations stabilize and make progress as they participate in the solution-building process. Like any other clients, clients in crisis improve by focusing on what they want to see different and drawing on their past successes and strengths. Consequently, solution-focused procedures are as useful to them as to anyone else.

We now outline an approach to interviewing these clients. This approach invites clients to draw on strengths and resources masked by their reactions to crisis events. As you will see, sometimes the interview develops as in any other first session; sometimes it calls for another set of questions—coping questions (Berg, 1994).

Getting Started: "How Can I Help?"

We suggest that you begin as you would in any first session, by asking the client how you might be useful. This approach immediately puts you into the posture of not knowing and begins to counter any preconceptions you might have about what clients in crisis are like and what they need from you. Like other clients, those who have recently experienced a trauma or disruption in their lives will usually begin by describing the traumatic event and their reactions to it. This is problem description, and your task, as usual (see Chapter 4), is to listen for the clients' perceptions and the words they use to describe these perceptions, for who and what are important to them, and for hints about what specific differences they want to see.

If clients seem frightened, angry, or tearful, use the skills of empathizing and affirming their perceptions that you studied in Chapter 3. Empathizing and affirming their perceptions will assure them that you genuinely care about their plight and are committed to understanding their experiences from their point of view. Empathic and affirming responses will also give them a chance to amplify and examine their own perceptions; this may both ease their sense of personal isolation, which often accompanies trauma, and foster a beginning sense of control, as a result of putting their experiences into words.

Sometimes, right after a traumatic event, clients are withdrawn; they are either reluctant or unable to speak. In such situations, you can pay attention to their nonverbals. It may be useful to ask what they are experiencing at the moment and to reassure them of your concern. You might say: "From the expression on your face, you seem very tense. I'm wondering if you're thinking about what just happened to you. I want you to know that I'm willing to listen to whatever you have to say." Some clients, feeling very disorganized, are unable to talk. In such circumstances, it can be helpful to simply sit with them without speaking. Just your physical presence and a periodic reassurance of your concern and patience can be comforting. Once a client begins to talk, you can proceed as you would in any solution-building conversation.

As you see, we begin cases involving trauma much as we would any other case. This approach is not only consistent with our belief in client competency and strengths; it also reflects our belief in the inevitability of change. Trauma in a person's life represents a change. Many problem-focused practitioners tend to view a crisis as a disruption of the person's equilibrium and crisis intervention as a restoration of that normal balance. We have found it more useful, however, to view traumatic change as an opportunity that calls for an extraordinary marshaling of strengths; it can lead in any of several directions, depending on the client's wishes, motivation, and capacities.

Reports from our clients about their experiences with trauma have shaped our approach. For example, clients will sometimes call us and insist on an appointment immediately, because they are "in a crisis and can't cope without help." By the time we see them, later the same day, they are often much calmer, however. When we engage them in a solution-building conversation, they are able to describe what they have done to improve their situation and what they need to do next. In fact, some of these clients do not even show up for their emergency appointments. In those circumstances, some practitioners might wonder whether such clients are personality-disordered persons who thrive on chaos, we prefer to assume that they probably have found a way to cope.

As a practitioner, you need to recognize that clients are always in the process of adapting to whatever they encounter in their lives. They will adapt to traumatic events as part of the same process. Neither you nor the client, for that matter, can know ahead of time what capacities and strengths a client will bring to a particular trauma, and so you can only proceed as you normally would—by adopting a posture of not knowing and assuming client competency until the client demonstrates otherwise.

"What Have You Tried?"

As we have seen, clients confronting trauma will almost always respond to your initial questions about what might be helpful with problem description. Once you believe that your clients have had an opportunity to express themselves about their problems and reactions, and you have had an opportunity to affirm those perceptions and to demonstrate your understanding and concern, you can proceed to ask what steps the clients have taken to deal with the situation. Many clients in trauma can describe coping strategies, even strategies that you may recognize from the professional literature. Some clients will say, "I deep-breathe to overcome the images in my head." Others may tell you that they called their best friends or family "to talk to someone I could trust." They might say that they sought out emergency services, such as a hospital crisis unit or the crisis hotline, to talk to someone who knew about "my kind of problem."

When your clients have already taken steps on their own behalf, you can respond as you normally would at this point in a first session. Compliment them directly and indirectly for what they have done. Explore where they got the idea to respond as they did, whether they have surprised themselves in the process, and how effectively they think they are handling themselves and their circumstances. As with any first session, expect to hear problem talk mixed in with a description of successes and strengths.

"What Do You Want to Have Different?"

In some cases, clients experiencing trauma can describe efforts to adapt; in others, they can do little except describe the trauma and its associated pain and terror. In either situation, it is important to ask the clients what they want to have different as a result of meeting with you. As you will recall, this question is intended to open a conversation about goal formulation. Although at first you may not feel comfortable about putting this question to someone who seems traumatized, we have found it useful for such clients. Asking clients to begin to consider where they want to go in their painful situation sends the message that they have some control over their future, however small it may seem at the moment. In addition, their answers will give you an idea of whether they have the capacity to work on goal formulation at that time.

We never cease to be amazed by clients' capacities, even in the toughest of circumstances. We cannot count the times that clients' problem talk suggested that they were overwhelmed and incapable of going to work on their inner emotional turmoil or circumstances and yet, when we turned to goal-formulation questions, they were able to begin useful work. Clearly, neither the depth of clients' pain nor the apparent severity of their trauma perfectly predict their capacity to start working on goals. Therefore, you must refrain from making assumptions on the basis of the severity of a traumatic event or your clients' symptoms. If clients are able to converse with you about their pain, begin to ask goal-formulation questions sometime in the first meeting and see what develops. Often, your clients' mood and degree of confidence will start to improve as they begin to perceive and shape possibilities for themselves.

Insoo adopted this approach with a client we will call Karen. Karen was a walk-in client who said that she had a crisis in her life and needed help. She said that, three days earlier, she caught her husband of four years sneaking out of their house with some of his things. He had not returned and she had "been doing nothing but crying since"; she was unable to eat, sleep, or function as she normally did. Although she seemed dazed, she was able to answer questions about her name, her address, her daily routine, and whom she lived with. She said she had been married for four years and had a daughter aged 2½. In the early stages of the interview, she stated repeatedly that her main problems at that moment were her inability to sleep and confusion about what to think.

Insoo was not surprised to hear that Karen was having difficulty sleeping; this is a common response right after a major upset. After gaining a sense of

Karen's perception of her immediate problems, Insoo opened a dialogue intended to help Karen start thinking about possible goals:

INSOO: I can tell from what you say that you have been having a very difficult time of it since your husband left. I'm wondering about how I can help. What would you like to have different as a result of our meeting together today?

KAREN: Sleep. I just have to start getting some sleep.

INSOO: So suppose you got some sleep. How would that be helpful to you?

KAREN: If I just knew why he left me, but he won't talk to me. I don't know where he lives, and I tried to call him where he works but he won't take the phone call.

INSOO: So this came as a complete surprise to you—his wanting to leave you?

KAREN: I never knew he would do this to me. We never fought; he never said he was unhappy. All marriages have their difficult times, so I thought we were pretty normal.

INSOO: If we were to pretend—I know he will not come here to talk to me, but if we were to pretend that he was here, and I was to ask him how likely it is that he will come back to live with you, what would he say?

KAREN: He would say that he will never come back to live with me. I was sleeping and I heard some noise and just woke up and saw him walking out the door with a bag. I begged him not to go, but he just walked out, saying he doesn't want to be married anymore. So, I don't think he will come back. If that's the case, I have to find a way to go on with my life and take care of my baby. But I am so tired all the time; I need some sleep.

In this exchange, though Karen seemed dazed, she was able to begin some solution talk about what she might want to be different in her life. To invite her to think realistically, Insoo asked about the chances of her husband returning. Again Karen rose to the task. Even though deeply distressed, she did not break down and return to problem talk; instead, she thought about Insoo's question and answered that her husband was unlikely to return. As we noted earlier, there was no way ahead of time for Insoo to know that Karen had the capacity to begin this goal-formulation work; to learn this about Karen, Insoo had to open the conversation and see what developed.

Listening to Karen's answers, Insoo noticed that Karen, although still confused about the end of her marriage, was able to think about the future and the needs of her baby. Clearly, her baby and parenting were very important to her and would play a big role in how she would eventually choose to organize her future. However, Insoo also listened to Karen's assessment of her immediate need—the need for sleep. To respect her client's priorities, Insoo followed up on that need:

INSOO: So, what happens when you try to sleep? What gets in the way?

KAREN: I can't sleep because, whenever I try to go to sleep, I get really mad that he is doing this to me and wonder if there is another woman in his life. And then I get even more mad and I start to cry. And then I have to get myself calmed down again.

INSOO: [*asking Karen to amplify solution talk*] So how do you get yourself calmed down at times like that?

KAREN: I try not to think about how mad I am. I read books, watch TV, do deep breathing. If only I could just stop thinking. . . . I am going round and round and get really mad and then start to cry. I've been crying a lot. Oh God, I didn't know I had so many tears in my body.

You can see that the conversation between Karen and Insoo is already taking on the familiar character of a first session. Karen is engaging in solution building by starting to converse about her difficulties in getting to sleep and what she is doing to overcome them. She mixes problem talk with solution talk. To focus the dialogue on more solution talk, Insoo has several options: (1) She could compliment Karen for her efforts; (2) she could ask which of Karen's ways of calming herself work best; (3) she could explore for any exception times to the sleep problem since her husband left; or (4) she could ask Karen to scale how well she is adapting to the problem and then return to goal formulation by asking what will be different when Karen is doing just a little bit better.

The remainder of the session with Karen proceeded very much as any other first session would. Insoo asked solution-focused questions aimed at goal formulation and exception exploration and then took a break to formulate feedback. It seemed to Insoo that, while Karen's efforts at relaxation were useful, she was still struggling to find ways to calm herself when she went to bed. In her feedback, Insoo suggested an additional strategy that might help Karen to calm herself:

Karen, first of all, I want to tell you that you did the right thing by coming here today, which I'm sure took lots of courage for you to do. You have had a big shock just three days ago, and I think the reactions you have been having are quite normal and to be expected. I can see how you would be crying a lot, be mad at him, and have difficulty sleeping. These are normal reactions to a terrible event, and maybe even more understandable in your case, because he hurt you even more by the way he left you. And, on top of all that, it is even possible that you may never find out why he did what he did because, as you say, he refuses to talk about it. I want you to know that I am very impressed with how you are handling all this because, despite all your pain and upset, you still have a clear idea about how you want to raise your daughter, and you can also give him credit for being a good father to your daughter.

I agree that the thing for you to do right now is to figure out how to get some good sleep. [Karen nods in agreement] So I have some suggestions for you.

First, since you already know the relaxation exercises, I suggest that you continue to use them. When you are in bed in a comfortable position, relax your entire body, using your relaxation techniques and your breathing techniques. And, second, after you have gone through your routine, there is one more thing you can do. As you lie in bed with your light off waiting for sleep to come, keep your tongue away from the roof of your mouth and keep your eyes open at the same time—until you quietly fall asleep. And last, between now and the next time we meet, I would like you to pay attention and keep track of all the things you do to make things just a little bit better.

At the end of the session, Karen and Insoo scheduled another meeting.

Asking the Miracle Question

Workshop participants and students often want to know if it is appropriate to ask the miracle question of clients in crisis. Certainly, it is not the first thing we would do; thereafter, it depends. If the conversation unfolds as it did with Karen, who was able to indicate generally who and what were important to her and what she was doing to overcome her difficulties, we might well ask the miracle question. As we described in Chapter 5, the miracle question allows clients to dream about their future or, as one client put it, "to paint a more colorful life for myself." If they are to work with the miracle question, clients need energy and at least some glimmer of hope that life can be different. If your client does have energy and a little hope, it can be useful to ask the miracle question.

However, the miracle question should be tailored to the particular client. With clients who have experienced a major disruption in their lives, it is important to scale down the miracle; perhaps the miracle is that the client wakes up tomorrow morning and is starting to put his or her life together or, in Karen's case, that she has slept a little better. When you ask what will be different as a result of the miracle, be prepared to hear answers that often do not seem related to the client's current perception of the problem. For example, Karen might answer: "I'd have more energy and take my daughter out to play." Although not apparently related to Karen's sleeping difficulty, more focus on her relationship to her child may somehow help Karen to calm herself.

In contrast to Karen, some clients in crisis seem utterly hopeless and helpless. They answer all your questions with problem talk; they describe at length their disorienting and painful reactions to the trauma in their lives. Their manner, too, may indicate that just to make it from one moment to the next is all they can handle. In our experience, these are a small minority of clients. Usually, it is not helpful to press these clients on goal formulation, much less to ask them the miracle question. For the moment, such clients are caught up in their suffering and feel doomed to suffer for a long time to come—perhaps even for the rest of their lives. Let's look at how you can interview clients who are feeling so overwhelmed.

Coping Questions

Coping questions attempt to draw clients' attention away from the fear, loneliness, and misery of life's ugly and horrific events and refocus it on what the clients are doing to survive their pain and circumstances. Coping questions are a form of solution talk that has been tailored so as to make sense to clients who are feeling overwhelmed (Berg, 1994). These questions help the client and practitioner to uncover together those times and ways in which the client struggles against his or her plight. As you gain experience, you will soon find that asking coping questions feels like a special case of exploring for exceptions.

The Case of Jermaine

One day Insoo's office received a call from a man who was very troubled. He said that he was having a "hard time of it lately" and finally agreed with his wife that he "better get some professional help." He reported that he was having "flashbacks and blackouts" and asked the secretary, "Could I please see someone right away?" Insoo was available later the same day.

When Jermaine walked into Insoo's office, he seemed visibly upset. He was hunched over; he looked very tired, with dark areas under his eyes, and he was rubbing his hands nervously. As Insoo began her meeting with him, he focused on his symptoms. He said he was waking up in the middle of the night with flashbacks; had difficulty falling asleep; was experiencing rapid heartbeat and sweaty palms; was fearful of leaving his house; and, when he did go out, was constantly looking over his shoulder to see if someone was following him. "Most of all," he said, "it's not getting any sleep that makes me so jumpy. If only I could get rid of these horrible nightmares." When asked, he assured Insoo that these reactions were "not at all like my normal self."

Insoo asked when these symptom had started. Jermaine said it had been about three weeks ago. One day, he had gone to withdraw some cash from an Automatic Teller Machine (ATM) in his neighborhood. After withdrawing the money, he returned to his car and climbed in. To his dismay, two men rose up from the back seat with guns pointed at his head. They demanded Jermaine's cash and told him to drive off to another ATM. In sheer panic, he did as he was told and drove from machine to machine until his withdrawal limit was reached.

To Jermaine's horror, the gunmen decided to hold him and locked him in the basement of a house. They also took his keys and wallet and therefore learned his name and address. The next day, under the threat of "blowing my brains out," they put him through the same experience; they drove him from ATM to ATM until his withdrawal limit was reached.

The longer Jermaine was with them, the more his abductors seemed to relax around him. Three nights into his ordeal, while his tormentors were partying upstairs, he banged on the locked basement door and moaned: "I'm sick in my stomach; I'm going to throw up." One of his abductors let him step out of the back door, and he ran, managing to escape. Since then, he said, he had been trying "to pull myself together, but I just can't." He added: "I'm exhausted and not able to go back to work, because I'm too scared and tired, and thinking about how much income I'm losing only makes things that much worse."

When Insoo asked him what he had tried so far to deal with this traumatic event and its consequences, Jermaine said he had talked to his wife about some of what had happened to him and some of its aftermath, but also said that he was "holding a lot back because I do not want to upset her." In the belief that all people who have been abused and assaulted have their individual ways of coping (Dolan, 1991), Insoo decided to respect and explore what he had done so far by asking coping questions.

Coping Exploration

The way to open a conversation around coping is simply to ask, "What have you found helpful so far?" This question suggests that you think the client has somehow found useful ways to begin adapting to his or her traumatic experiences. It also demonstrates that you respect the value of any client-generated coping strategies and you want to start with these and build any additional strategies around them. Here is how Insoo took this approach with Jermaine:

INSOO: I am sure it is quite scary to wake up in the middle of the night sweating and with your heart pounding. So, when you wake up from the nightmares and flashbacks, what have you found to help yourself calm down?

JERMAINE: [after a long pause] I lie in bed very still, because I can't tell if the nightmare is real or not. When I lie still—very scared—I can hear my wife's breathing in her sleep.

INSOO: OK, what about that—listening to her breathing is helpful?

JERMAINE: [pauses again] You know, I haven't thought about it before, but it helps to listen to her breathe in her sleep, lying there next to me. [pauses to think] Because, when I listen to her breathing next to me, it means I'm home with my family. It means I'm safe.

INSOO: I guess you are right.

JERMAINE: When I lie there for a long time, listening to her breathing, so peaceful; then, when my eyes get adjusted to the dark, I can look at her sleeping face.

INSOO: So what about that is helpful, looking at her sleeping face?

JERMAINE: When I can finally *see* my wife's face, it means I'm really safe, that I'm really home. I don't have to be so scared anymore. Knowing that my family is safe helps, too.

INSOO: What else have you found helpful?

JERMAINE: When I can't go back to sleep, I walk around the house in the dark, listening to classical music with my headphones on. That calms my nerves. I've tried watching TV, but it's terrible, with all the commercials. I also tried reading; I've been reading a lot, but you can only read so much.

INSOO: I guess you are right; you can only read so much. So, what else have you found helpful?

JERMAINE: I try to help around the house. It breaks my heart that my wife works so hard. She is really tired when she comes home; she has such a tough job. So, I try to be helpful to her by cleaning the house. [smiling faintly] We have the cleanest house in town, because I clean it everyday. I try to make sure dinner is ready, too, when she comes home tired.

INSOO: I'm sure she appreciates that.

JERMAINE: She is a good woman. I tell her I'm lucky that I have her. She is good at what she does, and she tells me that I should take my time getting better. I want to keep this marriage.

INSOO: I would imagine that she would say that you are a good husband, too.

JERMAINE: Yeah; she tells me that all the time.

Like other solution-building dialogues, those around coping usually lead to a process of mutual discovery. Insoo did not know how Jermaine was coping before he told her, but neither did he—or, at least, not to the degree that he did after he had worked to answer Insoo's questions. By sharpening his awareness of what he is already doing, Jermaine can become more confident that he is not stuck or overwhelmed, but is already on the way to recovery. Moreover, through the conversation, he comes to realize more fully that he himself is developing these strategies. We have come to think that this awareness, more than anything else, builds hope and motivation in clients to continue to work in the toughest of circumstances.

Connecting with the Larger Picture

To build coping momentum with clients, you will need to notice and compliment those connections they make to people and experiences that are important to them. These connections often provide the motivation for them to cope against heavy odds and serve as the access point to many of their most meaningful successes. Thus, when Jermaine mentioned that he copes in part by helping around the house, cleaning and preparing dinner, Insoo indirectly complimented him on this, and their dialogue soon incorporated Jermaine's supportive, successful marriage, which is a source of strength and hope in his life.

Using Coping Questions with Clients Who Talk Suicide

Most practitioners feel doubt and anxiety about interviewing a client who has threatened suicide. This is understandable, because of the finality of the act for the client and also the incredible suffering that the act can mean for those who survive the client. Anyone who has experienced a suicide of a family member, friend, or a client knows how devastating it is for the survivors; it may haunt them for years.

Many beginning practitioners lose their composure when clients talk of suicide. Their initial impulse may be to persuade such clients that suicide is illogical, dangerous, hurtful to others, or an otherwise distorted response to their situation. However, practitioners who give in to this impulse may unwittingly exacerbate the risk of suicide because, by contradicting the client's perceptions, they further isolate the client. Other beginning practitioners have been known to take an opposite but no less extreme approach: They minimize or refuse to believe what may be a client's desperate cry for help.

At a minimum, most beginning practitioners believe that suicide talk by clients probably calls for drastic solutions like medication and hospitalization. That may be the case. However, before you resort to drastic recommendations, you should engage such clients in a coping dialogue.

Shifting into Coping Talk

As with all difficult tasks, the toughest part for you will be getting started. Clients who are thinking about suicide will tell you about lives full of pain, suffering, and traumatic humiliation. They may speak of a profound sense of personal inadequacy and failure. As a compassionate listener, you may feel drawn into their apparent hopelessness.

We have found that the best way not to feel hopeless about a client's prospects is to tell ourselves that there is always another side to any coin and to set about exploring it. It is also reassuring to keep in mind that any client who is talking to you about suicide is still present with you, is still alive and breathing. Somehow the client has managed to survive, despite past traumas and present pain. In this sense, clients who talk suicide are no different than Jermaine, and your best chance of helping them to mobilize their strengths and reestablish a sense of control over their emotions and circumstances is to ask coping questions and to encourage them to amplify their answers.

To be sure, clients talking suicide are among the most overwhelmed. Therefore, we want to indicate some ways to phrase coping questions that respect clients' immediate perception of life's hopelessness but still invite them to think about how they are surviving.

"HOW DID YOU GET OUT OF BED THIS MORNING?" It is important to start small and to start with something that is undeniably real. This question satisfies both criteria. A client who made it to your office, or even got out of bed, dressed, and met you at his or her home, has done something requiring a lot of energy for a person who is deeply discouraged.

When you ask this question, in a sincere and curious manner, be prepared for your client to be puzzled and even disbelieving. Sometimes, clients will give you a look that seems to say: "Here I am telling you about all this suffering in my life, and you ask me how I got out of bed; I can't believe you're asking such a dumb question." At other times, clients take the question seriously and try to answer it. In either case, the question is a good place to engage clients in a description of their microsuccesses. Here is how a client we'll call Ruth responded to the question:

INSOO: [*after listening to, and empathizing with, several horrible events in Ruth's life*] With all that has happened to you and as discouraged as you have been lately, I'm amazed that you managed to get out of bed this morning and face another day. How did you do it?

RUTH: What? Getting out of bed? Anybody can do that.

INSOO: [*indirectly complimenting*] Oh, I wouldn't say that. When someone is as discouraged as you have been, some people can't even manage to get out of bed all day.

RUTH: Yes, I know; I've had days like that myself. I forgot about those days.

INSOO: [*quickly recognizing that today was somehow a better day and therefore an exception*] So what did you do different this morning so that you got up and came here today, instead of being in bed like those other, worse days?

RUTH: It started out horrible. I even took my guns out and looked at them, but then I put them away. I also thought about taking a bottle of pills but decided to call here instead because, I don't know, something inside me made me think that it is stupid to check out now.

As Ruth's responses demonstrate, asking the question about getting out of bed can lead to important information that may be useful in the first stages of solution building. You probably already have ideas about where Insoo might have gone next. She might have asked: (1) for more details regarding what was different about this morning, as for any exception; (2) about past worse days and how Ruth coped with these; or (3) about the something inside that had helped Ruth to decide that suicide was stupid for her right now.

In adopting any of these options, Insoo is back on familiar ground as a solution-focused interviewer. She explores (coping) exceptions and, in the process, hears about who and what are important to Ruth.

"**HOW DID YOU SURVIVE LONG ENOUGH TO GET HERE?**" This is a variation on the previous question. It may be appropriate when clients tell you they are surprised to be alive, because their pain is so overwhelming that they came very close to suicide "just yesterday" or "a few hours ago." After you respectfully listen to the clients' account of their pain and begin to appreciate its depth, you can start the transition to coping talk with this question.

"**HOW OFTEN DO YOU HAVE THESE THOUGHTS?**" It is surprising how often clients who experience suicidal thoughts discover that they are not preoccupied with these thoughts 100% of the time. Between periods of crying, clients report that they take their children to school, prepare food for their families, go shopping, function at their jobs, and go about other daily activities. We have often been impressed by how well people can function in the midst of being depressed. Thus, potential solution patterns exist side by side with problem patterns. Asking about the frequency of suicidal thoughts conveys to the client that everyone has periods when they are not thinking about suicide. Even with clients who report that they think of suicide 95% of the time, you can explore what they are doing the other 5% of the time, in the hope of identifying something that might help to reduce the intensity of the suicidal thoughts or even to make the thoughts go away for a while.

"**HOW HAVE YOU MANAGED TO COPE FOR SO LONG?**" Some clients have struggled with their painful feelings for years. At times, they feel overwhelmed and hopelessly out of control. At the point of contemplating suicide, many of these clients have a strong tendency to place overly high demands on themselves and others. They become preoccupied with a sense of failure, either their own or their significant others'.

When you encounter a client who talks this way, you can ask how they've managed to cope. This question, again reality-based, invites clients to recognize that, somehow, they have coped with seemingly insurmountable difficulties for a long time already. It implies that they have past successes and strengths worth talking about.

"**HOW COME THINGS ARE NOT WORSE?**" Sometimes, a client will describe to you past horrors—a brutal assault, repeated childhood molestation, a disfiguring degenerative disease—in such vivid, compelling detail that you feel amazed that this person is able to carry on with life at all. When you learn to ask this question with curiosity and a sincere desire to understand, you are likely to hear some inspiring accounts of courage and human dignity.

Peter once met with a client who had been sexually assaulted several times as a teenager by two co-workers. Her tormentors kept control of her for two years through threats to both herself and her sister. She described how, more than ten years later, she still suffered from flashbacks, disorientation, and periods of dissociation. As he listened, Peter realized that this woman relived her terror and humiliation almost daily and regularly had thoughts of ending her life. He was amazed that she was not overwhelmed:

PETER: I cannot imagine living with what you have had to live with all these years; I can see how you might have decided to give up a long time ago. Yet, I know that you hold a job and take care of a family. It seems like you should be overwhelmed, but obviously you are not. How come things are not worse?

LINDA: There are many times each week that I want to give in and end the images I still have in my head; they are so powerful and frightening. [she begins to describe them again and becomes more frightened and tearful]

PETER: Yes, I know, I know; from what you've been describing, they are truly horrible. So, let me ask you, what else is there about you so that these images and memories did not completely take over your life?

LINDA: It hasn't been easy, but I think I got lucky. I met a kind, gentle guy who just wanted to be my friend, and for several years that's all we were. [she describes their relationship] Then he asked me if maybe I would be interested in getting married and I got terrified. I was so mixed up and so close to losing it almost every minute of every day. But I prayed and prayed, and he stayed nearby and eventually I did it; I married a man. I never thought I could ever be with a man and love him.

This was the beginning of a coping dialogue in which Linda and Peter explored how Linda drew on other memories and images in her past and the present—those of her husband, her child, and her job—to struggle against the memories of her abuse.

Scaling Questions

As we have seen, clients' perceptions shift as they are encouraged to talk about their successes and strengths, however small these may seem at first. Once you have worked with clients to uncover coping strategies, you can use scaling questions to reinforce their coping successes. Scaling questions can also help clients to formulate a next step in their struggle. Let's look at some of the ways you can use scaling questions with clients in crisis situations.

Scaling Current Coping Ability

Most clients in crisis become at least a little more hopeful as they talk about their successes. Therefore, we find it very helpful to ask clients to express their perceptions of success more explicitly (Berg & de Shazer, 1993). We accomplish this by asking a scaling question, for example: "On a scale of 0 to 10, where 10 means you are coping with your situation as well as you can imagine anyone could, and 0 means you are not coping at all, how well would you say you are coping right now?" Sometimes the number that the client gives makes sense in view of the previous coping dialogue; sometimes it is a surprise. In either case, we follow up with questions that clarify the meaning of the number and thus further help the client to build confidence.

Peter once met with a man named Jim who had made "a serious suicide attempt" one week earlier, when the woman he was living with threw all his belongings on the front porch; she attached a note to say that she had found someone new and never wanted to see him again. Jim said he was "destroyed." He went to his parents' home, because they were away traveling. That evening, he said, "I got into my truck with the garage door closed, rolled up the windows, started the engine, laid down on the front seat, and closed my eyes." To his astonishment, "the next morning I woke up with my truck in the driveway, and the window was rolled down, and I was still alive."

Jim told Peter that he had asked for an appointment because "my relatives are scared I might try to kill myself again and said I should get checked out." Jim reported that he was doing better; in the last few days, he had begun to eat and sleep more regularly, and three days earlier he had returned to work. When Peter asked him how he was coming to terms with losing his girlfriend, Jim said he had "just made up my mind that I was not going to let it bother me." Peter complimented his determination and asked what was proving helpful in this process. Jim replied that he had returned to remodeling a house he had built and also to his hobby of building guns. After some 30 minutes of coping talk, Peter asked Jim to scale how well he was coping:

JIM: [long pause] You know, I feel like I'm an 8; yeah. Maybe even a 9!

PETER: [surprised] Wow! I was expecting to hear a 4 or 5, but you say maybe even a 9. So what's happening that makes it so high?

JIM: I know, 9 seems so high; that's why I was thinking so hard. [pause] Maybe it has to do with what happened yesterday at work. My boss and I never got along or said much to each other. He's real religious, and he doesn't like the way I live or my jokes or much of anything else about me. . . . Except I do my job and he can't do anything about that, can he? So yesterday, I thought, "What the hell! I almost did myself in; I'm going to clear the air." And you know, we did; we talked and talked a lot about what was bothering us.

Naturally, Peter immediately began to examine Jim's new experience with his boss as an exception. Peter asked for a description of what happened, exactly what Jim's part was in the important event, and how the conversation with his boss was helpful to him. As Jim talked, Peter became more and more amazed at how much progress Jim had made in the space of one week—even in the space of their hour together. Despite what his relatives wanted, Jim decided not to return for another visit because, as he said, "I'm OK now; I don't need to come back."

Scaling Presession Coping Changes

No matter how long it has been since the traumatic event, it can be useful to ask clients to think about how well they are coping now, as opposed to immediately after the shock. This can be helpful even a few hours after the trauma, provided the client is emotionally organized enough to converse with you. Of course, the first step is to establish a caring, understanding contact with someone who has just been traumatized. However, once that rapport is starting to develop and you have inquired about the client's efforts at coping, you can ask a presession scaling question. Here's an example:

PETER: Allen, I know it is just hours since you were mugged, and I know from what you said that you are starting to pull yourself together. I'm wondering if you can tell me how successful you are being at this? On a scale of 0 to 10, where 0 was how you were doing immediately after the mugging and 10 is you are coping better than you possibly could have imagined, how well are you coping right now?

After a major shock, almost all clients will begin to reorganize to some degree and will provide a number higher than zero. You can then explore what the client might have done to move from 0 to the present level.

Scaling the Next Step

Having begun a conversation about the scale number that represents how well the client is coping, you and the client have a foothold from which you can push off into goal formulation. You can point the client to the future by asking: "OK, you say you have things at about a 3; what is the most important thing for you to remember to do to keep things at a 3? What's the next most important thing for you to remember to keep doing?" Or, adapting the procedure for goal formulation in later sessions (Chapter 8), you can start to work your way up the scale with your client: "So, when you are coping at a level of 4, what do you suppose you will be doing to handle things that you are not doing now?" "What do you suppose your friends will notice that you are doing differently when you are coping just a little bit better?" "What will it take for that to happen?" In other words, depending on how engaged and energized your client becomes, you can adapt any of the goal-formulation questions we discussed in Chapters 5 and 8. In some cases, as we noted earlier, we have even used a modified form of the miracle question to explore possibilities for future coping.

Scaling Motivation and Confidence

Once you have worked on coping goals, you can ask your clients to scale how hard they are willing to work on achieving those goals and how confident they are that they will eventually find ways to successfully cope. To review this kind of scaling, turn back to Chapter 6.

Feedback: Doing More of What Helps

Once you sense that a client is close to being overwhelmed and you start asking coping questions, the interview will closely resemble any other solution-building interview. Coping exploration is a form of exception exploration. As we have seen, you can use scaling questions in the usual ways. The same is true of end-of-session feedback. In coping situations, the feedback is usually organized around the suggestion that the client continue to do more of what the coping dialogue reveals as helpful. Insoo adopted that principle in her feedback to Karen, which we considered earlier in this chapter.

As another example of end-of-session feedback, let's return to the case of Jermaine, the client who had been abducted at gunpoint and was experiencing flashbacks, nightmares, and fears of leaving home. The first thing Insoo did in her feedback was to compliment him:

> Jermaine, you have told me an incredible story of horror. You were not only forced at gun point to hand over your cash that first day, but you were held for three days and forced to do it again and again, all that time not knowing if you would be killed and never see your family again. I am amazed that you found the strength to endure that horror; certainly not everyone could. And not only did you endure it, but you kept your wits about you and you figured out a clever way to escape. You waited for a time when their guard was down and came up with something believable so they would let you out of the back door. And then you ran—you managed to escape. I want to congratulate you on being very strong and very smart.

Insoo formulated the rest of her feedback around an idea that emerged later in their session. Jermaine's wife had told him that his symptoms had a name—posttraumatic stress syndrome. He said he found that comforting, because having a name for his symptoms meant that there was an explanation for what he was experiencing and that he was not crazy. Recognizing that posttraumatic syndrome was now a part of Jermaine's frame of reference and the label was helpful to him, Insoo decided to incorporate it into her feedback:

> Because your reactions are a part of posttraumatic stress syndrome, and because what happened to you was so frightening and lasted for several days, I think that you may continue for a while to have nightmares, blackouts, and fears about leaving your house and who might be following when you are in your car. This kind of hypervigilance to make sure that you are safe is normal and a useful survival instinct. It is a big part of what helped to save

your life during the extraordinary and horrible experience that you told me about today. It is as though your mind is still trying to make sense of that horror by going over it again and again in nightmares and in other ways, and it may take some time for your mind to figure out that you are really safe now.

So, in the meantime, while your mind is continuing to figure things out, I suggest that you continue to do what you have found that helps, giving yourself time to heal. Continue to listen to your music, clean the house, cook, and talk to your wife so both of you can be reassured that you are continuing to get better. [he nods in agreement] And keep paying attention to what else you discover in the coming days that's helpful, and come back and tell me what's better.

Gathering Problem-Assessment Information

Earlier in this chapter, we mentioned that, when interviewing traumatized and overwhelmed clients, beginning practitioners tend to feel more comfortable asking problem-assessment questions, rather than solution-focused questions. Although we believe that solution building through coping dialogues is more helpful than detailed problem assessment, we also accept that there is a place for problem assessment. Let's look at how solution building and problem assessment would ideally fit together.

As we have seen, client perceptions and frames of reference can change as clients interact with practitioners. Problem assessments, whether administered as standardized paper-and-pencil tests or as a series of questions asked by a practitioner, amount to a snapshot of some aspect of a client's perceptions at one point in time. They give a static view; only a second administration allows us to evaluate change. In addition, as problem assessments, they do not measure client strengths; past coping successes; what and who are most important to clients; and client capacities for hope and for discerning next steps. In other words, they do not measure the materials of solution building. Consequently, even in crisis situations, we recommend that problem assessment take a back seat to solution building.

Nevertheless, it is very important for you to become familiar with the main criteria that are used to assess a person's basic needs for living. As you may know, Abram Maslow (1970) has identified and ranked human needs for living. At the most basic level, he identifies physical and life-sustaining requirements, such as the needs for food, water, air, and shelter. At the next level of his hierarchy, he identifies physical-safety requirements, such as the need for protection from attack and disease. These most basic needs are more concrete than others in his formulation, which include the needs for love, self-esteem, and self-actualization. In crisis situations, clients are generally dealing with threats to life-sustaining and physical-safety needs.

Individual clients differ in their perception of what they must have in order to satisfy these basic needs. Various researchers have formulated questions that provide information about clients' perceptions of whether they are having difficulties meeting these needs; other questions yield information about so-called objective indicators of problems in satisfying these needs. For an introduction to the criteria and measurement questions that can be used to assess clients' life-sustaining and safety needs, you can consult a variety of sources, which cover the assessment of, for example, the different aspects of a person's mental status; the type and degree of substance abuse; the likelihood of harm to self or another person; and the presence of child abuse or neglect (Gilliland & James, 1993; Lukas, 1993; Martin & Moore, 1995; Sheafor, Horejsi, & Horejsi, 1994). If you familiarize yourself with this information, you will more quickly understand and empathize with the fear and inner sense of losing control that clients in crisis experience; you will also sharpen your capacity to attend to the factual aspects of the events and personal reactions that clients describe to you. For the same reasons, it can be beneficial to read first-hand accounts by those who have experienced different crises. Novels can also be helpful; for example, Peter's students read Judith Guest's novel *Ordinary People* for one intimate view of a family's reaction to the crisis of losing a son and brother.

Once you are familiar with problem-assessment information around basic human needs, you will notice that much of that information spontaneously emerges as you explore the client's frame of reference and begin the solution-building process. As you ask your solution-focused questions, the client moves back and forth between problem talk and solution talk. The problem talk includes data on problem-assessment criteria, but often not with the specificity that you or your agency may require. It is simple enough to ask for more clarification and then to return to solution talk, as in the following dialogue:

PETER: So when the miracle happens, what else will you notice that's different?

EMMA: [pause] I guess another thing is that I won't think about ending my life so often. Right now my life is so miserable, with me having no money and Protective Services after me; they already took my kids and put them in foster care. I'm so sad when my kids aren't with me.

PETER: Yes, I can see you love them very much and wish they were with you right now.

EMMA: I sure do, and I keep thinking that I can't live without them, and I keep thinking about killing myself.

PETER: How long have you been having these thoughts?

EMMA: Ever since my kids were taken away two weeks ago.

PETER: Did you ever have thoughts like that before?

EMMA: I've been discouraged before, but never like this. I never really had thoughts like this, and they keep coming back.

PETER: I'm wondering . . . have you come close to actually doing it? Have you ever made an attempt to take your life?

EMMA: No, I couldn't do that. It hurts so bad not to have them with me, but I couldn't do that—leave my kids without their mom. [tearfully] I just want it to hurt less; it hurts so bad not to be with them.

PETER: Yes, it can feel unbearable to be separated from those you love. [pause] So, thinking about what you just said, it sounds more like you think about killing yourself as a way to stop the hurt than that you really want to be dead? Am I understanding you correctly?

EMMA: Yeah, that's right. I don't want to be dead; I want to be with my kids and for the hurt to stop. I'm so lonely without them.

PETER: I'm also wondering about one other thing. I think I know the answer, but it's our practice here at our agency to ask this question when someone has told us that they are in so much pain that they are having thoughts about taking their life. My question is this: Have you thought about *how* you might go about taking your own life if you were to change your mind and decide to do it?

EMMA: No, I never think about that. I only think about how to make the pain stop. I don't want my kids to have a dead mother.

PETER: You must love your children very much. Even though you're hurting so much, you seem determined to endure your pain so that you can be there for your kids.

EMMA: [nodding in agreement] Yes, they mean everything to me.

PETER: So getting back to this miracle, when it happens, what will be there instead of the pain and the thoughts of killing yourself?

You can also adapt scaling questions to get problem-assessment information. For example, Peter could have asked Emma, "On a scale of 0 to 10, where 0 means that there is no chance that you will take your life and 10 means that there is every chance, what would you say the chances are that you will really do it?" Once Emma gives a number, say 2, Peter can explore the meaning of 2 for her. This assessment dialogue could be amplified by formulating the scaling question with a relationship focus: "If I were to ask your best friend—on the same scale—what the chances are that you will actually take your life, what would she say?" Obtaining assessment information with scaling questions has the advantage of giving you a ready route back into solution talk. Once your client has explained what is happening that makes things a 2, you can easily shift into questions about why things are not so bad that the number would be a 4 or a 6 or even a 10.

Our experience of coping dialogues with clients in crisis has revealed a paradox: The best assessment information is the extent and type of clients' solution talk. By pursuing coping questions and scaling questions focused on formulating the next small steps with clients, we come away from our interviews with the best information about whether clients will be able to meet life-sustaining and safety needs in their current circumstances. Ironically, that is the ultimate purpose of problem assessment: The practitioner gathers details about the nature and depth of clients' current crisis or problem in order to evaluate whether clients can cope by drawing on their own resources or whether more drastic steps such as hospitalization are indicated.

When the Client Remains Overwhelmed

After engaging in coping exploration and asking scaling questions, you may come to the conclusion that your client is overwhelmed and does not have the inner or outer resources to cope. In such situations, which are not common in our experience, you would recommend the available community resources to your client. Information on such resources will form part of the orientation at the agency or clinic where you work, along with the agency's preferred procedures for making such recommendations to clients. We believe it is a good idea for you to call in your supervisor or a senior staff member when you decide to move to such recommendations, especially if you are new to the field or the agency.

As a rule, clients who feel overwhelmed will be more open to drastic measures like medication and hospitalization when you have first worked hard with them in coping dialogues. If you have engaged a client in a coping dialogue and the dialogue reveals few if any current coping capacities, the client often comes to realize that he or she needs more intensive care and monitoring. Moreover, the information gathered from the coping dialogue will allow you to feel more confident and assertive in your recommendations, as well as in your case documentation.

Conclusion

Clients in crisis are not as different from other clients as you might first have imagined. Even though the events that bring these clients to you are more immediate, terrifying, and horrible than those described by other clients, clients in crisis build solutions through the same process as all clients do. In the examples in this chapter, both Peter and Insoo interact with such clients in the same ways as with clients who have not recently experienced trauma in their lives. The major difference in working with clients in crisis is that fewer of them accept the invitation to engage in goal formulation; instead, they stay focused on problem description. In response, we set aside goal formulation for the moment and turn to coping questions. These questions serve to uncover the small, undeniable successes that a shaken, overwhelmed client is experiencing in day-to-day—even moment-by-moment—coping. As clients identify their microsuccesses and their energy and confidence start to build, we return to goal formulation on a more limited basis, by using scaling questions to help clients formulate their next steps in coping.

In a sense, then, whenever we set aside goal formulation and turn to coping questions, we are only changing the order and immediate scope of the solution-building process; we are not shifting to a different process. Consequently, whenever we interview clients who have recently experienced trauma, we think less about whether they are in crisis and more about discovering their immediate capacity to engage in goal-formulation work.

Outcomes

Beginning was useful. I only came one time and made a beginning, but it helped.

The question about the miracle was good. It was good then, and I've kept on thinking about it; it's still helpful.

My husband responded well to concrete goal orientation; he has never done well in therapy, but at BFTC he liked the focus on doing.

(Observations made by BFTC clients 7–9 months after the end of services)

Although some of the solution-building procedures described in this book may resemble procedures used in other approaches, most appeared in the past 15 years and are organized in an innovative fashion. Consequently, outcome data about their effectiveness are just beginning to appear. Adams, Piercy, and Jurich (1991) report the results of a study on one solution-focused message, the formula first-session task. In addition, de Shazer (1991) devotes a brief appendix to the findings of an unpublished follow-up study (Kiser, 1988; Kiser & Nunally, 1990) at the Brief Family Therapy Center in Milwaukee. This study found highly successful outcomes for clients treated with solution-focused therapy: "We found an 80. 4% success rate (65.6% of the clients met their goal while 14.7% made significant improvement) within an average of 4.6 sessions. When contacted at 18 months, the success rate had increased to 86%" (de Shazer, 1991, p. 162). These findings are impressive, but clearly the outcome research on solution building is in its infancy.

How helpful can you expect solution building to be for your clients? It's important to learn more not only about overall effectiveness but also about effectiveness with diverse clients and across different types of client problems. To address these issues, Peter, with the cooperation of BFTC staff,[1] designed and conducted a study to gather more outcome data on solution building. In

---

[1] Larry Hopwood, in particular, assisted in the design of the research and in making the necessary revisions in BFTC forms and procedures.

this chapter, we describe the study and report the data on overall effectiveness. In later chapters, we present the results related to human diversity and to types of client problems.

Study Design

BFTC is an agency that offers individual and family counseling services and trains practitioners from around the world. All of the practitioners who see clients at BFTC use solution-focused procedures. As a result, it is an ideal setting in which to gather data about the outcomes of a solution-building approach.

Participants

The participants in this study were the 275 clients who came for services at BFTC from November 1992 through August 1993. Most of these clients were seen by one of the eight practitioners employed by BFTC. A small minority of the interviews were done by trainees learning solution-focused procedures; in all cases, these interviews and the end-of-session feedback included the participation of a BFTC practitioner situated behind a one-way mirror.

Clients knew that they might be asked to participate in an outcome study. Printed information given to them when they first came for services indicated that BFTC would probably be contacting them in future months to ask about the usefulness of the services they received. Clients signed a form to grant permission for future contact for research purposes. The same procedure was used to obtain clients' permission for observation of their sessions through the one-way mirror.

BFTC is located in an economically and culturally diverse neighborhood and has chosen to serve a variety of clients. This diversity is represented in our data. Of the 275 clients in our study, 57% identified themselves as African American, 5% as Latino, 3% as Native American, and 36% as white. At the time they first visited BFTC, 43% of these clients were employed, while 57% were not. (By far the majority of those not employed were referred to BFTC by public welfare agencies and had their services paid through public funds.) By gender, 60% of the clients were female and 40% male. Children, teenagers, and younger adults are somewhat overrepresented among the 275 cases. In one-third of the cases, a child 12 years of age or younger was the identified client; in 15% of cases, the client was a teenager (13–18 years old). Altogether, 93% of the clients were 45 years of age or younger.

Outcome Measurement

We measured outcome in two ways. The first involved a scaling question. BFTC practitioners were requested to ask clients the following question in each session, as a measurement of ongoing client progress: "On a scale of 1–10, where 10 means that the problems you came to therapy for are solved, and 1 is the worst they've been, where are your problems now?" Practitioners were also requested to record this *progress score* in their session notes, which are included in each client's file. By comparing progress scores from first sessions to final sessions for each client, we obtained our first measurement of outcome. We have chosen to call this comparison a measurement of intermediate outcome. BFTC practitioners recorded client progress scores 80% of the time.

We also measured outcome on the basis of interviews with clients conducted 7–9 months after their final sessions at BFTC. First, we mailed former clients a letter with advance warning: "Within a week or two someone from the Brief Family Therapy Center will be calling to ask if our services have been helpful to you." The letter also gave a rationale for the telephone survey. ("We make these calls to find out how you are doing right now and to get your ideas about how we might improve our services.") It indicated that the interviewer would be someone other than their therapist and someone who was not employed by BFTC.

In all, 50% of the former clients were reached by telephone. All of those who were reached consented to be interviewed. If the clients were children or juveniles, a parent or guardian was interviewed, except in cases where the juveniles had come for services by themselves and where the parent or guardian preferred that the juvenile be interviewed. When two adults were identified as clients in the same case, as in couples and family cases, the interviewer asked to interview the first adult reached. Approximately one-third of the clients who could not be reached had unlisted telephone numbers; another 25% had had their telephones disconnected.

The telephone survey included several questions intended to measure outcome. One was the scaling question already used to measure progress during therapy sessions at BFTC; another asked clients how satisfied they were with their therapy. We have chosen here to form our second measure of outcome by combining the answers to two other questions, which seem, at face value, to measure the overall effectiveness of solution-focused procedures most directly. These questions were first asked in a follow-up study by Weakland, Fisch, Watzlawick, and Bodin (1974) and were also asked in the study by Kiser (1988). The first question is: "Overall, would you say your treatment goal was met or not met?" Clients who answered "goal not met" were asked the second question: "Would you say there was any progress made toward that goal?" Clients were given the options of answering "progress made toward treatment goal" or "progress not made toward treatment goal." By combining the responses to these two questions, we obtained our measurement of what we call final outcome.

We are comfortable with this way of measuring final outcome; we believe that it is consistent with the attitude toward client perceptions expressed

Table 10.1 Number of Interviews*		
Frequency of Interviews	Number of Cases	Percent
1	72	26%
2	80	29%
3	47	17%
4	31	11%
5	20	7%
6	10	4%
7	5	2%
8	4	2%
9	2	1%
10	1	0%
11	1	0%
13	1	0%
23	1	0%
Total	275	100%

* In Tables 10.1–10.3, percentages are rounded to the nearest full percent.

throughout this book. If client perceptions are the best indicator of worthwhile client goals and the best source of information for potential solutions to problems, it makes sense to base our estimate of the usefulness of the solution-building process upon client perceptions. The two questions that constitute our measurement of final outcome ask clients directly for their perceptions of whether they got the help they wanted from their practitioners at BFTC.

Results

Length of Services

Table 10.1 presents data on the number of interviews for the 275 cases studied. As you can see, many clients (26%) came for only one session. More than 80% came for four or fewer sessions. The average (mean) number of sessions was 2.9.

Intermediate Outcomes

We calculated our intermediate outcome measurement by subtracting the progress score for the first session from that recorded for the final session. For example, a client who came to BFTC for four interviews and said things were at a 2 at the first session and at a 5 by the final session received a score of +3 on

Table 10.2	Frequency and Percentage Distributions for Intermediate Outcome (I.O.)	
I.O. Value	Frequency	Percent
−3	2	1%
−2	3	2%
−1	8	6%
0	24	17%
1	24	17%
2	18	13%
3	27	19%
4	8	6%
5	15	11%
6	7	5%
7	4	3%
8	1	1%
Total	141	100%

intermediate outcome. Table 10.2 gives the distribution of scores on intermediate outcome. These scores range from −3 to 8. Fewer cases are represented in this table, because of incomplete data on progress scores and because clients had to come for at least two sessions for an intermediate outcome score to be calculated.[2]

Table 10.2 shows that scores on intermediate outcome range from −3 through 0. For ease of presenting data in later chapters, we have chosen to collapse and label intermediate outcome scores as follows: −3 through 0 as "no progress"; 1 through 3 as "moderate progress"; and 4 through 8 as "significant progress." Organizing the data this way indicates that 26% of the valid cases showed no progress on intermediate outcome, 49% had moderate progress, and 25% showed significant progress.

Final Outcomes

Clients seen at BFTC from November 1992 through August 1993 were telephoned 7–9 months after their last interview. Among other questions, they were asked whether their treatment goal was met and, if not, whether any progress was made toward that goal. Table 10.3 presents the results from

---

[2] The average number of sessions for the 141 cases on which we have data on intermediate outcome is 3.7. This figure is higher than the 2.9 sessions for the original 275 cases. The discrepancy is understandable, because the measurement of intermediate outcome, by definition, excludes all single-session cases.

Table 10.3   Frequency and Percentage Distributions for Final Outcome (F.O.)

Final Outcome	Frequency	Percent
Goal met	61	45%
Some progress	44	32%
No progress	31	23%
Total	136	100%

clients' answers to these two questions. The data show that 45% of contacted clients said that their goal for treatment was met. An additional 32% said that, even though their goal was not met, some progress was made, and 23% said no progress was made.

Comparative Data

The outcomes of solution-building procedures compare favorably with those of other approaches. After combing the professional literature to determine how many sessions clients spend with their practitioners, Garfield (1994) found that, across different approaches to practice, the median ranges from 3 to 13 interviews. The median we found for cases at BFTC is two interviews. Because the research reviewed by Garfield involved problem-solving approaches of one type or another, the BFTC data suggest that clients may be able to make progress more quickly through exposure to solution building.

Lambert and Bergin (1994) have reviewed a wealth of research on the effectiveness of different approaches. The studies they reviewed included clients from many racial, ethnic, and class backgrounds. They also included data about clients with any of the enormous number of problems for which individuals seek professional help. Some of the clients were severely affected, some less so. All of the major therapies were represented in these studies.

Seeking a summary statement about the overall effectiveness of psychotherapy, Lambert and Bergin came to two conclusions. First, therapy is effective. Most of the studies they reviewed used both control and experimental groups. The individuals in both groups had similar kinds of problems, but those in the control group did not receive therapy, while those in the experimental group did. Comparisons of the groups consistently revealed that those receiving therapy made more progress.

Their second conclusion is that the positive effect of therapy is significant. The data indicate that the positive effect is typically the same as, or larger than, that produced by medications for different psychological disorders—for example, the positive effect of antidepressant medications. Lambert and

Bergin (1994, p. 147) found that, on average, 66% of clients who receive therapy show improvement, while only 34% of those who do not receive therapy improve on their own.

Both intermediate and final outcomes for BFTC clients in our study compare favorably with the figures reported by Lambert and Bergin. Intermediate outcome data show that 74% of BFTC clients improved from their first to final session in therapy. The final outcome data indicate that 77% improved. These success rates, as Lambert and Bergin (1994) call them, are several percentage points higher than their figure of 66% for other, more problem-focused approaches. In addition, the BFTC success rates were achieved over fewer sessions: The median number of sessions in the studies reviewed by Lambert and Bergin is six; it is two in the latest BFTC study.

Professional Values and Human Diversity

The human person has intrinsic value.
(Biestek, 1957, p. 73)

In Chapter 1, we stated that the skills used in solution building represent a different paradigm for professional helping than do those used in problem-solving approaches. If you agree with this view, even partially, you may well be asking yourself a number of questions:

- How does solution-focused interviewing fit with the values intended to guide practice in the helping professions?
- Is this way of working equally helpful to clients from diverse backgrounds?
- If I decide to use solution-building skills with my clients, how will this be received by my colleagues, my supervisors, and the agencies or clinics who might employ me?
- I can see that solution building can be helpful to individuals and families, but can it be applied to other levels of practice, such as working with small groups and organizations?

Our students and workshop participants regularly bring such questions up for discussion. In this and the next chapter, we present our answers, which are informed by conversations with students and practitioners who have been incorporating solution-focused interviewing skills into their practice.

Solution Building and Professional Values

The bedrock of any profession is its values. Professional values encapsulate the fundamental commitments of a profession and provide the criteria according to which practitioners must evaluate the acceptability of their work with clients. In the helping professions, then, all practice procedures, new and old, must be continuously scrutinized for the extent to which they conform with the field's cardinal values.

In Chapter 1, we noted that there are several overlapping but distinguishable helping professions: counseling psychology, marriage and family counseling or therapy, psychotherapy, rehabilitative counseling, social work, substance abuse counseling, and so forth. These various professions and professional associations within the field are in close agreement about the principles that should guide interactions between practitioners and clients. This is evident from a comparison of the ethical codes of particular helping professions.[1] This comparison could also be based on practice textbooks throughout the field, which typically review the fundamental values of their respective approaches to practice (for example, Axelson, 1993; Egan, 1994; Hepworth & Larsen, 1993; Ivey, 1994; Lewis, Dana, & Blevins, 1994).

In our discussion of professional values and solution-focused interviewing procedures, we have chosen to draw on the list of values and practice principles formulated by Sheafor, Horejsi, and Horejsi (1994), because their formulation is more detailed than others and therefore permits a more complete discussion. In the following pages, we will address those values that apply to practitioner-client interaction across all of the helping professions.

Respecting Human Dignity

All persons, by virtue of their humanity, have the right to be treated as valued creatures. This conviction has several implications for how practitioners ought to relate to clients. Foremost among these is the belief that clients must be accepted as they are. According to Biestek (1957), all aspects of any client must be accepted—the client's strengths and limitations, positive and negative attitudes, seemingly healthy and unhealthy behaviors, and attractive and unattractive qualities and habits. As Biestek and others (notably Rogers, 1961) describe it, acceptance must be unconditional; it must not be based on past performance.

Both Biestek and Rogers, however, are quick to point out that acceptance is not the same as approval. A practitioner can accept client attitudes and behaviors as real without approving of them. For example, a practitioner can accept that a client prefers to watch films with graphic violence rather than family movies without approving of that preference. The focus of acceptance, then, is on what's real for a client and not on what's good for the client.

---

[1] Should you wish to make the comparison, several codes are conveniently reprinted in the Appendix of *Issues and Ethics in the Helping Professions* (Corey, Corey, & Callanan, 1993).

The commitment to respecting human dignity also demands that practitioners remain nonjudgmental. This attitude toward clients means that the practitioner has no interest in judging the client or the client's story. Judging involves making legal decisions about the guilt or innocence of a person or moral statements about the rightness or wrongness of a person's attitudes or actions; it amounts to placing blame or making moral evaluations.

While practitioners are committed to remaining nonjudgmental with their clients, they must also recognize that clients live in a family and community context that maintains standards for evaluating individuals' attitudes and actions. In solving their problems, clients must take into account the legal and moral standards of the families and communities in which they live. For practitioners to ignore such standards would leave clients with the impression that their practitioners are unrealistic and hence not helpful.

Respect for human dignity through acceptance and the nonjudgmental attitude is the foundation for the development of trust in the client-practitioner relationship. When a practitioner responds in a judgmental or evaluative way, clients soon sense that the practitioner has preferences (and even expectations) about how they will think and behave; the practitioner's acceptance is conditional. Recognizing this, clients begin to feel more awkward and less accepted unless their preferences match those of the practitioner. They come to doubt that the practitioner is fully committed to understanding them and therefore lose trust that the practitioner will be helpful.

We believe that solution building effectively operationalizes client acceptance and the nonjudgmental attitude through the use of solution-focused interviewing. Beginning with our treatment of the fundamental skills in Chapter 3, we have pointed out consistently that solution building is based upon accepting client perceptions and working within clients' frames of reference. Notions of client resistance and challenging or confronting client perceptions play no part in the approach.

The solution-building process also contextualizes any solution that emerges (De Jong & Miller, 1995). As clients answer the miracle question and describe what will be different in their lives when their problems are solved, they are asked how they know such differences can occur in their lives. In their answer, clients almost always describe the family and community contexts in which they live and explain how their goals make sense in those contexts. In addition, the relationship questions asked in solution-focused interviewing invite clients to amplify goals and describe exceptions in terms that take seriously their relationships to family members and other important figures in the community.

In general, human dignity is fostered by relating to others in ways that enhance their sense of worth. Solution-focused interviewing does so by inviting clients to be experts about themselves and their lives. By paying so much attention to client perceptions, this method of interviewing implicitly conveys to clients that their perceptions are the most valuable and important resource in the solution-building process. Consequently, we believe that the process itself not only respects but actually enhances any client's sense of personal value and dignity.

Individualizing Service

Each person is unique. As a result, each client wants to be treated not only "as *a* human being but as *this* human being with his [or her] personal differences" (Biestek, 1957, p. 25). All the helping professions emphasize that each person has his or her own constellation of attitudes, beliefs, wishes, strengths, successes, needs, and problems. Consequently, clients expect their practitioners to listen to and respect their concerns and to be sufficiently flexible to assist them in ways that honor their individuality.

Respecting the individuality of each client is fundamental to solution-focused interviewing. In taking the posture of not knowing and continuously seeking amplification and clarification within the client's frame of reference and in the client's own words, solution-focused interviewing uncovers each client's concept of his or her problems, goals, past successes, and strengths. Solutions, too, are individualized, because they are built from exceptions and coping strategies that arise out of specific events in each client's life.

Effectively individualizing client services requires optimum flexibility on the part of practitioners. The solution-building process allows practitioners to be very flexible, because it depends for specifics (particular goals, coping strategies, strengths, and so forth) on the enormous range of perceptions and experiences brought to the helping relationship by clients. It is not bound by traditional assessment and diagnostic categories, nor does it limit itself to preferred interventions for particular diagnosed problems. Instead, it follows each client from one step behind, as the client develops an individualized solution of his or her own making. It is our experience that, as a bonus, solution building buttresses the practitioner's faith in the inner and outer resources of clients, because most clients build realistic and impressive solutions.

Fostering Client Vision

Sheafor, Horejsi, and Horejsi (1994, p. 90) write that a basic goal of practitioners should be to "introduce and nurture a sense of hopefulness and offer a vision that change is possible and that there are new and better ways to deal with the situation." This value implies that practitioners must be careful not to raise false hopes or project unrealistic outcomes for clients.

Solution-focused interviewing fits well with this value, although in a different way than problem-focused interviewing does. A whole stage of solution building—the development of well-formed goals through amplifying answers to the miracle question—encourages clients to develop a detailed vision of what their lives might be like when their problems are solved. This emphasis on inviting clients to create the vision by drawing on their own frames of reference means that solution building relies less on practitioner suggestions than do problem-solving approaches. As well as fostering hope and motivation in clients, this approach complements other practice values such as individualizing services and promoting client self-determination.

Solution-focused interviewing also counters any tendency of practitioners to raise false hopes in clients. First, because clients define their own visions for change, the practitioner's preferences for client goals have less opportunity to emerge in the interview. Second, the solution-focused approach asks clients, as experts about their situations, to clarify what parts of their miracle picture can and cannot happen and in this way encourages clients to think about and explain what is realistic.

Building on Strengths

Sheafor, Horejsi, and Horejsi (1994) indicate that practitioners in the field tend to be preoccupied with client problems, limitations, or deficiencies. They note that client assessments by interdisciplinary teams are often negative and mention few or no client abilities. They lament this "negative way of thinking about clients," and point out that "it is the clients' abilities and potentials that are most important in helping to bring about change" (Sheafor, Horejsi, & Horejsi, 1994, p. 90).

Building on client strengths is a hallmark of solution building, as illustrated by the emphasis on exploring and clarifying client exceptions and the regular practice of complimenting client strengths and successes.

Encouraging Client Participation

In discussing client participation, Sheafor, Horejsi, and Horejsi (1994, pp. 90–91) repeat these well-known maxims of the field: "Help your clients to help themselves"; and practitioners should "do *with* the client and not *to* or *for* the client." In other words, the helping professions are committed to empowering clients.

We believe that solution building not only fits with this value but, as we explained in Chapters 1 and 2, gives added meaning to client participation and empowerment. By minimizing the role of traditional scientific expertise and maximizing the role of client perceptions, solution building moves toward a different and more complete way of helping clients to help themselves. Clients are asked to help themselves by defining a miracle future, by identifying exceptions, and by exploring how the strengths associated with past successes can be used to build solutions.

Solution-focused interviewing gives added depth to the notion of working *with* clients. To work with clients means to collaborate with them by engaging in dialogues about their concerns and experiences. To truly develop a dialogue with clients means exploring and affirming their otherness; it means acknowledging that, as people distinct from their practitioners, clients probably have different wishes and points of view. Solution-focused interviewing does just this. In drawing out a client's perceptions, the interviewer is continually respecting and affirming the client's otherness.

Maximizing Self-Determination

As you probably realize, the values that we have been discussing complement each other. For example, as you foster client participation, you will also be individualizing services and maximizing client dignity. Client self-determination belongs to this same constellation and is probably the most emphasized of all the values that should guide practice.

Biestek (1957, p. 103) defines self-determination as "the practical recognition of the right and need of clients to freedom in making their own choices and decisions." As Biestek notes, the helping professions are unanimous in their support of this value, because self-determination is not only a basic human right but also respects the way in which people develop. People mature and develop a sense of who they are through making their own choices. Even though people may get tired and discouraged at times as they struggle with their problems, client self-confidence and satisfaction emerge not when practitioners take over for clients but, rather, when clients exercise responsibility and live as best they can with the consequences of their choices. Even with clients of limited mental capacity, practitioners are expected to work in ways that maximize clients' self-determination.

Solution-focused procedures foster self-determination. Clients are encouraged to take responsibility for their own lives throughout the solution-building process: They are asked to identify their problems and to define what is happening in their lives that makes these events problems; and they are also asked for their perceptions regarding a more satisfying future, existing exceptions, their levels of motivation and confidence, and so forth. For example, in the conversations between Ah Yan and Peter, she told him that she wanted relief from her panicky feelings and that she wanted a future in which she felt happy on the inside as well as the outside and her son, sensing her new composure, would feel free to go outside and play on the swing set and ride his bike. She also described exception times in which she could breathe better with no shakes and no worry, and indicated that she had a 10 level of motivation to work and a 10 level of confidence that she would find solutions.

Throughout this process, Ah Yan was taking responsibility for defining her problem and making choices about what to do with her life. Peter invited her to be the expert about problem and solution content; his expertise was primarily limited to guiding the process of solution building through the questions he asked. We believe that working this way with clients brings client self-determination to a deeper level. It is definitely different from approaches in which clients' perceptions are the raw material for professional assessments and suggestions that clients can choose to adopt or to ignore.

Fostering Transferability

Ideally, practitioners work in such a way that clients can take what they have learned about resolving their problems during services and apply it to other problems in their lives. Vinter (1985) calls this ideal transferability. Sheafor, Horejsi, and Horejsi (1994, p. 92) identify an aspect of transferability:

> An important aspect of preparing clients for the future is to teach them how to identify and make use of resources and natural helpers that might be found in their immediate environment. Such resources may include family members, relatives, friends, service clubs, and church or synagogue groups.

Transferability involves increasing clients' awareness of their inner and outer resources. Solution-focused interviewing is able to do so (De Jong & Miller, 1995). By consistently asking clients to explore and trust their own perceptions about what they want and how to make that happen, solution-focused interviewers give clients the opportunity to sharpen their awareness of their past successes and strengths—in other words, their inner resources. For example, in Insoo's interview with the Williams family (Chapter 6), she affirmed Gladys's goal to be a good mother, and she complimented many things Gladys was doing to make that goal a reality. In so doing, she was inviting Gladys to put into words those inner resources that she could continue to use in the future.

In addition, the relationship questions in solution-focused interviewing give clients the opportunity to identify outer resources. For example, in exploring with Ah Yan what differences others would notice about her when she was doing better, Peter learned that Ah Yan's husband and sister-in-law were great supports to her. He also learned that she was learning to use these outer resources in new and more effective ways.

We have gathered outcome data that bear out the transferability of solution building. Our telephone survey (Chapter 10) included this question: "We are also wondering if our treatment program has helped you with personal or family problems besides the one(s) which you worked on with us at BFTC. Would you say that it has helped, hindered, or neither helped nor hindered with other problems?" One-half of the former clients responded that the services had helped with other problems; the other half said the services neither helped nor hindered. Kiser's (1988) study of BFTC clients reveals an even higher rate of transferability. When he asked former clients the same question, 67% reported that the services had helped with other problems.

Protecting Confidentiality

Confidentiality requires that the practitioner hold in confidence the private information conveyed in the course of professional services. Clients disclose to the practitioner matters and points of view that if revealed to others, could be awkward or damaging to the clients and those they know. Consequently, it is clients' right to expect confidentiality. When practitioners meet this expectation, clients are more likely to trust them, to feel respected, and to work productively with them.

The professional workplace regularly codifies its policies on confidentiality and orients new practitioners to them before they are permitted to see clients. These policies reflect, and often exceed, client protections included in governmental laws and regulations. As you might expect, solution-building procedures operate within the law and agency policies. For example, when a team approach is used, clients are fully informed, and the team is not used without signed consent.

Solution-focused interviewing protects confidentiality in one other way. There is a longstanding belief in the helping professions that, in order to make progress, clients must express feelings about deeply painful and embarrassing events in their pasts. Some practitioners feel that they must probe for such material, even against the client's understandable resistance. By contrast, solution building is committed to the idea, based on experience and outcome data, that clients can make as much or more progress by drawing on their own sense of what their problems are, what they want to be different, and what strengths and resources are available to them. Consequently, clients are not asked to talk about their problems in the same personal detail. They decide what content they need to talk about in order to build solutions. We have found that, when given control over content, clients almost always choose to protect—that is, not to reveal to us—the intimate details of past failings. This certainly seems to have been the case with Ah Yan and the Williams family.

Creating this context for a deeper protection of confidentiality has also resulted in advantages for us as interviewers. We no longer worry about helping clients to uncover underlying issues, nor do we encounter client resistance. Instead, we enjoy working with our clients more than ever, while we allow them to take more charge of how they will build their own solutions.

Promoting Normalization

The helping professions participate in delivering services to persons with physical disabilities, with long-term mental illnesses, with mental retardation, and with other disabilities. The tendency in society has been to isolate such persons; they have often been required to live in ways that reflect stereotypes of their disabilities and are beneath their capacities. In response, the field has promoted the ideal of normalization, which calls upon practitioners to assist such clients in achieving the best possible way of living (Sheafor, Horejsi, & Horejsi, 1994).

Solution-focused interviewing fits well with the ideal of normalization. It emphasizes the discovery of client successes and strengths through exception exploration. At the same time, it encourages clients to be realistic, by asking them how they know that they can repeat and move beyond past successes. We have found solution building to be applicable to clients with severe mental illness, those managing the consequences of a debilitating disease such as lupus, those who have recently been diagnosed with a terminal illness, and those with other physical disabilities. Even for clients who seem overwhelmed, solution-focused interviewing can be helpful. Such clients usually become more hopeful when asked coping questions (Chapter 9) and complimented on their coping strengths and strategies. They often come up with additional ideas about how to live with their pain or disability.

Monitoring Change

Because clients and their contexts are always changing, Sheafor, Horejsi, and Horejsi (1994, p. 94) state that practitioners and clients together must make a "continuous monitoring and evaluation of the change process," by regularly collecting data about the outcomes of the strategies used to assist the client. If these data indicate that the intended change is not occurring, it is the practitioner's responsibility to take other steps.

In solution-focused interviewing, change is regularly monitored; indeed, the client's answers to the monitoring questions are integral to the discovery of client successes and strengths. Scaling questions are most often used to gain client estimates of change. For example, Peter asked Ah Yan the presession change question and received an answer of 6, which suggested that she was doing considerably better by the time of their first session than at the time she called to make her appointment. In their second session, when he asked her to scale her progress she chose 7 or 8. In both instances, her answers to the scaling question became the springboard for exploring what was different in her life and what she and others might be doing to make this progress happen. Because scaling is integral to solution building, monitoring progress feels comfortable to practitioner and client.

Solution building also respects the field's commitment to taking other steps when monitoring reveals a lack of progress. In solution building, it is a maxim to try something else when what the client is doing is not working. De Shazer (1985) has identified this maxim as part of the basic philosophy of a solution-focused approach and formulated a special task around it: the do-something-different task (Chapter 7).

Conclusion

Solution-focused procedures fit very well with the values intended to guide client-practitioner interactions in the helping professions. In fact, as we have illustrated, the use of these procedures can often enhance practitioners' ability to bring these values to life in their work with clients. That should not be surprising. If you recall our discussion of the forces that gave rise to the strengths perspective and recent notions of empowerment (Chapter 1), contradictions between these values and the procedures adopted in the problem-solving paradigm are what has prompted the call for more collaborative and empowering approaches to practice (Weick, 1993).

Diversity-Competent Practice

Practice textbooks currently in use in the helping professions are calling for more sensitivity to human diversity; some have gone so far as to build their approach to practice around the concept (Axelson, 1993; Devore & Schlesinger, 1987; Lum, 1992; Sue & Sue, 1990). These books contend that, for too long, the helping professions have operated with built-in preferences for the traits and behaviors of middle-class white males. Such preferences have minimized or ignored the characteristics more common among poor people, women, and people of color. The field as whole is now more committed than ever to preparing diversity-conscious and diversity-competent practitioners.

Efforts to foster diversity-competent practice in the field mainly presume the problem-solving paradigm, in which the practitioner first assesses client problems and then intervenes on the basis of the assessments. The expert practitioner is expected to respect human diversity at the assessment stage and then again at the intervention stage. Practice textbooks (Ivey, 1994; Lum, 1992; McMahon, 1990) emphasize that aspiring practitioners must learn about the values, beliefs, and worldviews of different economic, ethnic, and racial groups, along with their different styles of communication and problem solving. They also call on new practitioners to actively examine their own assumptions, biases, and ethnocentric attitudes, so that these can be recognized as personal limitations for professional practice and steps may be taken to lessen their negative effects. Having acquired self-knowledge and expert knowledge about diverse groups, practitioners apply this knowledge sensitively in the assessment stage, so that cultural traits are not assessed as problems or deficits, and again in the intervention stage, so that recommended interventions will be inoffensive and effective.

We have definite reservations about this approach. Certainly, it is important for practitioners to learn about the worldviews and preferred lifestyles of different groups (although, in this postmodern nation of intermixing peoples, these are becoming less sharply distinguishable), and all practitioners need to become more aware of their own attitudes regarding diversity. However, our preference for a solution-building paradigm makes us uneasy with attempts to address diversity within the context of professional assessments and interventions. Instead, we regard cultural diversity as one aspect of the enormous differences between people and as further confirmation of the need to take a posture of not knowing when interviewing clients.

We believe that the field's current approach to increasing diversity competency is incomplete. Imagine that you are a white, middle-class male and that you are about to interview an African American female who is unemployed and on welfare. Suppose that you have worked hard to soften your class, racial, and gender biases and that you have studied the professional literature about the histories, customs, preferences, and patterns of diverse groups. Suppose, further, that you have several years of experience in working with African American clients. With all these competencies and experiences, you would rightly feel prepared to do the interview. However, this background is not enough to ensure that you will do a diversity-competent interview, because you cannot assume that the particular African American you are about to interview will correspond exactly to the characteristics of African Americans described in the literature or represented in your past experience. Moreover, each individual is a composite of several dimensions of diversity (class, ethnicity, gender, physical ability/disability, sexual orientation, race, religion, and so forth), and you have no way of knowing ahead of time how these may interact with one another in any particular client. Consequently, no matter how much experience you may have had with a particular population of clients, you can make few, if any, assumptions about your latest client. Instead, you must make every effort to relate to each client as a human being with particular strengths, experiences, and idiosyncracies. To do otherwise would amount to stereotyping.

Ideally, then, the helping professions need a way of working with individual clients that is effective across diverse groups. We believe that the solution-building process comes closer to this ideal than do problem-solving approaches. Solution-focused interviewing draws on client perceptions and works more fully within their frames of reference. Because the client's perceptions will be shaped, in part, by the histories, customs, and problem-solving styles of the groups to which the client may belong, the solution-building process integrates those aspects of diversity as it proceeds; each one is regarded as potentially a valuable resource.

Table 11.1 Intermediate Outcome (I.O.) by Age*					
I.O.	12 Years and Under	13–18 Years	19–30 Years	31–45 Years	46–60 Years	Total
Significant progress	24%	21%	29%	27%	13%	24%
Moderate progress	44%	58%	38%	56%	50%	49%
No progress	33%	21%	33%	17%	38%	26%
Number of cases	46	24	21	41	8	140

* In Tables 11.1–11.8, percentages are rounded to the nearest whole percent.

Outcome Data on Diversity

To examine whether solution-focused interviewing is effective across diverse groups, we gathered relevant outcome data. In Chapter 10, as you will recall, we presented data on both intermediate and final outcomes for all BFTC clients who received services between November 1992 and August 1993. Here, we present data on intermediate and final outcomes for four categories of diversity.

Age

We asked the age of each client on an information form that clients or their guardians completed on their first visit to BFTC. When two adults came for services together, we asked them to choose which one would be the identified client for purposes of record keeping and third-party (private insurance or Medicaid) reimbursement.

Table 11.1 presents data on intermediate outcome by different age categories. As we explained in Chapter 10, intermediate outcome is a measurement of progress at the time of services. Table 11.1 includes data only for cases up through 60 years of age, because there are too few cases in higher age ranges to permit analysis. The last row of Table 11.1 gives the number of cases in each age category.

If we compare across columns in Table 11.1 within given categories of intermediate outcome, we find that age of client is not significantly related to intermediate outcome. Similar percentages of clients show significant progress for all age groupings. The only exception is for clients of ages 46–60 years, where a smaller percentage (13%) show significant progress by their final session. However, this percentage is based on only eight cases and hence has little

Table 11.2 Final Outcome (F.O.) by Age					
F.O.	12 Years and Under	13–18 Years	19–30 Years	31–45 Years	46–60 Years	Total
Goal met	37%	42%	32%	52%	58%	44%
Some progress	40%	47%	36%	24%	17%	33%
No progress	24%	11%	32%	24%	25%	23%
Number of cases	38	19	22	42	12	133

influence on the overall result. When comparing across age categories for clients showing no progress, clients who are ages 13–18 and ages 31–45 show a lower percentage of no progress, but the differences are not large. Overall, these data suggest that the use of solution-focused interviewing procedures is equally effective for persons of all ages.

Table 11.2 presents the data for final outcome according to the different age groupings. Final-outcome data were obtained by contacting clients 7–9 months after their last session at BFTC and asking them whether their treatment goal was met or not met. Those clients who responded "not met" were also asked whether or not any progress had been made.

Table 11.2 shows that clients of ages 19–30 are somewhat less likely to state that their goal was met and somewhat more likely to say that no progress was made toward their treatment goal. Overall, however, there is little if any relationship between age and outcome. Consequently, our measurements for both intermediate and final outcome suggest that solution building works equally well for persons of all ages.

Employment Status

Data gathered when clients came for their first sessions at BFTC provide a rough indicator of their socioeconomic status. Specifically, clients (or their guardians) were asked about their current employment status. Those who were employed regularly came with authorization for services from private insurance companies; those who were not employed were, for the most part, on public welfare and their services were paid for under Title XIX. Tables 11.3 and 11.4 present data on employment status and outcomes.

The data on intermediate outcome indicate that the percentage of those not employed who show no progress from their first to their final sessions is somewhat higher than the corresponding figure for those employed, but the

Table 11.3 Intermediate Outcome (I.O.) by Employment Status			
I.O.	Employed	Not Employed	Total
Significant progress	22%	25%	24%
Moderate progress	59%	42%	50%
No progress	19%	33%	27%
Number of cases	63	76	139

Table 11.4 Final Outcome (F.O.) by Employment Status			
F.O.	Employed	Not Employed	Total
Goal met	50%	37%	44%
Some progress	27%	41%	33%
No progress	23%	22%	23%
Number of cases	74	59	133

difference is not great (33% versus 19%). In addition, the difference is not present in the data for final outcome. Here, virtually the same percentage of clients who were not employed and those employed show no progress (22% and 23%), although a higher percentage of the employed (50%) do report meeting their treatment goal than those not employed (37%). Overall, the data suggest a small tendency for the employed to have better outcomes with solution-focused procedures, but there is little, if any, difference in outcome.

Gender

Tables 11.5 and 11.6 present the data on outcomes for clients who are female and those who are male. Here again, gender is not correlated with effectiveness. Women and men show equally positive outcomes for both intermediate and final outcomes.

Table 11.5	Intermediate Outcome (I.O.) by Gender		
I.O.	Female	Male	Total
Significant progress	28%	20%	25%
Moderate progress	46%	53%	49%
No progress	26%	27%	26%
Number of cases	81	60	141

Table 11.6	Final Outcome (F.O.) by Gender		
F.O.	Female	Male	Total
Goal met	46%	44%	45%
Some progress	27%	40%	32%
No progress	28%	16%	23%
Number of cases	79	55	134

Race

When identified clients came for their first session at BFTC, they (or their guardians) were asked to complete the following question on the client information questionnaire: "What race do you consider yourself/your child to be?" They were given these options: "American Indian/Native American; Asian/Oriental/Pacific Islander; Black/African American; White/Caucasian; Latino/Latina/Hispanic; Other." Because there were fewer than five cases for both Native Americans and Asian Americans, we do not present the data for these categories. Tables 11.7 and 11.8 present our outcome data for the other three groups.

These groups show little difference on initial and final outcome. Latino clients deviate a little from the pattern set by African Americans and whites,

Table 11.7 Intermediate Outcome (I.O.) by Race				
I.O.	African American	White	Latino	Total
Significant progress	27%	21%	43%	26%
Moderate progress	45%	58%	29%	49%
No progress	28%	21%	29%	26%
Number of cases	78	48	7	133

Table 11.8 Final Outcome (F.O.) by Race				
F.O.	African American	White	Latino	Total
Goal met	48%	45%	36%	46%
Some progress	32%	26%	46%	31%
No progress	20%	30%	18%	24%
Number of cases	60	47	11	118

but this difference is small and the Latino group itself is much smaller than the other two.

Diversity and Satisfaction with Services

Additional data about outcome 7–9 months after services suggest the usefulness of solution building with diverse clients. We asked former clients the following question: "Overall, would you say that you are satisfied, dissatisfied, or neither satisfied nor dissatisfied with your therapy services at the Center?" Of the 137 who responded, 72% said they were satisfied, 16% said they were neither satisfied nor dissatisfied, and 12% said they were dissatisfied. The level of satisfaction did not change when we looked separately at satisfaction level for clients of different age, employment status, gender, and race.

Thus, we see that a wide range of clients make good progress with solution building. This means that, as an interviewer, you do not need to make assumptions about your clients on the basis of their backgrounds. Instead, if you have a basic knowledge of diversity differences and have worked to rid yourself of diversity biases, you can proceed from a posture of not knowing, in the awareness that, by its very nature, the solution-building process is respectful of diversity and sensitive to people's differences.

CHAPTER **12**

Agency, Group, and Community Practice

Solution Building and Agency Practice

As we saw in Chapter 1, the helping professions operate within a problem-solving paradigm. This has definite consequences not only for client-practitioner interactions but also for how agencies and mental health clinics conduct other aspects of practice. At base, the paradigm requires practitioners to use their expertise to gather case data about client problems and to use those data in *problem assessments,* which then provide the foundation for *problem interventions.* Once in agency practice, you will soon discover that this paradigm has clear implications for the content of your record keeping and for your interactions with agency colleagues and collaterals.

Record Keeping

Case records typically include information about client characteristics, identified problems and their assessment, goals, interventions, services rendered, and documentation of progress. They have several uses (Kagle, 1991). They help practitioners to stay abreast of case information and progress and to communicate with colleagues, supervisors, and collaterals about cases. They are also important to agencies as documentation of services and as sources of information for funding requests and research.

Agencies characteristically require their practitioners to prepare the following documents on each case:

1. An initial assessment. Sometimes called an individual or social history, this document includes identifying information about the client, information about the presenting problem(s), referral sources, the practitioner's assessment of the client and the problem, and (in mental health settings) a DSM IV diagnosis (American Psychiatric Association, 1994).
2. A treatment (or service) plan. This document is a statement of goals in the case and the planned interventions or services intended to accomplish the goals.

3. Progress notes. As its name indicates, this document is a brief, often hand-written statement included in the case record after each contact with the client. It describes the degree of progress accomplished toward the goals since the last contact. If new problems have arisen in the case, this document can also include reassessment statements and reformulation of goals.

4. A closing summary. This is a summary statement of the identified problems, goals, interventions, and progress in the case, along with the circumstances under which the client terminated services. In addition, it includes any recommendations for future services or referral to other agencies.

These documents reflect the stages of the problem-solving model. Sometimes, agency procedures go even farther in their commitment to a focus on problems; they may require practitioners to administer standardized assessment instruments once they suspect certain problems. Practitioners then incorporate the results into the initial assessment and treatment plan.

As you incorporate solution-building into your work with clients, you will probably find certain aspects of this record keeping irrelevant to your work with clients. While you will need some information about clients' perceptions of their problems, you will generally not find expert assessment or diagnostic information helpful. Practitioners who have become more solution-focused in their work tell us that they have become increasingly frustrated with their agencies' documentation requirements.

How can you deal with this situation? We cannot offer you a perfect solution, but we do have some observations and suggestions. Let's begin by looking at Peter's experience.

Peter worked for several years in a clinical mental health setting with a problem and pathology focus. His agency had a detailed protocol of categories and questions that practitioners had to follow, in order to generate information for incorporation into an initial assessment and treatment plan; the information was also used in a DSM diagnosis, which must be submitted with any application for third-party reimbursement for services. Because the initial assessment and treatment plan had to be completed by the end of the second session, Peter felt pressured into adopting an emphasis on problems when he began his work with clients.

He had to follow the protocol; it was an agency policy. He decided to present it to clients for what it was—an agency requirement. As he became more solution-focused in his work, he would begin by making the following proposal to his clients:

> At our agency, it's a requirement to do an initial assessment and treatment plan by the end of our second meeting. The initial assessment involves a lot of questions about the concerns and symptoms which brought you here, as

well as questions about your background, family, and personal history. You may find answering these questions helpful or you may not; it seems to be different for different people. The treatment plan involves talking about what you want different in the future and how you might go about making that happen. It's been my experience that this can be very useful to clients. So I have a suggestion. Let's work today on getting all this information about your concerns down, and next time we can work more on what you would like to have different. (By the way, it's important to get this initial assessment information down so that I can make a diagnosis, and then you can receive benefits from your insurance company.) Is this plan of action OK with you?

Because clients are usually focused on problems when they first come in, Peter's clients consistently agreed to his suggestion. He then showed them the form that the agency uses, and he and the client worked through the items one by one. If there was additional time toward the end of the session, he began asking about what the client would like to have different in his or her life. Frequently, he also ended the session by giving the formula first-session task, as a way to turn the client's attention toward solution building. In the next session, he turned to goal formulation in earnest, by asking the miracle question and its follow-up questions. He also did exception exploration, took a break, and gave feedback at the end of the session.

This agency also required that clients sign their treatment plans, as part of its effort to operationalize clients' right to be informed about their treatment. Consequently, during the break in the second session, Peter would write out goals based on the goal-formulation dialogue; after the break, he reviewed these with the client and asked if the client would be willing to sign them, once they were typed up. Thereafter, he gave his solution-building feedback. After the client had left, he used the information obtained in both sessions to dictate his initial assessment and treatment plan.

Peter is still less than happy with this compromise solution. First, clients are asked for problem details and history that are not necessary in order to build solutions. Second, committing goals to paper for the client's review and signature pushes clients toward closure on goals when it is more useful for them to be freely thinking about more possibilities. However, his compromise did allow him to distance himself somewhat from the agency's problem-focused approach, to incorporate goal formulation using solution-focused procedures, and to include all parts of solution building by the end of the second session.

Another way of dealing with problem-focused recording requirements is to intersperse problem-focused and solution-focused approaches. Thomas' (1995) students have incorporated competency-based questions into their interviewing as they proceed through the client-history and problem-assessment questions required by the agencies in their internship settings. For example, when collecting family history data about family problems such as divorces, unemployment, and alcoholism, the interviewer can ask questions such as these:

- Your parents were divorced and at odds with one another all through the years when you were growing up. How did you manage to cope?
- I see a lot of unemployment in your family history; yet you have always held a high-paying job. How did that happen?
- You say your mom was alcoholic and you're not. Does that surprise you?

Although this approach does not necessarily uncover past successes and strengths directly related to what the client might want to be different, it does introduce more balance into the interaction, by asking about competencies as well as problems. If the competency data are also included in the initial assessment, that assessment will give a more complete and positive picture of the client to any professionals who might have access to the case file in the future.

Some agencies have moved away from traditional problem assessments to a solution-focused approach and require fewer client-history and problem-assessment questions, except in cases where practitioners suspect physiologically based problems and referral to psychiatrists and physicians for diagnosis may be necessary. This shift changes their documentation requirements so that paperwork more closely approximates the stages of solution building. The agencies continue to require their practitioners to write an initial assessment document—in part to satisfy reimbursement and funding requirements—but the document has less assessment and personal-history data. Instead, it includes a brief statement of the concerns that brought the client to the agency, necessary identifying information (most of which comes from a brief questionnaire that the client completes at the time of the first visit, before seeing the practitioner), goal-formulation information, scaling information (which includes past successes and strengths related to what the client wants), and feedback given. The content of this document is based on client perceptions rather than the practitioner's interpretation of what the client needs or the goals that the client should be striving for. Later documents include progress notes that record client gains, how these were accomplished, and adjustments that clients are making to their goals. A closing summary reviews progress made and includes any follow-up arrangements or referrals to other resources in the community.

Relationships with Colleagues

If you choose to become more solution-focused in your work, you will encounter colleagues and supervisors who are unfamiliar and uncomfortable with your approach to clients. Our workshop participants and students in internship settings tell us repeatedly that this happens.

In encounters with skeptical colleagues, you may be tempted to defend your approach and to cast the conversation into either/or terms: "Either your way is right or my way is right." As in your work with clients, we do not recommend that you directly challenge your colleagues' frames of reference, which have probably been developed over long periods of time, are informed by experience, and deserve to be respected. Instead, we suggest that you take a posture of not knowing and explore their concerns. Pay attention to what they might want from your interaction. Frequently, they may just want to know more about your approach. At other times, they will definitely be skeptical and even critical. In that case, you might ask them what they do differently with their clients and how they know that this is useful. You can respectfully compliment their strengths and successes. If they are interested, you can indicate what you do when you engage in solution-building dialogues with clients and how you perceive these to be helpful. Often, as the dialogue develops, apparent differences become less extreme.

There will be times when differences remain between your views and those of your colleagues; after all, solution building is different from problem solving. According to our workshop participants and students, their skeptical colleagues' major concerns are that solution building deemphasizes the connection between problem and solution, emphasizes the importance of client perceptions, and deemphasizes expert assessments and interventions. You and your colleagues may decide to talk more about the content and consequences of those differences at your agency. You might wish to institute agency roundtable or brownbag discussions on, for example, the relative importance of problem-assessment and solution-focused interviewing in crisis cases at your agency or on designing a study to compare solution-building and problem-solving outcomes with your clients. Our point here, once again, is that differences are best handled through open and respectful dialogue; direct challenges of deeply held views are rarely helpful.

Of course, you may find yourself in circumstances where your supervisor insists that you follow certain problem-focused procedures. Here, you will have to determine how much leeway you have to also incorporate your solution-building procedures. We discussed a couple of possibilities for doing this in the previous section.

Relationships with Collaterals

Collaterals are professionals at other agencies who have an interest in the outcome of your work with a certain client because they are also working with the client, because they referred the client to your agency, or for other reasons. Collaterals can include probation officers, psychiatrists, teachers, religious practitioners, and others. They frequently have definite ideas about your clients' needs and how to go about working with them, and usually they operate within a problem-focused framework.[1]

We suggest that, as with colleagues, you assume that collaterals are competent and deserving of your respect. Use your interviewing skills to discover what they might want from you. If they have had contact with the client, find out what they have done that they think was useful to the client. Affirm the valuable work that they have done.

Let's illustrate this approach with an example from Peter's experience. Peter has worked with sex offenders referred to him for counseling by their probation officers. Here is a conversation between him and a probation officer named Jackson about a referred client:

PETER: Jackson, I see from the letter you sent that you are referring a Fred Wilson to me. He's on my schedule for tomorrow. How can I be helpful?

JACKSON: You can see from the information I sent that he pleaded guilty to a Fourth Degree CSCC [Criminal Sexual Conduct Code] violation. He had been hanging around the monkey bars in the park, offering to help young girls up and catching them when they jumped off. He also was touching their private parts. Two girls complained to their parents, and there were witnesses who put him at the park at the time the girls claimed the abuse. He touched them through their clothes and there was no penetration, so it's been processed as a misdemeanor. The guy needs counseling.

PETER: OK. Can you tell me anything more about what you'd like from me?

JACKSON: I met with him a couple of times. I think he is in denial because he said that he didn't do it. He said the only reason he pleaded was because his attorney told him the girls' stories corroborated each others' and would be pretty convincing to the court because they were so specific for an 8- and a 9-year-old. I'm worried he might do the same thing again if he doesn't get it together; he probably has done it before and just never got caught. If he's like the other guys I've dealt with, he's gonna need at least a year of counseling. That's why I recommended a year of it once per week as a condition of probation in my presentence report to the judge. He also has to see me at least once per month.

PETER: So what might tell you that he's coming out of denial? What would he be doing differently?

JACKSON: Well for one thing—admitting that he did it and getting to work on where those sick tendencies in him come from. If you can help him to do that, that would be worth a lot. I talked to him a couple of times, and I think he's got some potential. He still won't admit what he did and that he has to work in counseling, but he's got a family and a good job in sales.

---

[1] Note, too, that when you work jointly on a case with colleagues at your own agency, you will essentially be in a collateral relationship with them.

PETER: Knowing what you know about him, how do you think he will be different when he comes around to admitting it?

JACKSON: Like I say, I think he's got a chance. He's got a family and a job, but he's so tied into that job and beating his competition that he's out of touch with his family. He's on the road a lot. I don't know if he even has any friends; he never mentioned any. I think when he starts to see himself for what he has become and admit it to himself and maybe even to his wife, he'll make some changes. He'll get his job more in perspective and get more interested in his family—spend more time with his wife, maybe go to some school activities of his kids. He's got some teenagers in sports, but he doesn't go to their games. He might even make some friends. For sure, he won't go to the parks [cynically quoting the client] "for walks by myself."

PETER: OK, Jackson, that gives me some good information to start with. Seems like you've been doing some serious thinking about this case and what could happen; I think he's lucky you're handling his case. Is there anything else you want me to know right now?

JACKSON: No, I don't think so . . . except that I think that, even though he still denies it, I think he might work in counseling. He listened to me real carefully and says he cares about his family and is thankful that they have stuck with him through this. [pause] He knows I want to talk to you every two weeks at first. He'll sign your releases. Give me a call in two weeks when you have space in your schedule.

PETER: OK, I'll do that; I'll get back to you after I've seen him the second time. Thanks for the referral.

Peter accepted and explored Jackson's perceptions about his new case; he invited Jackson to share his expertise about the case. In the process, he affirmed Jackson for his concern and work and got some specific information about what Jackson would have to see Fred Wilson doing differently in order to gain confidence that he was making progress and becoming less of a threat to the community.

Peter's interaction with Jackson indicates that, anytime you work with a collateral, you have at least two clients whose perceptions you will want to explore—the identified client and the collateral. We recommend being solution-focused with both.

Group and Organizational Practice

Solution-focused procedures were developed in work with individuals, couples, and families and are still most widely practiced and discussed in that area. However, they are now catching the interest of practitioners in group and organizational settings.

Group Practice

In group practice, the interpersonal process that develops in small groups is used to assist clients to achieve their individual goals. Counselors, psychologists, and social workers all work with groups. There are groups for individuals with substance abuse problems, pregnant teens, people with AIDS, those recently divorced, children of alcoholics, those with eating disorders, battered women, men who batter, incest survivors, and many more. Some groups offer therapy for behavioral and emotional disorders (for example, an anxiety-disorder group at a mental health facility); others foster personal growth (such as an assertiveness-training group); and still others are self-help groups (Alcoholics Anonymous).

The organization and process in most small groups reflects the same problem-solving assumptions and procedures seen in most individual and family approaches. In theory, introducing solution-building assumptions and procedures into this form of practice could be very useful to group participants.

We know of several agencies where practitioners have introduced solution-building procedures into their group work after becoming proficient with them in individual and family work. Their groups are customarily set up on a time-limited basis (6–12 sessions) because experience has taught that change can occur in a short period of time and that the time limitation encourages more purposeful interaction among group members.

Selekman (1991) describes one application of solution-focused procedures to group work. He has established a solution-oriented parenting group to foster empowerment among parents who live with their substance-abusing teenage children. The group meets for six weekly sessions, each of 1½ hours. Selekman uses solution-focused interviewing to help these parents uncover exceptions and develop goals. For example, in early sessions, group members are asked about times that go better with their teenagers, what they might have done to make the exceptions happen, and what they have to do so that these better times will happen again. Solution-focused task assignments are given at the end of each session. For instance, at the end of the first session, parents are all given the formula first-session task of paying attention to aspects of what is happening between themselves and their adolescents that they want to continue. Their findings are discussed at the next session. At a later session, parents are assigned a behavioral task: to do something different in a situation with their teenagers that is still problematic for them. As in all solution-building work, the group interaction and homework focus on discovering and using strengths and resources rather than uncovering and analyzing pathologies and problems.

Selekman thinks that solution-building procedures and group process make an effective combination. The parents in his group, worn down by so many crises and power struggles with their children, frequently become immobilized and lose sight of their capacities and possibilities. The group process can amplify the benefits of solution building. For example, when one parent in the group is discouraged and at a loss about what to do next, the group leader calls on other group members to generate creative possibilities. These are listed on the blackboard and discussed. The parent who is at an impasse often becomes more hopeful and creative in the process.

In the group, parents often begin to spontaneously use solution-focused questions. They ask fellow group members who have stated an exception: "How did that happen? What will it take for it to happen again?" They also start to compliment one another for their successes. Selekman reports that, to further accentuate client affirmation, the last session of the group is a party to celebrate parent successes, featuring a cake with the words "Congratulations, solution-oriented parents!" Certificates of achievement are given, speeches are made, and parents compliment one another on their hard work and parenting achievements.

In personal communications and papers presented at conferences, practitioners report how easily solution-building principles and procedures can be adapted to a variety of client populations and practice settings. Donna Linz (personal communication, 1994), for example, describes her successful group work with incest survivors. She and her colleague at the Group Health Cooperative in Seattle have been surprised at group members' progress. They had previously used a traditional group model of sexual abuse treatment, in which group members participated for two years or more, but they believe that clients make as much overall progress in their 14-week solution-focused group. Linz and her colleague begin solution-focused group treatment by using an adaptation of the miracle question: Each group member must work at defining something to do in their daily lives that until now they had only wished they could do. Group members also are asked to define a beginning step to a different life that can start 14 weeks later, when the group meetings terminate. Of course, many clients begin on their different life soon after they begin defining it. Linz also reports that clients use scaling questions to measure progress and make estimates about motivation and confidence levels. Clients decide for themselves how much detail to reveal as they talk about the meaning of their individual scaling numbers.

Michael Durrant (1993) describes using solution-focused group process in residential settings in Australia. More specifically, he describes the activities of processing groups, in which members focus on what has been going right instead of what went wrong. The group leader begins by asking: "Who needs to brag first about yesterday?" When members slip into problem talk, the leader uses solution-focused questioning to return the group's focus to exceptions and solution building. Members scale where they see themselves in terms of particular goals; they use the scaling numbers to figure out next steps. Durrant (1993, p. 167) quotes the observations of one group leader: "We have found that, over time, the groups have become more success-focused. Group members seem to enjoy finding good things to say about one another!"

An Organizational Application

Sparks (1989) reports on her use of solution building in place of problem solving in the Vehicle Maintenance Division in a large metropolitan city. Acting as a management consultant, her purpose was to stimulate more openness between managers and subordinates and more teamwork among supervisors. She describes her approach as organizational tasking, in which she held five workshop meetings with supervisors and gave them solution-oriented homework assignments to be completed between meetings.

The first workshop was organized around developing rapport with supervisors and inviting them to express their hopes and fears for their work in the division. The session ended with a task assignment: Participants were asked to meet with subordinates and request that they think ahead 12 months to a much-improved work environment. The supervisors were to ask their subordinates to describe what would be different about the environment and, more particularly, which of these differences they would most like to see realized in the next year. The supervisors were also asked to record the results of the meeting and to bring them to the next session.

At the second workshop, these alternative futures were discussed among the supervisors in a goal-formulation session. At the end of the workshop, supervisors were given two tasks: First, they were to meet with two subordinate managers separately and identify an incident where they had worked successfully together to solve a problem or develop an opportunity. They were to write up the details of this exception for use at the next workshop. Second, participants were invited to do something different in their work with subordinates and to describe it at the next workshop.

Later workshops were devoted to identifying exceptions and using them to build solutions to the strained relationships in the organization. Sparks asked supervisors to identify subordinates with whom they felt comfortable. They were to request these subordinates to identify and describe incidents with their supervisors that had had positive effects on their work performance and morale. Another observational task was for supervisors to notice things happening in the workplace that they liked and wanted to keep the same.

Sparks discovered that, as a result of her workshops, supervisors listened more carefully to subordinates, interacted with subordinates in a more comfortable way, and addressed a greater range of work-related issues between them. Whether coincidental or not, the Division Manager reported to her that, on all their measures of work performance, the organization had its most productive year ever after her consultation. In addition, Sparks administered her own outcome instruments, which measured four dimensions of successful teamwork: trust, openness, realization, and interdependence. The data led her to conclude "that there was a continual perception of improvement in team functioning over time on all four dimensions of team functioning" (Sparks, 1989, p. 56).

Sparks' work is important because it suggests that a solution-building approach can be useful in realizing organizational objectives. Once problem description and analysis give way to solution-building dialogues among an organization's staff members, hopefulness and motivation seem to increase, and exciting changes can occur.

Theoretical Implications

In fact, we are such inveterate meaning-makers that when we do not have an explanation for something, we make one up.
(Saari, 1991, p. 14)

I thought I was depressed, but after my visits to BFTC, I came to realize that I was only having blue spells.
(A former client)

If you are like most people, you want to understand—and will go to great efforts to figure out—the *meaning* of life's events. If an event is important to you, you reflect on it, put your impressions into words, and talk about it with other people. To do so is our most obvious and unique human characteristic (Mead, 1934).

Clients are no different. They, too, want to know the meaning of what is happening in their lives. Immersed in a culture that emphasizes problem-solving thinking, clients typically want to talk to their practitioners about *why* they are having their problems; they regularly seek the meaning of their problems in supposed causes, in the same way that people in Western societies make sense out of diseases by trying to discover the agents that give rise to them. Ah Yan, whose case we followed in Chapters 5–8, is an example. When she first told Peter about her panicky feelings, her question was: "Why? Why is this?" She told him, "I gotta figure out what's wrong with me."

While working your way through this book, you may have noticed that, in solution building with clients, we never ask why. We do not ask the why of client goals or exceptions, much less of their problems. Experience has taught us that asking why is not useful. Clients build solutions more efficiently when practitioners do not encourage them to analyze why they have problems and why solutions might work. Similarly, experience has taught that it is generally not useful for practitioners to try to figure out why clients have their problems; clients build solutions more efficiently if practitioners remain not knowing toward client problems, goals, and exceptions, and deemphasize problem assessment. However, regardless of usefulness, clients and practitioners alike keep on trying to figure out the meaning of their experiences.

Back in Chapter 1, we made two points that may have struck you as odd. First, we indicated that solution-focused procedures were mainly developed inductively, by observing client-practitioner conversations and paying attention to what seemed to be helpful; they were not deduced from existing theory. Second, we noted Steve de Shazer's comment that, although he knows solution-focused procedures are useful, he does not know why. In this last chapter, although it will probably not make us any more effective as practitioners, we are going to reflect on the meaning of what happens in the solution-building process and on what that may teach us about how best to go about helping others.

Shifts in Client Perceptions and Definitions

Observers at BFTC noticed that, as clients talked about their problems and how to solve them, their perceptions of the meaning of both problems and possible solutions shifted regularly. Some clients came in with several problems and were not at all sure about which was their real or underlying problem; over time, their focus became clearer. Often, clients would begin to describe the characteristics of their problems in new ways. The observers noticed consistently that, over the course of several sessions or even just one, clients would redefine their problems.

Ah Yan's problem definitions offer a good example. At the beginning of her first session, she viewed her problem—feeling panicky—in biological and psychological terms. She said she thought that she was crazy, noticed her hair falling out, and sought out a physician to discover the causes through medical testing; the tests were inconclusive. Peter began a conversation with her about what she wanted to have different. He also worked with her on developing a vision of an alternative future and explored whether there were any exception times that resembled parts of her miracle picture. She was able to describe exceptions that were random—not deliberate—and she emerged from this conversation with a vague definition of her problem:

> Ah . . . maybe . . . I don't know. . . . I can't figure it out—what's wrong with me. I don't know what to do. . . . I got all these feelings. . . . I gotta figure out what's wrong with me.

In their second session, as Ah Yan and Peter talked about what was better, Ah Yan identified several successes. She indicated that, by leaving a dance for a short time, she had been able to recompose herself when she felt her panicky feelings coming on. She implied that her problem might be tied to situations with a lot of people, where it is too stuffy; this description is more circumscribed than the all-encompassing definition of her problem in the first session. As Ah Yan and Peter discussed additional exceptions, she was able to describe several successes and strategies she used to brush her problem off. In exploring these successes and what she might be doing to make them happen, Ah Yan seemed to shift her focus from figuring out the causes of her panicky feelings to figuring out more strategies that she could use to keep the problem under control. Toward the end of the second session, in discussing the next steps, she again reshaped her perspective: She told Peter she needed to find more ways to let her children "learn how to do things by themselves." Having started with a biological and psychological definition, Ah Yan seemed to be working her way towards a more interpersonal problem definition by the end of the session:

> Yeah, I felt alone. I felt trapped. I don't know. I just felt so lonely, and now that I'm talking—like, my sister goes, "I heard that you didn't feel good," and she says, "I told mom you worry too much. You think too much." You know, now that I talk to people, it's like I can talk to anybody, you know. . . .
>
> Yeah, it's different [now]. I'm always listening and never talking; maybe that's my problem too: I never talk, always keeping everything inside. And, now, I'm starting [to talk], . . . and it kind of makes me [think], "Oh, someone's listening to me." It makes me feel better.

In addition, by the end of the second session, she was coming to define herself as an important part of the problem; she was giving up the idea that the problem was some mysterious biological or psychological factor outside of her control. She said:

- You know, it's like I'm trying to figure out if I can control it, if it's just me.
- Now I'm noticing I can control it if I want.
- I feel like it's really me that's making myself feel like this. I feel it's me.

Note that this dramatic shift in problem definition occurred in the context of conversations about several other matters: what Ah Yan wanted to have different; the details of her miracle picture; occasions in her present life that resemble her miracle picture; what was better by the time of the second session; and the strengths she used to make her successes happen. As she and Peter talked about these other topics, her definitions of her problem shifted.

These different areas of conversation between Peter and Ah Yan seem to be equally important for successful solution building. Consequently, as her definition of her problems shifted, so did her perceptions and definitions of what she wanted to be different, her successes, and her strengths. If you review the dialogues with this in mind, you can pick up these shifts. First, regarding what she wanted, Ah Yan began by saying she wanted relief from her panicky feelings. By the second session, however, her attention had shifted to strategies that worked for her (such as leaving a stuffy place for a break, rolling down the window in a moving car, and deep breathing), to finding more ways to "let my kids go a little bit," and to talking more to others about what is going on inside of her.

Second, regarding her successes and strengths, she first talked about feelings of powerlessness:

> Yeah, last year for a while I thought I was crazy or something. I was gonna get up and get out of bed and my hair is falling out and, like, when I took a shower, there's a bunch of hair in my hand. And I went to the doctor and said: "Doctor, why? Why is this?" And they did tests, lots of tests.

By the end of her first session, however, she was talking very differently. Her sense of competency and strength was building. When asked to scale her level of confidence about finding a solution, she chose 10 and commented, "I'm not gonna stop until I'm all the way." In her second session, she said: "I read that book: 'Who's in charge, you or your mind?' . . . *I am.*" With further conversation, she was able to describe the successes and strengths that warranted her growing sense of competency.

The same pattern of shifting perceptions and definitions occurs in the conversations between Insoo and the Williams family. As an exercise, reread those dialogues from beginning to end and trace the shifts in perceptions and definitions.

In some cases, the shifts in clients' perceptions are dramatic and easy to pick out (de Shazer, 1991); in others, they are more subtle and difficult to identify. However, if you carefully review what clients say over the course of their solution-building conversations, you will always find examples of these shifts (Berg & De Jong, 1996). Note that your skill as a solution-building interviewer depends on learning to listen for these shifts and inviting your clients to explore them as they occur.

Social Constructionism

We have observed that client perceptions and definitions shift in the solution-building process. How are we to make sense of this observation?

The theoretical perspective that, we believe, comes closest to accounting for these shifts is social constructionism (Cantwell & Holmes, 1994; Gergen, 1985; Goolishian & Anderson, 1991; Laird, 1993). This perspective maintains that individuals' sense of what is real—including their sense of the nature of their problems, competencies, and possible solutions—is constructed in interaction with others as they go through life. In other words, people *make meanings* as they interact with others. Many authors (for example, Berger & Luckmann, 1966; Gergen & Kaye, 1992; Hoffman, 1990; Mead, 1934) have pointed out that, as human beings, we are always trying to figure out the meaning of our experiences. "We are such inveterate meaning-makers that when we do not have an explanation for something we make one up" (Saari, 1991, p. 14). In the conversations between Ah Yan and Peter and between Insoo and the Williams family, the clients' meaning-making tendencies showed again and again. For example, reflecting on her problem of feeling panicky, Ah Yan asked, "Why? Why is this?" She told Peter, "I gotta figure out what's wrong with me." As we've seen, she also came up with reshaped meanings for her problems, competencies, and solutions as she conversed with others—including her husband, her sister-in-law, and Peter.

What are the theoretical implications of the observation that client perceptions and definitions (or meanings) shift over time and in interaction with others? To answer this question is an enormous undertaking, which cuts across the fields of literary interpretation, philosophy, the social sciences, and the humanities. Central to any answer is an understanding of language, the means by which human beings converse. Theoretical writings are beginning to give more attention to the role of language in the helping or therapeutic process. For example, De Shazer (1991, 1994) works with the linguistic insights of philosophers including Derrida, Foucault, and Wittgenstein to analyze the interrelationships among the use of language, client meanings, and solutions in the therapeutic process.

Social constructionists emphasize that shifts in client perceptions and definitions occur in contexts—that is, in communities. Consequently, meaning making is not entirely an individual matter, in which clients can come up with private meanings (including solutions) without regard to others. Instead, individuals always live in ethnic, family, national, socioeconomic, and religious contexts; they reshape meanings under the influence of the communities in which they live. In solution building, relationship questions provide an obvious way in which the interviewer can explore clients' perceptions of their contexts.

Besides emphasizing that clients must develop their individual meanings in the context of community, social constructionists draw attention to the wide diversity of communities from which clients come. Clients' backgrounds reflect different racial groupings, ethnicities, nationalities, levels of socioeconomic status, and so forth. Individual clients will reflect the multiple realities of these communities.

What are the implications of social constructionists' views for practitioners in the helping professions? Ideally, the practitioner is a collaborative partner as clients reshape their meanings and create more satisfying and productive lives. As Goolishian and Anderson (1991, p. 7) write, working with clients becomes

> a collaborative and egalitarian process as opposed to a hierarchical and expert process. The therapist's expertise is to be "in" conversation with the expertise of the client. The therapist now becomes the learner to be informed, rather than a technical expert who knows.

As you begin to understand the social constructionist view of definitions of reality and how people acquire these definitions, you will see how these theoretical ideas make sense of the usefulness of solution-building procedures, which encourage clients to explore their definitions of reality (problems, miracles, successes, strengths, and solutions) as they struggle to create more satisfying and productive lives.

Shifting Paradigms

The recognition that client perceptions and definitions shift and that there are multiple definitions of reality among clients poses a challenge to the assumptions of a scientifically based, problem-solving approach to working with clients. If clients' definition of their problems and solutions changes over time and in collaborative interaction with others, how can those problems be real in an objective, universal, and scientifically knowable sense? As we explained in Chapter 1, the scientific approach to problem solving rests upon the assumption that client problems are objectively real and universally the same, much like a stomach tumor or air pollution. It also implies that client problems are as accessible to the systematic observations of the scientist as are the human kidneys or the planets. The problems that Insoo and the Williams family worked on and those that Ah Yan and Peter worked on do not seem to be real in that sense.

Once we start to think of clients' problems as a function of their current definitions of reality rather than as something that is objectively knowable, we must shed the role of experts about clients' problems and solutions. To quote Goolishian and Anderson (1991) again, "the therapist now becomes the learner to be informed, rather than a technical expert who knows."

As we saw in Chapter 1, reliance on scientific expertise is one of two fundamental aspects of the problem-solving approach to working with clients. The other is a problem-solving structure that assumes a necessary connection between a problem and its solution, as in modern medicine, where it is believed that a disease and its treatment are necessarily linked. This assumption underlies the field's emphasis on assessing problems before making interventions.

This second assumption, too, does not fit well with the observation that clients have multiple and changing definitions of reality. Nor does it fit with BFTC practitioners' finding that different clients build very different solutions to what seem to be the same problems. Nor, finally, does it fit with outcome data on this topic that we have recently collected.

Outcome Data

Practitioners at BFTC have observed that clients' answers to the miracle question sometimes seem logically connected to their problems, but at other times

Table 13.1	Intermediate Outcome (I.O.) by DSM-III-R Diagnosis*								
I.O.	300.40	309.00	309.23	309.24	309.28	309.40	313.81	314.01	Total
Significant progress	27%	20%	17%	14%	29%	8%	33%	6%	20%
Moderate progress	46%	80%	50%	43%	46%	62%	42%	47%	51%
No progress	27%		33%	43%	25%	31%	25%	47%	29%
Number of cases	11	10	6	7	24	13	12	17	100

* In Tables 13.1–13.3, percentages are rounded to nearest whole percent.

are completely unrelated. In later sessions, when clients begin to talk about what is going better in their lives and how they have made those things happen, these successes and strengths often have no apparent logical relationship with their problems (de Shazer, 1988, 1991, 1994). Many clients are as surprised about the solutions as any problem-solving practitioner might be. In this connection, de Shazer (1988, pp. 5–6) has written that clients' concept of solution often precedes a definition of problem; having figured out a solution, the client will go back and define (or redefine) the problem to fit the solution. If correct, de Shazer's observation gives insight into part of the process by which people develop their sense of reality.

In solution building, the practitioner works in the same way with each client, regardless of what the client might say the problem is. However, if solution building can be regarded as an intervention with clients, in traditional problem-solving terms, and if there is a necessary connection between problem and solution, then solution-building procedures should not work equally well with all client problems. To test this reasoning, we reviewed intermediate and final outcomes in terms of DSM diagnosis and client estimates of their problems.

DSM Diagnosis and Outcomes

Practitioners at BFTC have been trained in giving DSM diagnoses (in other words, diagnoses based on the American Psychiatric Association's *Diagnostic and Statistical Manual of Mental Disorders*), which they submit in order to receive third-party remuneration for services. Table 13.1 presents data for intermediate outcomes by diagnosis, and Table 13.2 gives the data for final outcomes by diagnosis. Diagnoses are given according to the revised third edition of DSM (DSM-III-R), which was current at the time the diagnoses were given. Only diagnoses for which there are more than five cases are reported. The names of the diagnoses corresponding to the DSM numeric code in Tables

Table 13.2	Final Outcome (F.O.) by DSM-III-R Diagnosis								
F.O.	300.40	309.00	309.24	309.28	309.30	309.40	313.81	314.01	Total
Goal met	33%	67%	14%	48%	33%	53%	18%	31%	39%
Some progress	17%		71%	35%	50%	40%	45%	54%	40%
No progress	50%	33%	14%	17%	17%	7%	36%	15%	21%
Number of cases	6	6	7	23	6	15	11	13	87

13.1 and 13.2 are as follows: 300.40, Dysthymia; 309.00, Adjustment Disorder (AD) with Depressed Mood; 309.23, AD with Work Inhibition; 309.24, AD with Anxious Mood; 309.28, AD with Mixed Emotional Features; 309.30, AD with Disturbance of Conduct; 309.40, AD with Mixed Disturbance of Emotions and Conduct; 313.81, Oppositional Defiant Disorder; 314.01, Attention-Deficit Hyperactivity Disorder.

Looking first at intermediate outcomes, the data in Table 13.1 indicate that a majority of clients receiving solution-building services showed improvement over the course of their services. The percentage of outcomes with no progress was highest for clients with diagnoses of Adjustment Disorder with Anxious Mood and Attention-Deficit Hyperactivity Disorder.

Table 13.2 on final outcomes by diagnoses indicates the same result: Diagnosis does little to predict outcome. The percentage of outcomes with no progress was somewhat higher for clients with diagnoses of Dysthymia (note the small number of cases) and Oppositional Defiant Disorder.

Clients' Self-Reported Problems and Outcomes

We also gave clients an extensive checklist of problems when they made their first visit to BFTC. Before they began their first session, they were asked to indicate each of the "problems that you feel apply to you." Among the problems on the list were: depression, suicidal thoughts, eating disorder, job-related problems, parent-child conflict, family violence, alcohol/other drug abuse, sexual abuse, death of a loved one, self-esteem problems, and blended-family issues. We analyzed the data for possible relationships between any of these self-assessed client problems and our measurements of intermediate and final outcomes.

In Table 13.3, we present a summary of these data. We have calculated a success rate on intermediate outcome and final outcome for each type of client problem for which we have more than five cases. The success rate for intermediate outcome is a combination of the categories "significant progress" and

Table 13.3 Success Rates on Intermediate (I.O.) and Final (F.O.) Outcomes for Different Types of Client Problems		
Type of Problem	I.O. Success Rate	F.O. Success Rate
Depression	75% (79)*	75% (60)
Suicidal thoughts	74% (34)	79% (19)
Anxiety	72% (50)	74% (42)
Panic attacks	80% (10)	50% (10)
Sleep problems	75% (59)	76% (49)
Eating disorder	80% (40)	73% (26)
Withdrawn behavior	67% (58)	80% (39)
Health problems	72% (18)	60% (10)
Job-related problems	84% (19)	80% (15)
Financial concerns	74% (43)	74% (31)
Parent-child conflict	71% (35)	76% (25)
Communication problems	65% (57)	76% (46)
Family violence (actual or threatened)	60% (20)	77% (13)
Sexual abuse	64% (11)	75% (8)
Physical abuse	67% (12)	89% (9)
Alcohol/ other drug abuse	67% (12)	63% (8)
Marital/ relationship problems	76% (45)	81% (47)
Sexual problems	72% (21)	89% (18)
Death of a loved one	72% (18)	79% (14)
Self-esteem problems	77% (48)	73% (40)
Brother/sister problems	78% (36)	78% (31)
Blended-family issues	74% (27)	71% (21)

*Figures in parentheses indicate the number of clients who indicated having the particular problem. The total number of cases is 141 for I.O. and 136 for F.O.

"moderate progress"; the success rate for final outcome is a combination of "goal met" and "some progress."

These data suggest that solution building with clients is consistently successful, regardless of the client's problems.[1] With a few modest exceptions—panic attacks and health problems on final outcome—Table 13.3 indicates that more than 70% of clients show progress on the two measurements of outcome.

The data on clients' estimates of their own problems and those on practitioner diagnosis and outcomes do not support the notion of a necessary connection between problem and solution; it does not appear from these data that clients need specialized interventions based upon professional assessments in order to make progress. In solution building, clients have successful outcomes when exposed to a uniform set of procedures, without regard for any purported connection between problem and solution.

These findings have some very important implications. First, they suggest that practitioner preparation could be greatly simplified. Currently the helping professions expend considerable resources on conceptualizing problems, devising problem-assessment procedures and instruments, developing specialized interventions, and then teaching all that content to aspiring practitioners. Our findings suggest that they could focus instead on observing more carefully how clients use personal strengths and environmental resources to make changes happen and then teaching new practitioners how to respect and foster self-determined change in clients. This conclusion brings us back to certain of the recommendations arising from the empowerment and strengths perspective that we cited in Chapter 1 (Rappaport, 1981, 1990; Saleebey, 1992).

Second, if solution-building procedures are equally effective across different problems, then learning to become an effective practitioner need not be such a complex undertaking. If you decide to become proficient in your use of solution-building skills, you can expect to be consistently useful to clients, for the most part, regardless of the problems that they bring to you.

Shifting Perceptions and Definitions As a Client Strength

Our observations and outcome data indicate that, when they come to us for professional assistance, our clients are teaching us some very important things about the nature of their humanity and, therefore, how we can best work with

---

[1] Although, strictly speaking, we did not have a probability sample of a larger population in the BFTC study whose data we are reporting, we still ran tests of significance. We ran the Pearson chi-square test for the bivariate relationships in Table 13.3 and for the other relationships in the tables in Chapter 10, 11, and 13. None of the differences were found to be statistically significant.

them. They teach us that, as they encounter life's struggles, other people, and a variety of experiences, they regularly reflect on these encounters; they conceptualize and organize their experiences through their capacities for abstract thought and language. In so doing, they create interpretations and frames of reference that make sense out of what they experience.

We have said that people create meanings or definitions of reality through their use of words and through talking to one another. We do not mean to imply by this that their experiences and definitions are not real. Several authors (Berger & Luckmann, 1966; Watzlawick, 1984) have emphasized that definitions of reality, although in a certain sense constructed or invented, are completely real to the person. For example, when Ah Yan was experiencing nervousness, shortness of breath, and physical tremors, her problem of panic was fully real to her. Ten days later, her sense that she was in charge of her problem ("I can control it if I want") was no less real. As Efran, Lukens, and Lukens (1988, p. 33) put it, "An invented reality—once it has been invented— is as real and solid as any other."

We have come to realize that clients' capacity to reshape and shift their perceptions and definitions of reality is a critically important resource in their efforts to deal with their problems. Clients' capacity to change is somehow bound up with their ability to see things differently. As George Kelly, an early constructivist practitioner, wrote, "There is nothing so obvious that its appearance is not altered when it is seen in a different light. . . . *Whatever exists can be reconstrued*" (cited in Efran, Lukens, & Lukens, 1988, p. 32). Somehow, Gladys' efforts to create a better life for herself and her children are bound up with her ability to expand her perception of her own childhood abuse from something ugly and despicable to something that could teach her how she wanted to treat her own children. And Ah Yan's ability to make differences in her life is bound up with her capacity to shift her perception of her panicky feelings from a sense of victimization ("I don't know. . . . I can't figure it out—what's wrong with me") to a growing sense of power ("Now I'm noticing I can control it if I want").

These shifts in client perceptions and definitions of reality, which are so much a part of clients' solution building, occur most readily in conversations about alternative futures and useful exceptions. Solutions seem to depend more on clients' capacity to develop and expand their definitions of what they want and how to make that happen than on scientific problem definition, technical assessment, and professional intervention. If that is so, the role for you as a practitioner is to be what Anderson and Goolishian (1992) call a conversational artist; by using your skills to sustain purposeful conversations, you allow clients to develop the expanded perceptions and definitions that they need to live more satisfying and productive lives. Strictly speaking, practitioners do not empower clients or construct alternative meanings for them; only clients can do that for themselves. However, what we can do as practitioners is to assume and respect clients' competencies and artfully converse with clients so that they can create more of what they want in their lives (Berg & De Jong, 1996).

In the end, believing is seeing. If you are to escape the longstanding belief in the field that client perceptions and definitions are not resources but a source of resistance that the practitioner must overcome, it will be through your experiences in solution building with clients. If your experiences are anything like ours, you will see your clients build solutions that you never could have envisioned, much less designed for them. You will see a Gladys transform past abuse into motivation to be a good mother, or a family create a spaghetti fight to reestablish connection and commitment to one another, or a Jermaine recover from a horrific experience by listening to his wife's breathing in the middle of the night. We believe that, in the end, if you remain patient and purposeful in your solution-building procedures, your clients will impress and even amaze you with their resilience, their creativity, and their competence.

References

Adams, J. F., Piercy, F. P., & Jurich, J. A. (1991). Effects of solution focused therapy's "formula first session task" on compliance and outcome in family therapy. *Journal of Marital and Family Therapy, 17,* 277–290.

Alcoholics Anonymous. (1976). *Alcoholics Anonymous: The story of how thousands of men and women have recovered from alcoholism* (The Big Book). New York: Alcoholics Anonymous World Services.

American Psychiatric Association. (1994). *The diagnostic and statistical manual of mental disorders* (4th ed.). Washington, DC: Author.

Andersen, T. (1987). The reflecting team: Dialogue and meta-dialogue in clinical work. *Family Process, 26,* 415–428.

Andersen, T. (Ed.). (1991). *The reflecting team: Dialogues and dialogues about dialogues.* New York: Norton.

Anderson, H., & Goolishian, H. (1992). The client is the expert: A not-knowing approach to therapy. In S. McNamee & K. J. Gergen (Eds.), *Therapy as social construction* (pp. 25–39). London: Sage.

Axelson, J. A. (1993). *Counseling and development in a multicultural society.* Pacific Grove, CA: Brooks/Cole.

Bateson, G. (Ed.). (1972). *Steps to an ecology of mind.* New York: Ballantine.

Bateson, G., Jackson, D. D., Haley, J., & Weakland, J. H. (1956). Toward a theory of schizophrenia. *Behavioral Science, 1,* 251–264.

Benjamin, A. (1987). *The helping interview with case illustrations.* Boston: Houghton Mifflin.

Berg, I. K. (1994). *Family based services: A solution-focused approach.* New York: Norton.

Berg, I. K., & De Jong, P. (1996). Solution-building conversations: Co-constructing a sense of competence with clients. *Families in Society: The Journal of Contemporary Human Services, 77,* 376–391.

Berg, I. K., & de Shazer, S. (1993). Making numbers talk: Language in therapy. In S. Friedman (Ed.), *The new language of change: Constructive collaboration in psychotherapy.* New York: Guilford.

Berg, I. K., & Miller, S. D. (1992). *Working with the problem drinker: A solution-focused approach.* New York: Norton.

Berger, P., & Luckmann, T. (1966). *The social construction of reality: A treatise in the sociology of knowledge.* Garden City, NY: Anchor.

Biestek, F. P. (1957). *The casework relationship.* Chicago: Loyola University Press.

The Big Book. *See* Alcoholics Anonymous (1976).

Cantwell, P., & Holmes, S. (1994). Social construction: A paradigm shift for systemic therapy and training. *The Australian and New Zealand Journal of Family Therapy, 15,* 17–26.

Carkhuff, R. R. (1987). *The art of helping* (6th ed.). Amherst, MA: Human Resource Development.

Carkhuff, R. R., & Berenson, B. G. (1977). *Beyond counseling and therapy* (2nd ed.). New York: Holt, Rinehart & Winston.

Cecchin, G. (1987). Hypothesizing, circularity, and neutrality revisited: An invitation to curiosity. *Family Process, 26,* 405–413.

Conrad, P., & Schneider, J. W. (1985). *Deviance and medicalization: From badness to sickness.* Columbus, OH: Merrill.

Corey, G., Corey, M. S., & Callanan, P. (1993). *Issues and ethics in the helping professions* (4th ed.). Pacific Grove, CA: Brooks/Cole.

Cowger, C. D. (1992). Assessment of client strengths. In D. Saleebey (Ed.), *The strengths perspective in social work practice* (pp. 139–147). New York: Longman.

De Jong, P., & Miller, S. D. (1995). How to interview for client strengths. *Social Work, 40,* 729–736.

de Shazer, S. (1984). The death of resistance. *Family Process, 23,* 79–93.

de Shazer, S. (1985). *Keys to solution in brief therapy.* New York: Norton.

de Shazer, S. (1988). *Clues: Investigating solutions in brief therapy.* New York: Norton.

de Shazer, S. (1991). *Putting difference to work.* New York: Norton.

de Shazer, S. (1994). *Words were originally magic.* New York: Norton.

de Shazer, S., Berg, I. K., Lipchik, E., Nunnaly, E., Molnar, A., Gingerich, W., & Weiner-Davis, M. (1986). Brief therapy: Focused solution development. *Family Process, 25,* 207–221.

Devore, W., & Schlesinger, E. G. (1987). *Ethnic-sensitive social work practice* (2nd ed.). Columbus, OH: Merrill.

Dolan, Y. M. (1991). *Resolving sexual abuse: Solution-focused therapy and Ericksonian hypnosis for adult survivors.* New York: Norton.

Durrant, M. (1993). *Residential treatment: A cooperative, competency-based approach to therapy and program design.* New York: Norton.

Efran, J. S., Lukens, R. J., & Lukens, M. D. (1988). Constructivism: What's in it for you? *The Family Therapy Networker, 12,* 27–35.

Egan, G. (1994). *The skilled helper: A problem management approach to helping* (5th ed.). Pacific Grove, CA: Brooks/Cole.

Epstein, L. (1985). *Talking and listening: A guide to the helping interview.* St. Louis: Times Mirror/Mosby.

Freud, S. (1966). *The complete introductory lectures on psychoanalysis* (J. Strachey, Trans.). New York: Norton.

Furman, B., & Ahola, T. (1992). *Solution talk: Hosting therapeutic conversations.* New York: Norton.

Garfield, S. L. (1994). Research on client variables in psychotherapy. In A. E. Bergin & S. L. Garfield (Eds.), *Handbook of psychotherapy and behavior change* (4th ed., pp. 190–228). New York: Wiley.

Gergen, K. J. (1985). The social constructionist movement in American psychology. *American Psychologist, 40,* 266–275.

Gergen, K. J., & Kaye, J. (1992). Beyond narrative in the negotiation of therapeutic meaning. In S. McNamee & K. J. Gergen (Eds.), *Therapy as social construction* (pp. 166–185). Newbury Park, CA: Sage.

Germain, C. B., & Gitterman, A. (1980). *The life model of social work practice.* New York: Columbia University Press.

Gilliland, B. E., & James, R. K. (1993). *Crisis intervention strategies* (2nd ed.). Pacific Grove, CA: Brooks/Cole.

Goldstein, H. (1992). Victors or victims: Contrasting views of clients in social work practice. In D. Saleebey (Ed.), *The strengths perspective in social work practice* (pp. 27–38). New York: Longman.

Goolishian, H. A., & Anderson, H. (1991). An essay on changing theory and changing ethics: Some historical and post structural views. *American Family Therapy Association Newsletter,* No. 46, 6–10.

Guest, J. (1976). *Ordinary people.* New York: Ballantine.

Guralnik, D. (Ed.). (1972). *Webster's new world dictionary of the American language* (2nd ed.). Cleveland: Collins + World.

Haley, J. (1973). *Uncommon therapy.* New York: Norton.

Haley, J. (1987). *Problem-solving therapy.* San Francisco: Jossey-Bass.

Hepworth, D. H., & Larsen, J. A. (1993). *Direct social work practice: Theory and skills* (4th ed.). Pacific Grove, CA: Brooks/Cole.

Hoffman, L. (1990). Constructing realities: An art of lenses. *Family Process, 29,* 1–12.

Hopwood, L., & de Shazer, S. (1994). From here to there and who knows where: The continuing evolution of solution-focused brief therapy. In M. Elkaim (Ed.), *Therapies familiales: Les approches principaux* (pp. 555–576). Paris, France: Editions de Seuil.

Ivey, A. E. (1994). *Intentional interviewing and counseling: Facilitating client development in a multicultural society* (3rd ed.). Pacific Grove, CA: Brooks/Cole.

James H. (Ed.). (1920). *The letters of William James* (Vol. 2). Boston: Atlantic Monthly Press.

Kagle, J. D. (1991). *Social work records* (2nd ed.). Belmont, CA: Wadsworth.

Keefe, T. (1976). Empathy: The critical skill. *Social Work, 21,* 10–14.

Kiser, D. (1988). *A follow-up study conducted at the Brief Family Therapy Center.* Unpublished manuscript.

Kiser, D. & Nunally, E. (1990). *The relationship between treatment length and goal achievement in solution-focused therapy.* Unpublished manuscript.

Kuhn, T. S. (1962). *The structure of scientific revolutions.* Chicago: University of Chicago Press.

Laird, J. (1993). Family-centered practice: Cultural and constructionist reflections. In J. Laird (Ed.), *Revisioning social work education: A social constructionist approach* (pp. 77–109). New York: Haworth.

Lambert, M. J., & Bergin, A. E. (1994). The effectiveness of psychotherapy. In A. E. Bergin & S. L. Garfield (Eds.), *Handbook of psychotherapy and behavior change* (4th ed., pp. 143–189). New York: Wiley.

Lewis, J. A., Dana, R. Q., & Blevins, G. A. (1994). *Substance abuse counseling: An individualized approach.* Pacific Grove, CA: Brooks/Cole.

Lukas, S. (1993). *Where to start and what to ask: An assessment handbook.* New York: Norton.

Lum, D. (1992). *Social work practice and people of color: A process-stage approach.* Pacific Grove, CA: Brooks/Cole.

Martin, D. G., & Moore, A. D. (1995) *First steps in the art of intervention: A guidebook for trainees in the helping professions.* Pacific Grove, CA: Brooks/Cole.

Maslow, A. (1970). *Motivation and personality* (2nd ed.). New York: Harper & Row.

McClam, T., & Woodside, M. (1994). *Problem solving in the helping professions.* Pacific Grove, CA: Brooks/Cole.

McMahon, M. O. (1990). *The general method of social work practice: A problem-solving approach* (2nd ed.). Englewood Cliffs, NJ: Prentice Hall.

Mead, G. H. (1934). *Mind, self and society.* Chicago: University of Chicago Press.

Miller, S. D., & Berg, I. K. (1995). *The miracle method: A radically new approach to problem drinking.* New York: Norton.

Modcrin, M., Rapp, C. A., & Poertner, J. (1988). The evaluation of case management services with the chronically mentally ill. *Evaluation and Program Planning, 11,* 307–314.

O'Hanlon, W. H., & Weiner-Davis, M. (1989). *In search of solutions.* New York: Norton.

Okun, B. F. (1992). *Effective helping: Interviewing and counseling techniques* (4th ed.). Pacific Grove, CA: Brooks/Cole.

Parad, H. J. (1971). Crisis intervention. In R. Morris (Ed.), *Encyclopedia of social work.* New York: National Association of Social Workers.

Pincus, A., & Minahan, A. (1973). *Social work practice: Model and method.* Itasca, IL: Peacock.

Rapp, C. A. (1992). The strengths perspective of case management with persons suffering from severe mental illness. In D. Saleebey (Ed.), *The strengths perspective in social work practice* (pp. 45–58). New York: Longman.

Rappaport, J. (1981). In praise of paradox: A social policy of empowerment over prevention. *American Journal of Community Psychology, 9,* 1–25.

Rappaport, J. (1990). Research methods and the empowerment social agenda. In P. Tolan, C. Keys, F. Chertak, & L. Jason (Eds.). *Researching community psychology* (pp. 51–63). Washington, DC: American Psychological Association.

Roberts, A. R. (1990). *Crisis intervention handbook: Assessment, treatment, and research.* Belmont, CA: Wadsworth.

Rogers, C. R. (1957). The necessary and sufficient conditions for therapeutic personality change. *Journal of Counseling Psychology, 21,* 95–103.

Rogers, C. R. (1961). *On becoming a person: A therapist's view of psychotherapy.* Boston: Houghton Mifflin.

Saari, C. (1991). *The creation of meaning in clinical social work.* New York: Guilford.

Saleebey, D. (Ed.). (1992). *The strengths perspective in social work practice.* New York: Longman.

Saleebey, D. (1994). Culture, theory, and narrative: The intersection of meanings in practice. *Social Work, 39,* 351–359.

Satir, V. (1982). The therapist and family therapy: Process model. In A. M. Horne & M. M. Ohlsen (Eds.), *Family counseling and therapy* (pp. 12–42). Itasca, IL: Peacock.

Schon, D. A. (1983). *The reflective practitioner.* New York: Basic Books.

Selekman, M. (1991). The solution-oriented parenting group: A treatment alternative that works. *Journal of Strategic and Systemic Therapies, 10,* 36–49.

Sheafor, B. W., Horejsi, C. R., & Horejsi, G. A. (1994). *Techniques and guidelines for social work practice* (3rd ed.). Boston: Allyn and Bacon.

Sparks, P. M. (1989). Organizational tasking: A case report. *Organizational Development Journal, 7,* 51–57.

Sue, D. W., & Sue, D. (1990). *Counseling the culturally different: Theory and practice* (2nd ed.). New York: Wiley.

Talmon, M. (1990). *Single session therapy.* San Francisco: Jossey-Bass.

Thomas, F. (1995). Genograms and competence: Fashioning meaning through an alternate use. *News of the Difference, IV,* 9–11.

Vinter, R. (1985). Components of social work practice. In M. Sundel, P. Glasser, R. Sarri, & R. Vinter (Eds.), *Individual change through small groups* (2nd ed., pp. 11–34). New York: Free Press.

Walter, J. L., & Peller, J. E. (1992). *Becoming solution-focused in brief therapy.* New York: Brunner/Mazel.

Watzlawick, P. (Ed.). (1984). *The invented reality.* New York: Norton.

Weakland, J. H., Fisch, R., Watzlawick, P., & Bodin, A. (1974). Brief therapy: Focused problem resolution. *Family Process, 13,* 141–168.

Weick, A. (1992). Building a strengths perspective for social work. In D. Saleebey (Ed.), *The strengths perspective in social work practice* (pp. 18–26). New York: Longman.

Weick, A. (1993). Reconstructing social work education. In J. Laird (Ed.), *Revisioning social work education: A social constructionist approach* (pp. 11–30). New York: Haworth.

Weick, A., Rapp, C., Sullivan, W. P., & Kishardt, W. (1989). A strengths perspective for social work practice. *Social Work, 34,* 350–354.

Weiner-Davis, M. (1993). *Divorce busting: A revolutionary and rapid program for staying together.* New York: Simon & Schuster.

Weiner-Davis, M., de Shazer, S., & Gingerich, W. J. (1987). Building on pretreatment change to construct the therapeutic solution: An exploratory study. *Journal of Marital and Family Therapy, 13,* 359–363.

Zeig, J. K., & Lankton, S. R. (Eds.). (1988). *Developing Ericksonian therapy: State of the art.* New York: Brunner/Mazel.

Solution-Building Tools

These forms were prepared by Peter De Jong, Calvin College,
and Insoo Kim Berg, Brief Family Therapy Center.

Goal-Formulation Protocol

Role Clarification

(Working with a team; team may interrupt with a question; break then feedback.)

Problem Description

How can I help?

How is this a problem for you? (Get problem description; if more than one, which is most important to work on first?)

What have you tried? (Was it helpful?)

Goal Formulation

What would have to be different as a result of our meeting today for you to say that our talking was worthwhile?

Miracle question (Once asked, focus on *what will be different* when the miracle happens.)

Regarding client: What will you notice that's different? (What will be the first thing that you notice? What else?)

Regarding significant others: Who else will notice when the miracle happens?

What will s/he notice that is different about you? What else?

When s/he notices that, what will s/he do differently? What else?

When s/he does that, what will be different for you?

(*continued*)

Goal-Formulation Protocol *(continued)*

Moving toward a Solution

(Use when client can answer the miracle question)

> If you were to pretend that the miracle happened, what would be the first small thing you would do?

> How might that be helpful?

> **Or:** What's it going to take for a part of the miracle to happen?

> Is that something that could happen? If so, what makes you think so?

Ending

1. If the client is concrete and detailed in answer to the miracle question, give compliments and suggest: "In the next week, pick one day and pretend that the miracle has happened and look for what difference it makes."

2. If the client is *not* concrete and detailed in answer to the miracle question, give compliments and suggest: "Think about what's happening in your life that tells you that this problem can be solved. And I'll do some thinking too."

(If a second session is a possibility, you can ask the client to meet with you again to continue working on the problem.)

Questions for Developing Well-Formed Goals

To the interviewer: When using these questions, remember that you most want to explore for the client's perception of what will be different when either the miracle happens or the problem is solved. Remember too that developing well-formed goals is hard work for clients. Be patient and persistent in asking the interviewing questions.

The Miracle Question

Suppose that, while you are sleeping tonight, a miracle happens. The miracle is that the problem that brought you here today is solved. Only you don't know that it is solved because you are asleep. What difference will you notice tomorrow morning that will tell you that a miracle has happened? What else will you notice?

Amplifying around the Characteristics of Well-Formed Goals

Small

Wow! That sounds like a big miracle. What is the first small thing you would notice that would tell you that things were different?

What else would tell you that things were better?

Concrete, Behavioral, Specific

You say that the miracle is that you'd feel better. When you feel better, what might others notice different about you that would tell them that you feel better?

What might you do different when you feel better? What else?

Start of Something Different/Better

You say that the miracle is that you'd weigh 50 pounds less. OK, what will be different in your life when you lose that first pound? What else?

Presence of Something Different/Better

You say that, when the miracle happens, you'll fight less with the kids. What will you be doing *instead*?

Amplifying around Perceptions of Significant Others

When the miracle happens, what differences will your husband [children, co-workers, teachers, friends, etc.] notice around your house? What differences will your husband notice about you? What else will they notice that's different?

(continued)

Questions for Developing Well-Formed Goals (continued)

Amplifying around the Client's System of Relationships

When your husband [children, co-workers, teachers, friends, etc.] notice _____ [the difference that the client mentions in answering the previous question], what will your husband do differently? What else? And when he does that, what will you do? How will things be different around your house?

Tips

If clients say "I don't know," say:

Suppose you did know, what would you say?

Or, go to significant other questions, for example:

If I were to ask your husband [children, etc.], what would he [they] say?

If clients struggle with the questions or say they are tough, agree with them and say:

I'm asking you some tough questions; take your time.

If clients cannot work with the miracle question, work with questions phrased along the lines of "when the problem is solved."

When clients get unrealistic ("I'd win the lottery!"), just agree with them by saying:

That would be nice wouldn't it.

If they persist, ask: What do you think the chances are of that happening?

Or:

What tells you that _____ could happen in your life?

When clients give you a concrete piece of the miracle picture or potential solution (for example, "When the miracle happens, I guess I'd be taking more walks"), take it one more step by asking:

What's different for you when you take more walks?

Part of respecting the client's perceptions is to respect the words that they use for their perceptions and adopt them in your interviewing questions. Thus, the preceding question picks up on the client's reference to taking more walks.

VERY IMPORTANT: If, despite your best efforts, clients are unable to work with the miracle question or to define how things will be different when the problem is solved, ask:

How do you know this problem can be solved?

(continued)

Questions for Developing Well-Formed Goals *(continued)*

Goal Formulation in Later Sessions

Work from the scaling question about progress:

> On a scale of 0 to 10, where 0 is where you were at when we began working together, and 10 means that the problem is solved (or the miracle happens), where are you at to-day?

> OK, so you're at a 5. What is happening in your life that tells you that you are a 5?

> So when you move up just a bit, say from 5 to 6, what will be different in your life that will tell you that you are a 6? What else? What will be different when you move on to a 7?

Thereafter, amplify just as you would for the miracle question, for example, around significant others. For example, when you move up to a 6, what will your co-workers notice that will tell them that you are doing just that much better? What else?

Protocol for Formulating Feedback for Clients

Finding the Bottom Line

Is there a well-formed goal? What is it?

Are there exceptions. What are they?

If yes, are they deliberate or random?

What is client's relationship to services? (Visitor, complainant, or customer type?)

The Feedback

Compliments

Bridging statement

Task

Common Messages
(End-of-Session Feedback for Clients)

Visitor-Type Relationship

Here's an example of a message to a client who was sent for services by his probation officer (Berg & Miller, 1992, p. 99):

> Curtis, we are very impressed that you are here today even though this is not your idea. You certainly had the option of taking the easy way out by not coming. . . . It has not been easy for you to be here today; having to give up your personal time, talking about things you really don't want to talk about, having to take the bus, and so on. . . .

> I realize that you are an independent minded person who does not want to be told what to do and I agree with you that you should be left alone. But you also realize that doing what you are told will help you get these people out of your life and you will be left alone sooner. Therefore, I would like to meet with you again to figure out further what will be good for you to do. So let's meet next week at the same time.

Complainant-Type Relationship

1. Client cannot identify exceptions and does not have a goal

   > Pay attention to what's happening in your life that tells you that this problem can be solved.

   Or, since the client does not have well-formed goals, use the formula first-session formula task (de Shazer, 1985, p. 137):

   > Between now and next time we meet, we [I] would like you to observe, so that you can describe to us [me] next time, what happens in your [pick one: family, life, marriage, relationship] that you want to continue to have happen.

2. Client can identify exceptions

   > Between now and the next time we meet, pay attention to those times that are better, especially what is different about them and how they happen — that is, who does what to make them happen. Next time, I'd like you to describe them to me in detail.

   When the client says that the exceptions are due to someone else doing something different, propose a variation of the same observation task:

   > Alice, pay attention for those times when your boss is more reasonable and open. Besides paying attention to what's different about those times, pay attention to what he might notice you doing that helps him to be more polite, reasonable, and open toward you. Keep track of those things and come back and tell me what's better.

(continued)

Common Messages *(continued)*

A final variation adds the element of prediction:

> Alice, I agree with you; there clearly seem to be days when your boss is more reasonable and open and days when he is not. So, between now and the next time that we meet, I suggest the following: Each night before you go to bed, predict whether or not tomorrow will be a day when he acts more reasonable and open and polite to you. Then, at the end of the day before you make your prediction for the next day, think about whether or not your prediction for that day came true. Account for any differences between your prediction and the way the day went and keep track of your observations so that you can come back and tell me about them. (de Shazer, 1988, pp. 179–183)

Customer-Type Relationship

1. **Client has a clear miracle picture but cannot identify exceptions**

   Between now and the next time we meet, pick one day and pretend the miracle has happened. Go ahead and live that day as if the miracle has happened — just as you described it to me. Then come back next time and tell me what's better.

2. **Client seems highly motivated but does not have well-formed goals and cannot identify exceptions**

   We are so impressed with how hard you have worked on _____ [the client's complaint] and with how clearly you can describe to us the things you have tried so far to make things better. We can see why you would be discouraged and frustrated right now. We also agree with you that this is a "very stubborn" [client's words] problem.

   Because this is such a "stubborn" problem, we suggest that, between now and next time we meet, when _____ [the client's complaint] happens, that you *do something different*—no matter how strange or weird or off-the-wall what you do might seem. The only important thing is that whatever you decide to do, you need to do something different. (de Shazer, 1985, p. 123)

3. **Client has well-formed goals and deliberate exceptions of his or her own doing**

   Ralph, I am impressed with you in several ways: First, by how much you want to make things go better between you and your children. Second, that there are already several better times happening like _____ [give examples]. And third, that you can describe to me so clearly and in such detail what you do to do your part in making those times happen, things like _____ [give examples]. With all that you are doing, I can see why you say things are at a 5 already.

   I agree that these are the things to do to have the kind of relationship with your children that you want to have. So, between now and when we meet again, I suggest that you continue to do what works. Also, pay attention to what else you might be doing—but haven't noticed yet—that makes things better, and come back and tell me about them.

(continued)

Other Useful Messages

When a client complains of a compulsion

Pay attention for those times when you overcome the urge to [overeat, drink, hit your child, use pornography, get panicky, etc.]. Pay attention for what's different about those times, especially what it is that you do to overcome the urge to _____. (de Shazer, 1985, p. 132)

When there are competing views of a solution. There are two possible situations here. In the first, individuals have different views; for example, if parents disagree about how to handle a child who steals, you might say:

We are impressed by how much both of you want to help your son "not to steal." The team is also impressed by what different ideas the two of you have about how to help your child through this difficult time. We can see that you were brought-up in different families and learned different ways to do things [the parents had said they could see their different family backgrounds at work in their conflicting views].

The team is split on which way to go—one-half feels like you ought to go with John's ideas and the other half feels like Mary's might work best. Therefore, we suggest that each morning, right after you get up, you flip a coin. Heads means that Mary is in charge and you do things her way with Billy while John stays in the background. Tails means John is in charge that day. And also—on those days when each of you is not busy being in charge—pay careful attention to what the other does with Billy that is useful or makes a difference so that you can report it to us when we meet again.

In the second, an individual is aware of more than one option and cannot decide which is best; for example, if a client is struggling with the decision whether to leave her boyfriend, Bill, you might say:

Like you, I am unsure about whether it would be best for you to "stay with Bill or leave him and begin a new life." I agree that this is a tough decision and figuring it out is going to take more hard work. As you continue to work on it, I suggest that each night before you go to bed, you flip a coin. If it comes up heads, live the next day as much as possible as though Bill is no longer a part of your life. Don't contact him and start to take the first steps toward the things you said you would do differently if you were on your own, such as spending more time with your friends and family and so forth. If it comes up tails, live the next day as though he is still a part of your life—all those things you described to me about what that means for you. Then, as you do these things, keep paying attention to what's happening that tells you that you are becoming more clear about whether to leave him or stay in the relationship. Remember, though, that usually a person cannot be 100% sure. And then come back and tell me what's better.

Protocol for First Sessions

Client Name(s): _____ **Date:** _____

Complaint/History: (How can I help? What tells you that _____ is a problem? What have you tried? What has been helpful?)

Goal Formulation: (What do you want to be different as a result of coming here? Dialogue around the miracle question.)

Exceptions: (Are there times when the problem does not happen or is less serious? When? How does that happen? Are there times that are a little like the miracle picture you describe?)

Scaling:

Presession change:

Willingness to work:

Confidence:

(continued)

Protocol for First Sessions *(continued)*

Compliments:

Bridge:

Task/suggestions:

Next time:

Protocol for Later Sessions

Client Name(s): _____ Date: _____

What's better?

Elicit: (What's happening that's better?)

Amplify: (How does that happen? What do you do to make that happen? Is that new for you? Now that you are doing _____ , what do you notice different between you and _____ ? Or: What's different at your house?)

Reinforce/compliment: (Not everyone could have said or done _____ . So you're the kind of person who does _____ ?)

Start again: (What else is better?)

Doing more: (What will it take to do _____ again? To do it more often?)

If nothing is better: (How are you coping? How do you make it? How come things aren't even worse?)

Scaling Progress:

Current level:

Next level(s): (When you move from _____ [number for current level] to _____ [one number up the scale], what will be different? Who will be the first to notice? When s/he notices, what will s/he do differently? What would it take to pretend that a _____ [one number up the scale] has happened?)

Termination: (How will you know when it's time to stop seeing me? What will be different?)

(continued)

Protocol for Later Sessions (continued)

Compliments:

Bridge:

Task/suggestions:

Next time:

Exception-Finding Questions

To the interviewer: When exploring for exceptions be aware that such questions can be phrased to ask for the client's perceptions of exceptions (individual questions) and the client's perception of what significant others might notice (relationship questions). Examples of each are included below.

Exceptions Related to the Miracle

1. **Elicit**

   So, when the miracle happens, you and your husband will be talking more about what your day was like and hugging more. Are there times already that are like that miracle—even a little bit?

   If your husband was here and I were to ask him the same question, what do you think he would say?

2. **Amplify**

   When was the last time you and your husband talked more and hugged more? Tell me more about that time. What was it like? What did you talk about? What did you say? What did he say? When he said that, what did you do? What did he do then? How was that for you? What else was different about that time?

   If he were here, what else might he say about that time?

3. **Reinforce**

   Nonverbally: Lean forward, raise eyebrows, take notes. (Do what you naturally do when someone tells you something important.)

   Verbally: Show interest. (Was this new for you and him? Did it surprise you that this happened?) and compliment (Seems like that might have been difficult for you to do, given everything that's happened in the relationship. Was it difficult?).

4. **Explore how the exception happened**

   What do you suppose you did to make that happen?

   If your husband were here and I asked him, what do you suppose he would say you did that helped him to tell you more about his day?

   Use compliments:
   Where did you get the idea to do it that way? That seems to make a lot of sense. Have you always been able to come up with ideas about what to do in difficult situations like this?

5. **Project exceptions into the future**

   On a scale of 1 to 10, where 1 means no chance and 10 means every chance, what are the chances that a time like that [the exception] will happen again in the next week [month, sometime in the future]? What will it take for that to happen?

   (continued)

Exception-Finding Questions *(continued)*

What will it take for that to happen more often in the future?

Who has to do what to make that happen again?

What is the most important thing for you to remember to do to make sure that that [the exception] has the best chance of happening again? What's the next most important thing to remember?

What do you think your husband would say the chances are that this [the exception] will happen again? What would he say you could do to increase the chances of that happening. If you decided to do that, what do you think he would do? If he did that, how would things be different for you [or around your house or in your relationship with him]?

Exceptions Related to the Problem

If the client cannot define a miracle and relates to you only in terms of problem talk, phrase your questions in terms of the *problem* instead of the miracle:

Can you think of a time in the past day [week, month, year] when you and your husband fought less or not at all?

Then proceed with the five steps given for exceptions related to the miracle.

What's Better?

You can begin all later sessions with this exception-exploration question. Be sure to follow all five steps and to use both individual and relationship questions.

Always ask "What else is better?" after you finish exploring an exception.

Coping Questions

In rare cases, the client cannot identify any exceptions and seems overwhelmed. You can then ask coping questions to uncover what the client is doing to make it in such difficult circumstances:

I'm amazed. With all that's been happening, I don't know how you make it. How do you do it? How do you get from one minute to the next?

If a client describes a longstanding depression and one discouraging event after another, you might say:

I can see that you have many reasons to feel depressed; there have been so many things that haven't worked out the way you wished. I'm wondering how you have managed to keep going? How have you been able to get up each morning and face another day?

If the client says she has to keep going for her kids, you might say:

Is that how you do it? You think about your kids and how much they need you? You must care a lot about them. Tell me more about what you do to take care of them.

Index

TO THE OWNER OF THIS BOOK:

We hope that you have found *Interviewing for Solutions* useful. So that this book can be improved in a future edition, would you take the time to complete this sheet and return it? Thank you.

School and address: ————————————————————————————

Department: ——————————————————————————————————

Instructor's name: ————————————————————————————————

1. What I like most about this book is: ————————————————

——

——

2. What I like least about this book is: ———————————————

——

——

3. My general reaction to this book is: ————————————————

——

4. The name of the course in which I used this book is: ——————

——

5. Were all of the chapters of the book assigned for you to read? ——————

   If not, which ones weren't? ——————————————————————

6. In the space below, or on a separate sheet of paper, please write specific suggestions for improving this book and anything else you'd care to share about your experience in using the book.

——

——

——

——

Optional:

Your name: _____ Date: _____

May Brooks/Cole quote you, either in promotion for *Interviewing for Solutions* or in future publishing ventures?

Yes: _____ No: _____

Sincerely,

Peter De Jong
Insoo Kim Berg